W9-BGX-478

INSIDE
JOAN COLLINS

INSIDE
JOAN COLLINS
A BIOGRAPHY

BY JAY DAVID

Carroll & Graf Publishers, Inc.
New York

Copyright © 1988 by Carroll & Graf Publishers, Inc.

All rights reserved.

First Carroll & Graf edition 1988

Carroll & Graf Publishers, Inc.
260 Fifth Avenue
New York, NY 10001

Photographs by courtesy of Globe Photos and Photo Trends
Cover photo by courtesy of Photo Trends

Library of Congress Cataloging in Publication Data
Adler, Bill.
  Inside Joan Collins.

  Bibliography: p.
  1. Collins, Joan, 1933–   2. Motion picture actors
and actresses—Great Britain—Biography.   3. Television
actors and actresses—United States—Biography.   I. Title.
PN2598.C66A64   1988   791.43′028′0924[B]   88-2562

ISBN: 0-88184-396-2

Manufactured in the United States of America

TABLE OF CONTENTS

Chapter One

Odds Against

Ascot is a pretty little village some twenty-five miles west and slightly south of London. It is known mostly for the Ascot Gold Cup, run at the racecourse constructed on Ascot Heath. The two-mile course dates back to 1711, when it was opened by Queen Anne. Every June the Ascot Races feature probably the largest assemblage of English royalty during the calendar year.

On Saturday, August 2, 1980, a nine-year-old girl named Katyana "Katy" Kass was visiting her best friend, a girl named Georgina, who lived in Ascot. Although Katy usually traveled with her mother and father when they were on the Continent, this time Katy's mother and father had taken along only Katy's older sister, Tara, on their weekend trip to Paris.

But Katy didn't mind. She and Georgina were free to move about the Ascot house and yard, going wherever they fancied, as long as they stayed within sight of the nanny watching them. Outside in the garden, however, a twelve-year-old boy began teasing them unmercifully.

For some reason, the nanny was distracted at the same time the two girls began chasing away the bothersome boy. They pursued him down to the bottom of the garden. The gate at the end of the garden pathway was broken. The gateway led out into what appeared to be a country lane and not a busy public street.

Continuing their chase of the boy, the girls stepped out only a few feet into the lane and——

An eighteen-year-old youth was driving the family car down the country lane passing by the house, taking his father home from a medical checkup for a heart murmur. Suddenly he saw two girls run out of a garden alongside the lane so fast that he could not avoid hitting them. He braked to a stop immediately.

Georgina was hurt; she had a broken leg. Katy was in a much worse way. Hit by the fender and bumper of the car, she had been thrown hard against the concrete curb and had landed on the right side of her head.

A neighbor saw the accident and rushed out with a blanket to cover Katy. Almost immediately two police constables appeared on the scene. One called for an ambulance. The two policemen could not revive Katy at all. Then the ambulance driver recognized Katy's symptoms as brain injury.

Another ambulance followed to attend to Georgina; Katy was rushed to the local Ascot hospital. Her hair was cut off and her skull examined. The doctors on duty felt her case was hopeless and telephoned the Central Middlesex Hospital in Acton, a suburb of London. Middlesex is one of the top neurosurgical hospitals in Britain. Within thirty-five minutes Katy was in Central Middlesex Hospital.

It was determined immediately that she had suffered a skull fracture, with severe injuries to the brain stem. Several hours after the accident, she was still in a deep coma. In fact, the doctors who took charge of her case were not sure that she could survive more than a few hours.

They tried to notify her father and mother, but Georgina's parents had misplaced the name of the hotel in Paris where

Katy's mother and father were staying. Almost frantic with grief, Georgina's mother telephoned Katy's grandfather, show-business impresario Joe Collins—but Collins was with his wife and youngest daughter on the south coast of England, enjoying the weekend.

The only person who could be contacted was in London. He was Bill Collins, Katy's uncle. But Bill had not been notified of his older sister's Parisian itinerary. Where were Joan Collins and her husband Ron Kass? Bill had no idea— but once he learned of the tragic circumstances of Katy's accident, he determined to find them.

Methodically he dialed each hotel in the Paris telephone book until he finally located them. It was two o'clock on Sunday morning, August 3, when Bill reached his brother-in-law Ron Kass at the Hotel Lancaster.

"There's been an accident," Bill told him clearly. "It's Katy. She's been badly hurt."

Kass shook his head to clear it. "An accident? Katy? How bad?"

"I'm afraid it's critical," Bill said slowly.

By now Joan Collins was awake in the bed beside her husband.

"What is it?"

"It's Katy. She's been hit by a car," her husband told her. "She's . . . critical . . . a head injury."

"No!" Joan screamed. "Not my baby—not Katy!"

Here was irony indeed. Joan Collins was an actress whose profession was the portrayal of deep emotion. Here, her own life had overtaken her art. Quite suddenly she found herself involved in a play whose story line she never would have chosen.

Not only was it difficult for Joan to envision her daughter's comatose condition, it was even more difficult to figure out why she and her husband had not brought Katy along with them to Paris, rather than leave her at her friend's house in Ascot.

"We have always taken Katy on our travels, but this one

time we left her behind," she said later. There was no question that Joan was feeling that old bite of guilt deep within her. Why had she left Katy home to be hurt—perhaps killed?

The Kasses had left London on Friday night and were spending the weekend in Paris to meet the costume designer Erté to discuss a new selection of clothes for Joan to wear in her appearance in the play *The Last of Mrs. Cheyney,* which was about to open in London's West End.

Alerted to the cries of her mother, Tara rushed into the bedroom to try to comfort her. So did Ron. More information came over the line. Katy's schoolmistress had been located and was with her at the hospital. But the doctors would say nothing more about her condition than that stunning and terrifying word: critical.

"I got hysterical," Joan Collins admitted later. The problem was that when Ron Kass begun calling the airports for transportation, he discovered there were no flights out of Paris until the middle of the morning—something like seven hours away. That was not good enough.

Finally Ron managed to locate Joan's father on the south coast. Joan got on the phone, weepy and shaken. "Daddy," she cried, "we've got to get back to Katy and there isn't another plane for seven hours. Can you think of anything—please, Daddy?"

Joe Collins knew a friend—Roger Whittaker—who could fly and had a plane. Learning of the crisis from Joe, Whittaker immediately promised to fly to Paris and pick up the Kasses. He telephoned Joan himself to tell her he was on his way.

"Joan, it's Roger. Be at Le Bourget at five-thirty. I'm coming to get you!"

Soon he was loading his three travelers into the plane to fly back to London.

"I was so upset, I fell against his chest and burst into tears," Joan wrote later. "He shook me like a Dutch uncle and told me to shape up, to think positively."

They were rushed through customs at London Airport and drove out to Central Middlesex Hospital, where they found Katy in intensive care. A terribly upset Joan Collins finally got in to see her daughter, lying there all bluish white, as still as a stone, with her eyes closed.

"You cannot envision what it's like to see your child lying in a coma in an intensive-care ward, with her head shaved, tubes coming out of everywhere, eyes closed, not moving at all, and one arm bent way back because of a contracted muscle."

It was a terrible shock for Katy's mother and father.

"Katy, darling," Joan called. "Mummy's here. If you can hear me, squeeze my hand."

And, indeed, Katy *did* squeeze her hand. "I knew she had heard!" Joan said later.

But now came the bad news. Dr. Lionel Balfour-Lynn, Katy's pediatrician, had been called, had examined Katy, and then had talked with the physicians in attendance.

"What are her chances?" Joan asked him in a hushed voice.

She was startled and disconcerted to see tears fill the man's eyes. "Of survival, sixty-forty *against*." He admitted that they had not even expected her to survive the night.

The odds were *against* survival! Joan realized. Katy did not even have an odds-on chance. Ron was with Joan now, and the two of them broke down.

"We fell on each other and cried," Joan recalled.

But shortly after that, they made a vow with each other. "Katy's not going to die. She's not. She's absolutely not!"

Joan wrote later: "We would pour into her our love, faith, strength, and optimism. Katy would receive from us our firm belief that she was going to live and to recover."

What the doctors wanted to do first was explore the wound in the brain with a bore, but decided against that and instead subjected Katy to a more conventional brain scan. Roger Illingworth, the neurosurgeon in charge, studied the scan and decided that an operation to relieve the pressure on the brain would not be necessary. There was another way to approach the problem.

Illingworth discussed the alternate procedure with Joan and Ron carefully, pointing out that he could give Katy steroids to reduce the swelling in the brain around the wound, and use other drugs as well. To reduce any strain on the brain, Katy would be put on a respirator, which would take care of her breathing. Then, if the steroids worked, Illingworth would use other drugs to reduce the swelling even more.

It was a risk—but everything was a risk. Illingworth felt that if Katy survived the first forty-eight hours, she might recover. But now came the very serious news. Illingworth warned Joan and Ron of one more scary possibility:

"Katy *could* be in a coma for four to six weeks."

When Joan Collins heard that, she almost collapsed again. Six weeks! An eternity!

But then Joan braced herself and thought about it. Although she was no physician, she could understand the need for communication between the conscious and the unconscious. It seemed to her that if communication ceased, the comatose victim would lose interest and simply die. But if constant voice communication could be maintained, the unconscious person might try to break through the wall set up by the wound in the brain.

And so Joan Collins determined to keep up a constant voice contact with her daughter—with help from her husband, her other daughter, and others.

"We decided to talk to Katy *all* the time and try to keep active that part of her brain that was still working." That would reassure Katy that the people who loved her were with her.

But how could this be done? How could Joan Collins and Ron Kass get on with their professional lives and always be there? The answer was a simple one. Their professional lives were going to consist now of keeping Katy in communication with the living—until she returned to normal.

And that was exactly what they did. Ron Kass rented a trailer, parked it in the lot next to the hospital, and there he and Joan Collins stayed when they were not in Katy's hospital room.

"I spent every waking minute at Katy's beside," Joan said. "I threw myself with utter desperation into not only her survival . . . but her return to normality and out of coma as soon as possible."

Not one minute did she waste on anything else during the following six long weeks. And while she was in the hospital room with her daughter, she was spending her time *willing* the child to live.

"We decided we would constantly talk to her, touch her, turn her, and play music for her, and each of us took bedside shifts from morning to night." They would talk to her all the time, saying anything that entered their minds. They would play records of all kinds, from the sound track of *Grease* to *Peter and the Wolf*.

In addition, through a friend of Ron Kass's, Joan Collins got in touch with the Institutes for the Achievement of Human Potential in Philadelphia. This is an organization that advocates a method of helping keep comatose patients alive by stimulating their senses of touch, sound, smell, sight, and taste. There are many ways to do this: by clapping blocks together to create sound, by dabbing mustard on the tongue, and by constantly touching the face and hands.

"If ever I believed in *will* and faith and hope and prayer, I used every ounce of it on that child," Joan said later. And she was determined not only that Katy would survive, but that she would live her life as a normal child.

Joan allowed herself only four or five hours of exhausted sleep each night, and then she would get up again and sit by Katy's bed. During those four or five hours, Ron would pace outside the room, keeping an endless vigil on his daughter.

As crises usually have a way of doing, this crisis in the life of Joan Collins and Ron Kass came at the worst possible time. Both of them were quite aware that their marriage was in a very bad way. In addition, Ron Kass's income had been severely curtailed, and it had been largely on that that the Kass family (including two children from Joan's earlier marriage) had subsisted.

Kass had more or less become a general manager and agent for his wife, Joan Collins, who was now on the comeback trail after having almost completely given up her acting work in show business for the better part of a decade.

Joan knew she had to earn enough money to support the family because her husband had been unable to get work since a big job in California had folded under him five years before. She herself had made a substantial sum by writing her autobiography—a big success in Britain—and had made two movies that had earned her good money if nothing in the way of prestige.

She had opted for stage work, and with her husband's help, she had toured the provinces in Britain in a revival of the old play, *The Last of Mrs. Cheyney*. Now that show was scheduled to open in the West End in London.

Joan had also signed on to do a tour of the provinces in a new, untried play titled *Murder in Mind*, although it was a minor production and would probably lead to little income.

Nevertheless, in spite of the fact that some money was coming through, she and Ron Kass knew that their days together were numbered. She was too restless a woman to put up with a loser as a husband. She had left an earlier husband who had lost his initiative. She would leave this one, too, when the chance presented itself.

Now, with Katy's life hanging in the balance, Joan dropped all thoughts of separation. The two of them pitched in together to try to save the life of their child.

Yet the future was a problem that could not be solved overnight. Joan knew it would be a difficult thing to change her style of acting enough to move from films and television to the London stage. But that was where she had decided to

go. And she had two jobs ahead of her: to finish up *Mrs.
Cheyney* and do *Murder*.

But not now.

Now was Katy's time. And in characteristic fashion, Joan
Collins immediately channeled all her energies into that one
aim: to keep in touch with Katy and bring her through her
illness.

She allowed nothing to impinge on her from the outside.
It was as if her exclusive function in life was to stay beside
Katy's bed and talk to her, keeping her alive.

The weeks began to unroll—monotonous, exhausting, de-
bilitating . . . and yet, always invigorating because of that
tiny hope that Joan kept in the front of her mind.

The First Week

It was the sixth day of the first week after the accident—a
Friday—and the bad news began to pile up all around Joan.
Katy was running the risk of serious infection. Because of the
way the respirator worked, it could only make any infection
worse.

Katy had to be taken off the respirator.

There was a great deal of argument among various members of the team working on Katy. Some felt that she should
have an immediate tracheotomy—a hole cut in her throat to
allow her to breathe—but others felt that she did not need
such an operation.

Finally, she was ordered off the respirator while a team
stood by waiting to perform the tracheotomy if it were
needed. Illingworth felt such an operation was not needed;
he thought she could breathe without the respirator.

When Katy was removed from the respirator, Illingworth
was proved right. Katy gasped and heaved and twisted about
in terrible stress for a few moments. "We heard raspy sounds,"

Joan recalled. But eventually Katy gasped and finally began breathing on her own. It was said at the hospital that Illingworth smiled for the first time in fourteen years.

The Second Week

On the eighth day, the big breakthrough came. Joan had gone out to purchase the Sunday newspapers, and when she returned to the hospital room, Ron was there, excited and waving his arms. "She's opened her eyes!"

"It was like Christmas and birthdays all at once," Joan wrote later. "I rushed to the intensive-care ward, and her eyes were indeed open—but completely blank. They weren't following me!"

Although Katy was not looking at Joan at all, but simply staring vacantly into space, it was a marvelous sign.

But other signs were not so good. That same day, Katy stopped breathing quite suddenly. No one knew why. Illingworth decided that she must have suffered a muscular spasm that had paralyzed her respiratory system.

She was still attached to the life-support machines, which set off an alarm. The resuscitation team was immediately on the scene to save her.

"Ron and I decided we must watch her constantly," Joan said later. "He will be with her at night and I will do the day shift."

On the ninth day Katy was moved to the children's ward, where it was a lot more cheerful.

By the tenth day after the accident, Katy was down by at least twenty pounds from her normal weight of seventy. She resembled, as Joan wrote, "a little skeleton from a concentration camp with her cropped hair and skinny arms and legs."

In fact, while Joan sat with her, she could hear Katy

making little sounds in her throat—like a lonely animal moaning. But that grisly sound was another good sign; it meant that her vocal chords worked.

"You mustn't get too optimistic, you know," one of the doctors told Joan. "The chances are strong that she will have some disability."

Friends who visited Katy in the children's ward would look at her emaciated body and then go off and cry in the parking lot. "I cried every day myself," Joan admitted, but she never let herself go in front of Katy.

On the twelfth day, material arrived from the Institutes for the Achievement of Human Potential in Philadelphia. There were instructions on stimulating each of the five senses of the comatose child.

For sound: ringing bells, blowing whistles, banging blocks of wood together loudly, and playing tapes of familiar voices and sounds.

For smell: making the child smell strong odors like ammonia, perfume, and garlic.

For feel: applying hot and cold compresses, tapping, pinching, and poking the body, and brushing the skin with objects like feathers, silk, and velvet.

For taste: putting strong tastes on the tongue—lemon, honey, and mustard.

For sight: shining a flashlight into the eyes.

The instructions were to stimulate one of the senses every ten minutes, six times an hour, for as long as feasibly possible during Katy's waking hours.

The Third Week

Joan had a theory that she must be positive about Katy and not allow any negative thoughts to interfere with her daughter's recovery.

"I refused to allow anybody to be negative around her," she said.

Once an intern warned Joan that she was making herself sick. "She's not going to get any better," he said.

Joan was furious. She grabbed him by the arm and hauled him out into the corridor. "Don't you ever speak in front of my daughter like that again. She can hear!"

She rushed out into the trailer and screamed for ten minutes, punching the wall so hard that she sprained her wrist.

Joan had Katy's riding teacher make a tape for her. Then Joan turned on the television to a horse race and played the tape. Joan was enthused by what Katy did.

"Katy got very excited and hot. I know she was *reacting*."

On the eighteenth day, Joan noticed that Katy seemed to be trying desperately to lift her head from the pillow. She was also beginning to move her legs around. Spraying water on her cheek, Joan saw her wince at the cold.

The Fourth Week

One Catholic visitor announced that Katy was "going to recover." She then urged Joan to give thanks to God by giving up one of her cherished bad habits.

"I gave up chocolates, an addiction of mine," Joan said. She confessed that she could never give up cigarettes or wine— they were the only things that kept her going through her ordeal.

Katy now appeared to be passing through a spell of appearing restless and excitable—moaning a bit in that animal-like way, and even trying to cry. No tears, however. Joan learned that comatose people cannot cry because it is impossible to stimulate the flow of tears.

Finally Katy began to eat food—potatoes, peas, and chicken. She seemed to be actually tasting the food.

"Each new thing that she does is a miracle," Joan noted.

The Fifth Week

Katy's coma began to lighten in the fifth week. During that period, Joan and Ron took Katy home for a short visit. Katy could not speak yet, but she seemed to follow things with her eyes. As they drove down their street, Katy looked excited and began to move her head, body, and legs. Once inside the house, she was propped up in her chair, facing the television set. She looked around as if she knew where she was. She even ate some mashed food. Sam, her cat, climbed up on her lap and went to sleep. Katy seemed relaxed and almost happy.

In fact, when Ron lifted her from her chair to carry her down the stairs, she made a face as if she wanted to cry. But she was not able to. There were no tears yet for her eyes.

The doctor who had warned Joan not to be too optimistic said that Katy was really doing quite well.

"She's a very determined person," Joan told him.

The doctor smiled. "Like her mother."

The Sixth Week

During the sixth week, on the forty-second day after her accident, Katy was brought home for good. The doctors felt that there was nothing more they could do for her at the hospital. Whether she continued to improve was up to her father and mother. Besides, the physicians felt that Katy's progress would be hastened by a familiar environment.

Joan told her in the morning, "Today we are going home." And Katy smiled! Joan hugged her—it was the first time she had smiled in six weeks.

Once Katy was home, it was like working with a newborn

baby. Katy had to learn everything from scratch. It was necessary to have day nurses and night nurses.

She was still supported by people as she was walked about the room.

The Seventh Week

One morning during the seventh week—forty-seven days after the accident—Katy was placed in the middle of her parents' bed, as usual. Her eyes were just staring into space— also, as usual.

"Ron and I, standing on either side of the bed, were sharing a joke," Joan recalled. "We were both laughing when suddenly Katy laughed, too—though sounding like a person with laryngitis."

That was enough for Joan and Ron. They kept on talking together and laughing, and told more jokes. Katy followed suit, laughing along with her parents.

It was slow going after that first start, but gradually Katy began to improve. One day Joan brought in a horseshoe to show Katy. Horsemanship was Katy's favorite sport. And now Joan heard what she thought was a faint whisper:

"Horseshoe."

It was the first word Katy had spoken since the accident in August.

Now Joan and Ron kept with Katy every minute of the day.

The Tenth Week

Finally Katy began taking her first steps, some four weeks after being moved to her home.

And in October she managed to write her first words since the accident:

"Dear Mommy and Daddy, I love you very much."

It was time for Joan and Ron to get on with their life. In fact, on the day Katy had spoken her first word—"horseshoe" —Joan had begun rehearsals for *Mrs. Cheyney*. This kept her busy. She had been smoking and drinking a great deal during the ordeal—and now she cut out both, cold turkey.

On opening night, Katy appeared backstage. She brought with her the note she had written in October.

It was Joan's most memorable gift that year.

The following January, Katy returned to school. Her speech was still a bit slow, she had a memory problem, and one of her eyes was dilated a bit. Joan urged her daughter to practice running and dancing.

"She does lash out in frustration once in a while," Joan reported, "but she also has this most extraordinary spirit. In six months—or a year, or maybe two—I hope she'll be exactly as she was."

Katy had come far: from the almost-dead to the living.

"She has been to a place that none of us will see until we die," Joan wrote. "It's like she was there—and was called back."

And now it was time for Joan to begin rebuilding her own life, which was in pretty much of a mess. Her personal life. Her professional life.

After *Mrs. Cheyney* closed, the Kasses went to Marbella, Spain, on the Costa del Sol, for a short rest in the sun.

There the call came through that began the next chapter of Joan Collins's life. . . .

Chapter Two

Early Collins

She was born Joan Henrietta Collins in a north London nursing home in Bayswater on May 23, 1933. Bayswater is a London neighborhood just north of Kensington Gardens and Hyde Park, one of the largest park areas in the city.

Her father was Joseph Collins, a theatrical agent, and her mother Elsa Bessant Collins. The Collinses were perfect examples of the ancient English adage that opposites attract. In appearance, in attitude, and in spirit, each was the direct antithesis of the other.

Joe Collins was darkly handsome, with brown eyes, curly hair, and European features. Engaged as a theatrical agent in show business, he was typically outgoing, quick-witted, and energetic. He was the unputdownable impresario. He represented hundreds of performers of all shapes, sizes, and talents. In his time he represented such later superstars as Peter Sellers, Shirley Bassey, and Vera Welsh, a singing favorite whose professional name was Vera Lynn. He was also a friend of actor Roger Moore and of other luminaries.

Elsa Collins, the daughter of a south London railway porter named William Bessant, was blonde and fair. She had blue eyes and the clean-cut features of an Anglo-Saxon fairy-tale princess. Brought up to be a woman in the traditional mold—childbearer, cook, and nurturer—she was as gentle and soft as her husband was rough and harsh. "She had beauty, she had charm, she was easy to talk to," wrote Joe Collins years later.

Joe Collins had been born into a show-business family, and although he had left theatrical work to try other fields, eventually he returned to it on a permanent basis. At the time of Joan's birth, he was in partnership with Lew Grade in the theatrical agency of Collins and Grade. Later Grade would become "Lord" Grade of Elstree, but he was always "Uncle Lew" to Joan. Grade had begun his show-business career as a hoofer but had joined Collins in the 1920s as agent in the "Collins and Grade Agency" on nothing more than a handshake and a promise.

For several generations, the Collinses had been in the entertainment business. Will Collins, Joe's father, had come from a long line of fishmongers in London until he had been drawn into vaudeville in the 1890s to become a top stage impresario. In fact, when Joe Collins began his career he had used the name "Will" in order to utilize his father's clout in the business.

It was Joan's grandfather, the original Will Collins, who had usurped the name Collins. His real family name was Hart, his given name Isaac. In fact, Isaac Hart was a relation of Ernest Simpson, the second husband of Bessie Wallis, who became the Duchess of Windsor. He was also related to Sir George Faudel Phillips, the Lord Mayor of London in 1896. The name Collins? In 1891, Joan's grandfather became entranced by Lottie Collins, a beauty in the London music halls. He was so impressed with her that he decided to take her last name as his own—and so became Will Collins. No one ever knew how he had decided on Will for his first name, but perhaps it was because of the pleasant repetition of the double "l" in Collins.

Joe Collins's mother was Henrietta Collins, formerly Henrietta Assenheim, a singer who had become a star on the musical comedy stage as a teenager in *Aladdin* at the Theatre Royal in Bristol. Will Collins made her change her name to "Hettie" Collins, so it would sound like his favorite, Lottie Collins. Will formed traveling companies of vaudeville entertainers and toured South Africa, where prospectors were making fortunes mining gold. The Boer War soon put a stop to that, but the traveling companies prospered in the war atmosphere as well. After Will Collins married Hettie in Cape Town in 1901, two of Hettie's sisters, Hannah and Bessie, joined Hettie to become the "Three Cape Girls."

To Joan, her grandmother Henrietta, after whom she was named, became "Grandmother Hettie"—a bouncy, brassy, saucy woman. It was Hettie who took Joan under her wing at an early age and taught her the fundamentals of dance: high kicks, splits, and other important moves. She was loud, she was effervescent, and she was *fun*.

More than that, as Hettie's first grandchild, Joan was doted upon by her grandmother. Later Joe Collins would recall:

"I think it was Mother [Hettie] who, from Joan's earliest years, fostered her determination to be a big star. Joan had certainly inherited many of my mother's qualities: her talent, her charisma, her springy, hip-swaying walk, the provocative twinkle in her eye."

Joe also remembered catching his elder daughter in front of a mirror poking at her eyes with matchsticks. Berating her for "playing with matches," he learned that it had something to do with his mother's "tricks."

"Granny taught me this," Joan told him. "She says if you balance matchsticks on your lashes it makes them longer and stronger."

The Collinses were quite a contrast to the Bessants, and of course, to Joan's mother, who was the ultimate ice-maiden

blonde of the prewar world: beautiful, proper, and uneman-
cipated. Joe would shout back at anybody. Not Elsa. She was
too gentle, too peace-loving ever to shout back, even at Joe.
"It wasn't in her makeup," Joe said. Even when she accepted Joe's proposal of marriage, she was low-keyed and
cool.

"They say two can live as cheaply as one," she told Joe.
"We might as well get married. But for goodness' sake, don't
let's make a fuss!"

From the very start, these two warring instincts—the fire
of the Collins tribe and the ice of the Bessants—were at
work in Joan, pushing her in one direction and trying to pull
her back in the other.

In Joan's youth, Joe, who was then using his father's name
"Will" professionally, prospered even though others were
out of work and suffering. People sought out entertainment
to combat the blues in their lives. The Collinses were affluent enough to live in a very nice apartment in Maida Vale,
just a few blocks from Regent's Park in north London. Joan
spent her first years surrounded by near-luxury and the
excitement of show-business personalities.

There were always parties at which scores of Joe Collins's
clients were present—theatrical people of all kinds, a noisy,
spirited group, which suited Joan just fine. She loved to
show off in front of people and tell stories the way the
performers did, without inhibition and without any shyness
at all. From the beginning, she knew she was going to be an
actress, like her grandmother Hettie.

When Joan was about five, the family moved to the border
of Hampstead, between Kilburn and Cricklewood. It was
there that Joan's little sister, Jackie, was born. Elsa and Joe
decided they would stick with the letter "J," and they named
number two Jacqueline—and what better middle name than
Jill, from Jack and Jill? Eventually there would be three
children—the third a boy named Bill, after Will, Joe's father.

It was 1939, and world events were about to overtake the
Collinses. For the first years of the war, Joe had continued

to take the family on automobile rides to Brighton, where they would spend their time at the seaside resort. Joe had been there when he was growing up, too; in fact, Joan's grandmother Hettie lived in Brighton during the first years of World War II, which began in earnest in 1940.

In August 1939, the family moved to Bognor, on the Sussex coast, where Joan's maternal grandmother, Ada Bessant, was living. But once the Blitz began in earnest in 1940, it turned out that Bognor was too dangerous. Ada told Joe, "As the Germans fly in over our coast, they're even shooting at innocent people walking on the promenade."

Joan and Jackie were returned to the west of London, in Maidenhead, Berkshire. But that was only for a short time. When the Blitz languished, the Collinses moved back to Maida Vale in London—only to be caught in a raid that completely destroyed the apartment complex in which they lived!

The was enough for Joe. He moved the family to Ilfracombe, located in the southwest of England, on the Bristol Channel, almost two hundred miles from London. But this constant moving around was an example of the kind of life Joan had. In spite of the seemingly settled existence of the family, the day-to-day life was one of constant change—change that began to take its toll on Joan herself. She began to withdraw into a shy, rather intense little person, unbelievable as that image of her may seem today.

Encouraged by her grandmother Hettie, Joan had been enrolled in a dancing school at the tender age of three. Soon after that, she was moved to another dancing school, and then a third. By the time she was in her teens, she had attended at least ten different dancing academies.

The same unsteadiness was evident in her regular schooling, and may be the reason she did not do as well as a person of her intelligence and willpower might have done. She was always dissatisfied, and would move from one friend to another as casually as her family would move from one place to another. On weekends the family was constantly on the

move, too: to Brighton before the war started to visit Grandma
Hettie, to Bognor to visit her maternal grandmother Ada, or
to the other parts of England to visit people her father
knew.

It was the show-business associates who were fascinating
to Joan—and who were fascinated by her. She was a very
pretty child, and would dance at the drop of the hat, or sing,
or show off in any one of a dozen ways for anyone. The
remark she usually heard from her father's friends was: "Of
course, you really *must* go on the stage."

Nevertheless, even though Joe Collins was flattered that
his friends should consider his firstborn a potential stage
talent, he did not want his daughter—or any member of his
family—to go into show business permanently. He knew too
much about its inner workings and how frequent rejections
could destroy even the most confident person.

Joan's life changed dramatically during the war years. Her
being first out of London, and then back in it, and then
somewhere else, was all part of the mix-up of those tense
and trying years. Even at Ilfracombe, life was unsettled. It
was so far away from the action of the city that Joe was
constantly frantic about losing touch with his clients and with
the entertainment business.

Finally Joe decided to stay in the city by himself. There
was a tremendous *need* for entertainers and for entertainment of the troops and refugees from Hitler's Europe.

Life may have been exciting, but it was not any picnic. In
fact, it was horrible, as Joan once confessed, with all the
constant moving about, and the changes in schools, and the
new people she had to meet for the first time everywhere.
And so the outgoing, confident, effervescent Joan suddenly
became Shy Joan, Retiring Joan. "New children at school
whispering and giggling in the corner at the nervous new
girl made me feel an outsider."

As the perennial "outsider," Joan retreated in the classic
psychological manner, going into a fantasy world of books,
film magazines, and motion pictures. The real world was a

pain; she could enjoy herself only in the one she created for herself.

But another calamity occurred in those years. Suddenly Joan and Jacqueline had a new little baby brother, Bill. Now there were *two* people to compete with Joan for her mother's attention. The growing girl was overwhelmed by it all.

As she entered her teenage years she was, as she put it, "awkward, spotty, gawky, shy, boy-hating, and introverted." To combat her own hateful self-image, she determined to become what she now felt her father had always wanted her to be: a boy!

She would force herself to go with her father to his favorite outdoor sport—football—every Saturday afternoon. She hated the freezing weather, the noise, and the yelling. But, valiantly, she would jump up and down, yelling whenever one of the locals would score a goal, as she put it, "trying to please him."

Secretly, she confessed, "I couldn't understand the fascination of twenty-four unkempt, dirty men kicking a ball around a muddy field, while thousands of raucous blokes in caps and mufflers cheered and screamed."

Her antics failed to fool Joe. "She pretended it was all very exciting, yelling when I yelled, but she didn't fool me," he wrote later. "I could see she was bored."

In fact, Joan hated most sports, except for swimming. She loved to swim. After all, she knew she looked good in a bathing suit. But she put up with football for years, silently resolving to get out of all that by becoming a successful actress.

Beginning with her father, there were any number of people opposing her dream of a theatrical career. There was Grandma Hettie, who, although she was one of the main reasons that Joan wanted a theatrical career, did not want Joan hurt by it. And there were two formidable aunts—sisters of her father named Lalla and Pauline. Both were figures in the world of show business; they did not want Joan bruised by it any more than she was already.

Lalla was the oldest of Joe's sisters, who at sixteen had played in *Joy-Bells* with the Original Dixieland Jazz Band at the London Hippodrome. Later she opened on Broadway in *Andre Charlot's Revue of 1924* with Jessie Matthews and Marjorie Robertson, both of whom became future screen stars (Robertson under the name of Anna Neagle). She was also "romantically" involved with England's dancing star, Jack Buchanan, also a member of the *Revue* cast.

Pauline was featured as a double for the great Gracie Fields in a motion picture produced by Fields's second husband, Monty Banks. She danced in musicals like *Rose Marie* and Noel Coward's first revue, *London Calling*. She later became a successful theatrical agent, exactly like her brother and father.

These three formidable ladies would draw unflattering and sordid pictures of what went on backstage behind the façade of glamour and excitement out front. They would do everything they could to discourage Joan from going on to become an actress, even though they themselves were perfect examples of arguments *to* do so.

Those years were mixed up enough, what with the moves from one place to another and the bombing raids and the stress of wartime life. But before anyone actually realized it, the war was over and the vast rebuilding process to a peacetime life-style was under way.

Now Joan and Jackie (and Bill) moved back to London proper, where Joan was enrolled in a high school to finish her education. She went to a private school for girls—called "public" in England—named Francis Holland School. It was during her studies there that she made her actual stage debut in a West End stage production at the Arts Theatre—a production of Ibsen's *A Doll's House* in which she played one of the two children. Joan had one line.

When her cue came up, she failed to appear. She had become so engrossed in reading a teenage magazine called *Girl's Crystal* that she had forgotten to listen for her cue. "To Joan, acting was just a game," her father once said.

There was one person in Joan's life who did not make a "big thing" out of her desire to be an actress. Surprisingly enough, given her attitude and personality, it was Joan's mother.

"Some people are domestically inclined, others aren't," Elsa Collins once said. "And Joan did *not* inherit my love for housework and cooking!"

"You know, Mummy," Joan had told her, "you chose to be a housewife. I didn't. You chose your career. I have chosen mine."

So be it, her mother decided. She knew about her daughter's obsession to get on the stage; secretly, she supported it.

In spite of her fiasco at the Arts Theatre, Joan began her campaign for a stage career in earnest when she was fifteen years old. Her big obstacle was her father. Joe would have nothing to do with trying to initiate a show biz life for Joan.

"You don't know what you're letting yourself in for!" he told her. "You could be famous at twenty and forgotten at twenty-seven. You could get very hurt. If you do become a big name, everyone will want to know you, invite you to their parties, butter you up . . . and a year or two later, once you're not doing so well, they'll walk right past you in the street as if you were a stranger."

He pointed out the dangers of high unemployment, the rigors of the life, the never-ending hours of work.

"It's a profession where you'll meet lecherous men who try to take advantage of you. The very word 'actress' attracts all kinds of hangers-on."

Joan listened and argued. Part of her argument concerned the actual steps she might take.

"Daddy," she told him, "I'm aware of the pitfalls, and I'd still like to do it. I want to audition for the Royal Academy of Dramatic Art. If I get in, will you let me train there?"

The Royal Academy of Dramatic Art was the country's premier training school for actors and actresses, with only 20 applicants in 250 chosen to study. And suddenly Joe Collins's arguments ceased. When Joan asked his permission to try out for the RADA, he agreed.

"I was pretty well floored to hear him agree immediately," Joan's mother admitted later. When the two of them were alone, Elsa asked him why he had changed his mind so quickly.

"I think it's a fine idea," he told her somewhat smugly.

"After all the years you've been objecting?"

"Don't you see?" Joe replied craftily. "This will be the finish! Let her take the exam. She'll never pass it. It will be the end of it!"

He knew the odds. Only a handful survived. Else felt sorry for Joan. In order to help her daughter through what she now considered as a crisis of rejection, Joan's mother took her shopping for a special dress—one with blue polka dots. It was to be her good-luck dress.

Dressed up in her lucky costume, Joan went to the audition where she did a scene from the American play *Our Town* by Thornton Wilder, and read a scene from George Bernard Shaw's *Cleopatra*. Then she came home for the long wait.

When the letter finally came, some weeks later, Joan discovered that she had been accepted at the prestigious drama academy and would be enrolled in the fall.

"There was no prouder man in the whole of the British Isles than one Joe Collins," Joan's mother said.

Joan was fifteen-and-a-half when she joined the Royal Academy. By then she and her father had struck a bargain between them. If she showed no progress after two years of dramatic training, she would agree to give up acting and go to a secretarial school. During the training, Joe would give his daughter a subsistence allowance to live on.

It was at that time, Joan confessed in her autobiography, that she "discovered the opposite sex for the first time." But in those days, sexual contact was not the casual thing it became in the revolutionary 1960s. Then it was limited to petting, necking, kissing, and cuddling. A girl saved her virginity for the man she would marry.

"I suddenly became aware of my sex appeal," Joan wrote later, in a nontypical throwaway line.

David McCallum, the British actor who later made a big hit in American television on "The Man from U.N.C.L.E." as the "Russian" partner, was a member of Joan's RADA class.

"You were the first girl in that class that the rest of us noticed," he told her later.

This was a new experience for Joan. To be noticed, to be desired, to be "in." Yet it was all still a game to her. She was, of course, a young woman with a very definite father complex. Wishing to be desired by him, she was looking—in dime-store psychological terms—for affirmation of her desirability by attracting males.

Joan was never particularly interested in any of them, but she enticed them one by one, won them one by one, and discarded them one by one. "Most of the men and boys I chose were difficult, sometimes unable to love, or to be giving, and that was *always* what intrigued me. Not for me to be wooed and won; I was the wooer, and in being so I was wounded many times."

But sexual games were only part of Joan's life at that time. She was indeed working very hard at learning her trade on the stage. Although she was taken out most of the time for dinner by her dates, she supplemented her subsistence allowance by doing an occasional job modeling.

Once she was even on the cover of *Reveille,* a magazine aimed at the working class, specializing in sexy shots of screen personalities and beautiful models.

Not that she was strictly a magazine-cover type; her forte was posing for the steamy photographs in the women's confession magazines. In one, she was the hunted teenager in a turtleneck about to be raped by a sex maniac in a haunted house. She also modeled teenage clothes for several of the women's magazines. Usually she wore tight blue jeans and bulging plaid shirts. She would wear heavy eye makeup and thick black eyebrows.

In a national magazine she appeared in a picture story on

jazz clubs dressed in an outrageous costume: gold gypsy
earrings, flat ballet shoes, and black polo-necked sweater.
With heavy eye makeup and hair in straight bangs and
ponytail, she was a standout. She appeared with a male
partner in a picture captioned: "The couple who dress *très*
jazz."

At this time, Joan began hanging out in the smoky dives in
Soho, listening to the ragtime and jazz outfits with friends
from RADA. Actually, she was becoming somewhat discour-
aged and disenchanted with RADA. She was not making as
much progress as she had hoped to. The problem was not in
her *appearance*, but in her *speech*.

"With so much in her favor," one of her report cards said,
"this student is hampered by the weakness of her voice. She
seems to lack the confidence to project and make use of the
amount of voice she does possess. If she will make up her
mind to cast away all fear and self-consciousness and *speak
out*, she will find her confidence increasing, and the unsure
element in her acting will disappear. Otherwise it is 'The
Films' for her and that would be such a pity!"

In effect, she did not have the proper English *accent*.
Although the critic speaks of her *tone* and *confidence*, it is
quite obviously something else at fault here. It was, of
course, her delivery that bothered the powers that be. She
was supposed to learn to speak with the conformist and
accepted *accent* of the West End stage.

It was Joe Collins, working in the background, who actually gave that extra added push to his daughter's languishing
career—that little something that made it begin to take off.
When she had been accepted at RADA, her father confessed: "I made a total about-turn and decided to back her
every inch of the way."

He approached Leslie Bloom, Collins and Grade's drama
agent, and asked Bloom to put together a dramatic stock
company for a repertory season. "I'm really doing this to
help my daughter," he told Bloom. "She can play small parts
and help backstage."

And thus Eros Players opened at the Palace Theatre in Maidstone, Kent, in March 1950. During Joan's summer vacation from RADA, she was a member of the company. Her father paid her £3.10s. a week (this was before the modern English coinage had been adopted). Joan appeared onstage in only the last production of the season, playing the maid in Terence Rattigan's comedy *French Without Tears*.

Yet that was enough. Actually, Joe had lost money almost every week the repertory operated, but he was really setting up his daughter in the business. She herself later confessed that it was her father who "bought her a rep." The real reason for her repertory experience was to give the dramatic property "Joan Collins" a chance to list her stage credits.

To do this Joe took out a page in *Spotlight*, Britain's casting directory, with her photograph printed alongside a notice that she was appearing at Maidstone and was available for work.

Soon Bill Watts, a film agent, telephoned him. "She's a great-looking kid," he said about Joan. "Who is she?"

Joe Collins confessed that she was his daughter.

"Well, I may have something for her," Watts said. "They're looking for a girl to play the lead in a film about beauty queens. They want a new face. Can I put your daughter's name forward?"

Of course, Joe said.

And so Bill Watts took over from there. He took Joan to lunch at a posh London restaurant, explaining that he was an agent who represented pretty models—Joan knew who he was, of course—and that he felt she might work out in motion pictures.

Joan, still imbued with the Royal Academy of Dramatic Art's prejudice against film work, and in spite of her discouraging days at RADA over her accent, made her usual half-hearted protest. "But I want to be a *serious* actress." She told Watts that her plans were for a stage career. She would finish her two years at the Royal Academy, do a few seasons in repertory theater, and then try out for the West End.

But naturally Joan was simply echoing the eternal snob-
bery of RADA against "the films." She knew she was not
making good at RADA. She *let* Watts persuade her to try
several roles under his supervision.

It was only a week after she signed with him that she got
her first role. Actually, she tried out for the lead in a film
called *Lady Godiva Rides Again.* It was a story about a
beauty queen and her adventures on the way up and on the
way down.

"The makeup man and the hairdresser who painted and
coiffed me for *Lady Godiva* had learned their craft in the
Dark Ages," Joan reported later.

She did not win the role of Lady Godiva, but she did get
signed on for a bit part. She played one of the beauty
contestants. Dressed in black knit suit, she worked for three
days before the cameras in Folkstone Town Hall, where the
film was made. In the picture, although certainly not in any
of her scenes, were the great Stanley Holloway and Diana
Dors. Also playing was Jean Marsh, who soon afterward was
hired to portray the maid Rose in "Upstairs, Downstairs,"
and later in the series "Nice to Fair."

Two weeks later Joan was hired to do the part of a maid in
a film titled *The Woman's Angle,* with Cathy O'Donnell and
Lois Maxwell, who later was Miss Moneypenny to Sean
Connery's James Bond. Big bucks for the job—£50!

In spite of the minimal money, Joan was suddenly getting
reviews in the press. "Britain's Best Bet Since Jean Simmons." One reviewer wrote: "She has the come-hither eyes
of Ava Gardner, the sultry look of Lauren Bacall, a Jane
Russell figure, and more sex appeal at her age than any other
film actress I've met." At nineteen, too!

The head of the Royal Academy of Dramatic Arts was not
amused. "What's all this *filming* nonsense?" Sir Kenneth
Barnes accosted her one day.

JOAN: It's nothing, sir. I'm just trying to make some
     extra pocket money.

SIR KENNETH: Well, just don't get carried away by it,
my dear. When all is said and done, there is only
one thing that matters, and that's the *theatah*.
JOAN: Right, sir!

In spite of Sir Kenneth's admonitions, Joan continued her
film work. Her third part was Lil in *Judgment Deferred*, a
Southall Studios Thriller—"an exacting and emotional role of
a one-time beautiful young girl, a convict's daughter, ruined
by the colorful and dangerous crowd in which she has sought
pleasure"—according to the script.

The reviews weren't bad. *Evening News:* "Although so
young for her emotional role, Joan comes through with flying
colors!"

At that point she was called to Ealing Studios for a test for
the role of Norma, a runaway juvenile delinquent for the J.
Arthur Rank picture, *I Believe in You*. Ealing was the home
of the marvelous comedies of Alec Guinness, and of many of
the best actors around. Basil Dearden and Michael Relph
were a time-tested producer-director team—they had made
The Blue Lamp and *Kind Hearts and Coronets*—and promised that whoever played Norma would become a star. Besides that, she would also become a member of the Rank
Organization—one of the film plums of the time.

Joan tested with Dirk Bogarde, in a pink baby-doll night-
gown, on an acre-sized bed, wallowing about and kissing. It
wasn't all that simple, however. In all, Joan made three tests
for the role of Norma, meanwhile stalling one of the top-
level principals at Ealing who had high hopes that Joan
would be "nice" to him, if he was "nice" to her. As Joan
wrote later, tongue only partly in cheek:

"I gloomily realized that I had probably blown the part—if
not the producer!"

In spite of the contretemps, Joan *did* get the part. It was
her first role in a major film at a major film studio. She was
now in the big time—even if only in a minor way. She was
billed with such big stars as Laurence Harvey, Celia John-

son, Cecil Parker, and Harry Fowler. Celia Johnson had made a hit playing with Trevor Howard in Noel Coward's *Brief Encounter*.

But it was Larushka Skikne at Rank who intrigued Joan the most—or, as he was known by his non-Lithuanian name, Laurence Harvey. Harvey took full charge of Joan and taught her how to dress, how to order wine, how to read a French menu, how to smoke with elan—and even how to swear like a trooper.

The only thing he did *not* teach her was how to . . . well, Joan would have used the proper four-letter word, even at that tender age. Fuck. Nor would she have minded if he *had* tried to teach her the fundamentals of the act.

At that point in her life, Joan considered her virginity one of those troublesome bits of personal baggage she was required to carry along with her everywhere she went. To her, it merely pointed up her own inexperience in life.

Determined to lose her virginity and acquire a veneer of sophistication and worldliness as soon as possible, she had tried to seduce one of her fellow students at RADA during her first months there. Unknown to her, he was a latent homosexual who was even then not quite sure *what* he was. In the British edition of her autobiography, Joan described her attempts to lose her virginity to this man as "a sado-masochistic relationship."

Later she explained: "I was a girl of sixteen who felt the time was ripe to 'do it,' as we used to say in those days, and the chap I wanted to do it with was unable to do it. Of course, I didn't know."

Quite possibly, her "target" had not fully acknowledged his homosexuality. Because he could not fulfill Joan's expectations, he turned sadistic. He took out all his frustrations on her—bit her, punched her, kicked her—and, true to form, she thought it was all *her* fault.

"Ten years later," Joan related, "he became an actor, did fairly well, had a nervous breakdown onstage one day. He was carried off screaming and yelling. He was sent to a mental home for a year."

Then, with typical off-the-wall humor, Joan wound up her remarks about him: "Probably all to do with the fact that he realized he had missed his chance with me."

Thus the status of Joan's persona at the time she met Laurence Harvey was one of brooding anticipation—about something of which she had no inkling. The problem was that Harvey was then living with Hermione Baddeley, the actress, who was some years his senior. When Harvey introduced Joan to his live-in lover, the dialogue went something like this:

BADDELEY: So this is the one you're seeing, Larry, is it? This is "the new Jean Simmons"?
HARVEY: Well, uh——
BADDELEY (to JOAN): Let me tell you something, my dear. Jean has absolutely nothing to worry about. You don't have her looks, you don't have her talent— and you certainly don't have half the overblown things the newspapers have been saying you have.
JOAN (bursts into tears and rushes off).
BADDELEY: That's right—leave! No guts! That's the trouble with you young ones today! No guts at all!
HARVEY (catching up with JOAN in the street): Don't worry, darling, she doesn't mean it! Come back to the party! I really want you to be friends.
JOAN: Oh, Larry! I'm so humiliated. I can't face that woman. Please take me home.
HARVEY (flagging a cab): Here's her fare. Would you please deliver her home? (Kissing JOAN on the forehead) Love you, darling! Must get back to Totie's. (Exits)
JOAN: Oh! (bursting into tears again).

Joe Collins knew his daughter was getting a good start in the profession, and he was pretty much aware of her personal problems as well. "She was flung suddenly into the environment she had craved since childhood, without having a chance to recover her balance." And of course, it was not easy for her—none of these confrontations with the old pros like Hermione Baddeley were any *fun*.

Joan did not finish her two-year course at RADA. Instead, she learned her dramatic craft the hard way—through hands-on experience in front of the camera. Later on, when Joan Collins had become an international symbol of glamour and beauty, her father said, "It was not luck which brought Joan to where she is today; it was hard graft." "Graft" in the British idiom does not imply dishonesty at all, but simply means grueling sleeves-rolled-up labor.

She would be learning about life and work the old-fashioned way—on the firing line.

Chapter Three

Joan and the Beautiful Beast

Although Maxwell Reed, who died prematurely in 1974, at the age of fifty-five, is today more or less relegated to footnotes in cinema textbooks or in histories of film, he had his day in the late 1940s and early 1950s when he was one of the real heart-throbs of the screen.

Called an "Irish leading man," he came originally from Larne, in Ireland, but spent most of his growing-up days in south London. He served in the Royal Air Force and the merchant navy before being "discovered" by a talent scout.

He affected an American tough-guy attitude and accent to accentuate his basic features of smoldering lust and machismo, but was actually a product of the English repertory system. After acting in repertory at Scarborough, he joined the Rank Organization's Company of Youth—known popularly as the "Rank Charm School"—and soon became a much-sought-after actor.

His heyday was the early postwar years, with most of his pictures made for British film companies, although he did several American movies as well. His roles were patterned after the rough-tough heart-of-gold heroes of the postwar era—and not the tongue-lashing society-baiting angry-young-man type that superseded them.

One of his best-known efforts was *The Brothers,* a story set in a Scottish community, with Reed and his "brother" in love with a Scottish girl from Glasgow, played by Patricia Roc. He was also assigned roles as underworld characters, professional fighters, and so on. Rank's publicity mavens liked to call him "The Beautiful Beast."

By the time Joan Collins had made it up through the minors to the J. Arthur Rank Organization in *I Believe in You,* Maxwell Reed was an established young star being groomed by the company for bigger and better things. In its own way, the Rank brass was following the basic outlines of the American studio system of the late thirties, which had trained young actors and actresses in the ways of acting *and* promoting themselves, as well as in carrying on as "stars" in their own right.

Joan Collins now joined that exclusive club—or "Charm School"—where she and the rest were taught the basics in posture, in carriage, in attitude, in charm, and in elegance. In that same school were two who, like Joan, went on to greater things: Petula Clark and Honor Blackman.

Reed captured Joan's attention totally. She had always had a schoolgirl crush on him, pinning his pictures up in her bedroom and mooning over them. Although he was fourteen years older than she, he was a personable young man, six feet four and a half inches in height, sporting thick wavy black hair, pool-deep black brooding eyes, and the sadistic mouth so fashionable in the rapacious heroes of the postwar era.

Ironically, it was Laurence Harvey—an honest and decent man who had no dishonorable intentions toward Joan Collins at all—who introduced Joan to Reed. The introduction did not take place within the confines of the studio, but at La Rue, a nightclub favored by the young and the bright and famous.

Harvey and Reed had played together in a recent B picture and had been friends for some time.

Joan did not hide her admiration for Reed, and Reed was caught by something in the young actress that fascinated him. Although he did not know of her, he was impressed. At La Rue he ditched the date he had brought with him and joined Harvey and Joan for drinks at Harvey's table.

Joan outdid herself in being being scintillating. Reed was even more impressed by her effervescence and her smarts than he was by her obvious beauty. Although he was then thirty-three and Joan was still in her teens, the two seemed destined for one another. Joan was somewhat put off by Reed's affected American accent, but she paid no attention to any warning bells in her head. She was in the clouds.

The next morning at work Reed telephoned her while she was in the makeup department getting ready for shooting. When he asked her for a date, she accepted immediately. She knew she would be causing trouble at home. Even dates with Harvey had caused consternation with her mother and father—and Harvey was only in his twenties. This man was over the hill!

The best thing to do would be to keep it quiet. Joan agreed to meet Reed on a Sunday at the underground station at Bayswater Road. He zoomed up in a big flashy powder-blue American Buick, instructed her to "Get in, baby!" and waited for her to jump in before he swooped off in high gear. After driving around and around Hyde Park he suddenly headed for Hanover Square, where he pulled up in front of an old Georgian house.

Now warning bells began flashing in Joan's mind. It was Reed's apartment. She swallowed her fear and put on an air of nonchalance; after all, she was always a good actress. Perhaps, after all, this was only a friendly get-together before dinner, or perhaps the theater, or perhaps the opera. Perhaps?

Reed knew Joan's favorite drink was Scotch and Coke,

and he mixed her a huge one in a goblet and handed it to
her. Then he passed over a slim book wrapped up in a plain
brown dust jacket.

REED: Make yourself at home, baby, and have a read
    while I have a bath. I won't be long.
JOAN: (!)

As Reed flowed out of the room into the bath, Joan blinked
and took a deep swallow of the drink to steady her nerves.
What brand of Scotch was that? she wondered. It didn't taste
at all like any Scotch she had ever had.

Casually she opened the book Reed had given her—to be
startled out of her wits. It was filled with erotic drawings of
men and women in interesting sexual positions. At that
point, after leafing through the book with growing apprehension, Joan finished her drink and decided to leave. When
she rose, however, she felt so dizzy she . . .

As she related in her autobiography, the next thing was
"total oblivion"—she was out cold. When she came to, she
found herself and Reed entwined together on the sofa—her
clothes strewn through the apartment, her stockings ripped,
her sweater in tatters.

Joan passed out again. The experienced Reed, taking his
cue from Harvey, who had said that Joan was indeed a
virgin, had concocted a scenario to seduce her with knockout
drops to make the seduction smooth and silken. Besides, he
did not believe for one moment that she *was* a virgin.

Now he grinned at her and asked her how she liked it.

"*Like* it?" Joan cried out. "I *hated* it. . . . It was horrible,
degrading, and demeaning."

There was nothing that could be done about it at that late
moment, and so she finally got out of Reed's flat after he had
tried again and again with her. It was after three in the
morning when she finally got home. There, she was forced to
lie her way through a network of probing questions. The odd
thing was, her parents believed her impossible fibs.

Had she learned her lesson? Hardly. The very next afternoon Reed invited her to a party—and she accepted! Reed was smooth and easy to take, and that night he left her at home with only a chaste kiss on the cheek. And so the dating began.

About this time she told her parents: "Larry introduced me to Maxwell Reed. He *is* gorgeous."

Her father's reaction was uneasy. "Now don't go silly over him. He's a lot older than you and a big star, and he makes the most of it. I've heard he makes scenes in nightclubs. He had a bad reputation around town. The man's a roué, and he's not for you!"

"We fell in love," Joan wrote later. In spite of that, she still detested sex with him, but "gritted" her teeth, and "tolerated it." Her private life was developing into a real whirl with Reed, but meanwhile her professional life was progressing satisfactorily. She continued to shoot *I Believe in You* day by day, and the studio was quite elated at the rushes. Joan's role began to look like the making of her. Even Hollywood had begun rapping on her door, according to Bill Watts.

As was inevitable, her parents found out what was going on between Joan and the thirty-three-year-old Reed. They were appalled at this mismatch. But Reed was a smoothie, and he was able to convince them that he was simply "educating" Joan about stardom. Essentially, he said, he was her mentor, not her lover. They believed him.

Reed wanted Joan to move in with him, but she resisted, knowing that she could never explain away all that to her parents. But ironically, while her romance with him was heating up, his romance with her was cooling off. He had slipped a disc, been forced to have an operation, and the operation had left him momentarily numb below the waist. Panicked that he was to be a cripple for life, he began blaming Joan for his misery.

Reed was in a psychological cul-de-sac, too. His career was definitely on the wane. Joan was beginning to be noticed;

he was beginning to be ignored. Their relationship was a seesaw: one moment warm and passionate, the next cold and cruel.

Joan later speculated, "Because of his disability, Max would only get aroused by sadism. . . . I went along with the beatings and the perversions he thought up. He insisted I pose for some nude Polaroid photographs which he thought might turn him on."

Hoping that his sadistic lapses were only temporary and would vanish when he recovered from the operation, she forced herself to tolerate him. It was at this period that Reed began making strange and offbeat remarks to Joan about sex—pointing out that with Joan's looks, he could make a fortune if she would drop out of the film business and become a high-class courtesan. The unvoiced suggestion seemed to be that he would then act as her "manager"—a cleaned-up term for "pimp." Joan pretended not to hear any of these kinky remarks.

I Believe in You was released and became a blockbuster hit. Joan received accolades for her work. "Joan Collins makes a tremendous impression as the wayward girl," one critic wrote. "She has a dark luscious kind of beauty which puts her in the Jane Russell class, but Joan already seems to be an actress of greater ability. On the showing of this first big film part, she looks like the most impressive recruit to British films for many a moon."

The U.S. critics liked her as well. *Variety* wrote that she had given a "strong dramatic" performance as Norma, the reformed streetwalker. "A dozen of my darkest red roses to Joan Collins," *News of the World* said. "Fire and spirit in her acting and that odd combination of allure and mystery that spells eventual world stardom."

Joan Collins became the first actress that the Rank Organization had put under contract for over a year. The buildup began. No film was in the offing to follow up the popularity of *I Believe in You*. With Reed pounding at her and blaming her success for his failure, Joan finally gave in and agreed to appear with him at the Q Theater, in the stage version of *The Seventh Veil*—the hit that had made James Mason a superstar opposite Ann Todd. Reed played the sadistic piano teacher, and Joan the Ann Todd role.

Reed's sadism surfaced in one scene when he threw her to the stage floor with such force that she was black and blue for days. It was a one-week engagement; Joan was happy when it was over. But immediately they planned to do a follow-up: an adaptation of *Jassy*, another film starring James Mason, this time with Margaret Lockwood.

Then one night Reed changed course and suddenly asked Joan if she would marry him. When she told him he would have to ask her father, he agreed.

Her mother recalled the scene. "Her father and I objected vigorously [to Reed's suggestion of marriage]. They'd met such a short time before, and Joan was only eighteen, entirely too young to take on the responsibility of marriage."

The discussion went on for days. "I was the first to give in," Elsa admitted. "I knew that if we didn't give our permission, they would most certainly elope, and I felt as all mothers feel, that a girl's family must be with her on her wedding day, that the wedding should be a happy, memorable occasion."

Joan's father was opposed to Reed from the beginning. "Mr. Reed," he told the actor, "I have to tell you that you are not the type of husband I envisage for my daughter."

Besides, he felt that Joan was too young to know what she was doing. He blamed Reed for his hand in the affair. "You've got an absolute cheek in coming to my home and confronting me with what you have in mind. I'm telling you here and now that I will not agree to this marriage. Is that clear?"

Joan was beside herself with grief. "Daddy, please!" she interrupted. "I *do* want to marry Max."

Joe Collins turned on Reed once again. "If you want to know the truth, Reed, you're nothing but a dirty——" At this point Collins's language, as he wrote later, "got less polite." It made no difference. Reed was cool and persistent.

"Mr. Collins, Joan and I love one another. I am well able to provide for your daughter. I have a very nice flat in the West End——"

"Reed! Will you please get out of here?"

Then Joan's mother broke in. "Stop it, Joe! Please stop! Be reasonable. Lots of young girls get married and it all works out. Why are you so sure this marriage is wrong for Joan?"

It stunned Joe Collins to have his wife turn on him like that. He did not know that Elsa had already capitulated in order to keep her love for her daughter intact.

The obvious split between Elsa and Joe gave Reed his opening. And he used it. "Well, Mr. Collins," he said, assuming that aggressive, hooded, smoldering attitude he was so good at, "if you don't agree to us getting married, we'll just go off and live together."

That did it. Joe Collins began shouting. "I've had enough of this! You can go on talking it over as much as you like. I am not going to be browbeaten!"

He glowered at Reed and spat out: "You're a lunatic and you can go to hell!"

Beside himself, Joe Collins left the house and wandered disconsolately around the London streets for over six hours. When he returned, Elsa sought him out.

"You heard what Maxwell Reed said, and he meant it," she told him, referring to Reed's threat to set up house together. "If you refuse them permission to marry, she'll go and live with him. You can give children as much advice as you like, but interfering is another matter. It doesn't work. In the end they go their own way."

By now Joe Collins was of a slightly different mind than he had been when he left the house.

"All right," he told Elsa. "If you think it's the only way, *you* can tell them they can be married. I'm not going to get involved in this. *You* can handle it."

The wedding took place at the register office at Caxton Hall, Westminster, on May 24, 1952, the day following Joan's nineteenth birthday. Afterward there was a reception at Ciro's Club. Joan's headmistress from Francis Holland School was among the guests. There were wedding pictures in the paper the next day.

In spite of all the promises, the marriage was doomed from the start. As Joan's mother recalled: "At first everything went well. They set up housekeeping in a penthouse apartment, and Joan tried her hand at cooking. They bought a boat and spent their weekends sailing. They had their careers in common and starred in several plays together."

But it was not all quite that idyllic on the inside. Joan and Reed went to Cannes together for their honeymoon, in Reed's powder-blue Buick. Cannes was a nightmare, with Reed suddenly slipping out of his Dr. Jekyll role into his Mr. Hyde personality.

They were on the beach one day when a couple of French photographers started to snap pictures of Joan. Reed immediately flew into a rage and dragged her back to their quarters, where he proceeded to rough her up. He told her in no uncertain terms that he owned her now that they were married, and that she would not be permitted to look at any other men unless he told her she could.

Throughout the honeymoon Reed continued to make her life miserable. She was finding this "other" side of his nature less than attractive now. There had only been a hint of it earlier; a perceptive woman would have anticipated trouble, but Joan had not. In fact, even his outer image now somehow came into focus for what it was.

She had known that he dyed his hair black and then permed it to give it that sleek quality it had on screen. She knew that he usually wore eyebrow and eyelash makeup— thick with mascara—to photograph well. But even in private he would dress up in a pair of shorts and wear black thong sandals that laced up the sides. When he walked anywhere, the three gold medallions around his neck clanked together loudly.

"He got more wolf whistles in the south of France than I did," Joan said.

For her next job, Joan reported to Segovia, Spain, where she would shoot her scenes for *Decameron Nights*, a collection of Boccaccio's tales linked together by the box-office casting of Louis Jourdan and Joan Fontaine. Joan Collins would play Fontaine's handmaid in one segment and Jourdan's lover in another. This was not a Rank film; Joan was being lent out to an American group for about $25,000. Joan, of course, got her usual £50 a week during shooting; Rank pocketed the difference in the manner of all film studios at the time.

After about a week, Reed tired of the Riviera and drove over to Spain to join Joan on the set. He was in a nasty mood. His mood clouded Joan's own and she began scrapping with the director, Hugo Fregonese, who felt that actors and actresses were a necessary evil in an otherwise bearable world.

She was glad to get back to London to start another picture for Rank. Actually, the critics were not at all savage to the Boccaccio anthology, mentioning Joan and several of the supporting actors by name. It was pointed out that the director and the writer had failed to elicit any spicy comment or excitement in the production.

In *Cosh Boy*, Joan's next film, she played the usual delinquent teen-ager, this time named Renée, the girlfriend of the lead. The picture was released in the United States as *The Slasher*. There were a number of very obvious sex scenes in the picture, the first a brutal seduction. Later, when Renée discovers herself pregnant from the rape, she tries to commit suicide. The picture became the first of Britain's X-rated films—the new rating system had just been established.

At home with Reed, Joan was being treated to the downside of his nature once again. He was unable to get work. His screen persona was a bit old-fashioned at this juncture, and he had trouble getting the familiar macho roles. The swashbucklers were not making as much money at the box office as formerly.

Finally he did get a job on *Sea Devils*, to be shot in Jersey by Raoul Walsh, the American director. This was a story, modeled loosely on Victor Hugo's epic sea novel, *Toilers of the Sea*, in which Reed played a piratical and muscular heavy. He was the baddie to Rock Hudson's hero.

After they finished the pictures they were both working on, Joan and Reed played another local repertory production, Thornton Wilder's *The Skin of Our Teeth*. Joan was Sabina, the eternal vamp. Reed played the sixty-year-old Mr. Antrobus. Under a heavy makeup job, he looked reasonably aged.

Again the pair were teamed in a Rank film, *The Square Ring*, a boxing picture. This was Reed's vehicle, not Joan's. She played a cameo role in it. And yet there were repercussions at home after shooting. Now Reed was blaming his wife for upstaging him on the set!

Joan got a juicy role in her next picture, *Turn the Key Softly*. This was a story about the parole system in Britain. The script followed the lives of three women just released from prison. *The New York Times* reviewer, identified only as "A. W.," took special notice of Joan:

"There also is Stella Jarvis, a Cockney lady of the evening and no stranger to durance vile, who is anxious to start a new life with an honest and loving bus driver." As for her, "Joan Collins is properly lush and brassy as the Cockney charmer who almost, but not quite, reverts to her gay way of life." A. W.'s use of the word "gay" did not refer to homosexuality, but simply to the basic meaning of the word in a traditional sense.

Enthused by notices like that one about Joan's acting abilities, the Rank Organization began giving her a big publicity buildup, calling her "Britain's Best Bad Girl," and similar compliments. On the strength of all this good publicity, an Italian company decided to borrow her to play Juliet opposite Laurence Harvey's Romeo. Tests were made, even though neither Joan nor Harvey thought she was young enough or callow enough to do the part.

The director looked at the test and decided he wanted her—but he demanded one thing. She did not have the right kind of nose. To be Juliet, she must have a *Roman* nose. In other words, she had the role, but she must get a nose job to keep it. At this point Joan finally balked, called in Bill Watts, and let him do the screaming and yelling.

Somebody else got the part.

Her next picture was another loan from Rank, this time for a picture called *Our Girl Friday*, an adaptation of Noel Langley's novel of the same name, produced by Langley and George Minter. Joan was the star, Sadie, the stereotypical spoiled brat of that era. The story involves the shipwreck of a pleasure cruise that casts four of the passengers on a de-serted island—where Joan lives with three men for the dura-tion of the picture.

The scenes were shot on the Island of Majorca in the Mediterranean just off the coast of Spain. The three men opposite Joan included Kenneth More, who had just come off a huge success in *Genevieve*, George Cole, and Robert-son Hare as a grim and proper old economics professor.

Although the picture was a big success and made a lot of money both in Britain and in the United States, not all the reviews were pro-Collins. "A. W." in *The New York Times* hedged his good notice by taking a swipe at Joan in this manner: "As the sought-after damsel Joan Collins is perfect for the bikini suit in which she swims and in which she undulates across the beach. And she doesn't make a bad impression in a properly tattered dress, either. She makes no impression as an actress."

Nevertheless, the public loved it. And so did one Ameri-can out in Hollywood: Darryl Zanuck, the head of Twentieth Century-Fox Pictures.

Part of Joan's rapture at working on this picture was being away from Reed. She was quite aware that her marriage was not a success. It was only a matter of time before something drastic had to happen. In order to forestall whatever that was to be, Joan begged Bill Watts to get her a play somewhere out of town.

And so it was that she moved from film to the stage for *The Praying Mantis,* in which she was lent out by Rank. She was a Byzantine empress whose interesting sex wrinkle was to seduce a warrior, and then send him off to be executed. The play was not well received, but it went on tour for three weeks in seaside resorts—and that was it. Not a success. But Joan enjoyed the camaraderie of playacting.

Reed was in and out of town trying to get work in the action pictures he thrived on. At that time, Rome was into the spaghetti-Western mode, and there were swashbucklers galore coming out of that country. But Reed was worried about his overall career. It was going nowhere. Program pictures were not exactly the answer to a sagging career.

On one of his home visits, he took Joan out to Les Ambassadeurs, a nightclub in London. This was then a very "in" place for the acting fraternity, with actors and producers and directors using it as a home away from home and a place to meet, eat, and cheat. It occupied a moldering old Georgian house in Hamilton Terrace.

At this time, Joan was involved in rehearsals for *Claudia and David,* a stage comedy from America about a child bride and her husband. During drinks, Reed began chatting with an Arab who was seated near him. Even then oil money was enabling the lucky few in charge of the Persian Gulf countries—never a people to eschew the sybaritic life anyway—to enjoy life among the beautiful people in London and Paris and on the Riviera.

Reed's new friend was Sheik Abdul Ben Kafir, according to his introduction to Joan. He was an aged, baggy-eyed man with a thick accent and a lascivious glitter in his deep-set eyes.

The scene that followed could have come right out of one of the motion pictures that Reed and Joan made. He pulled Joan onto the dance floor and began whispering in her ear.

REED: Ten thousand pounds! He'll pay you ten thousand pounds for *one night!*

JOAN: You must be kidding!

REED: What's more—I can even watch!

JOAN: I beg your pardon, Max. Are you *seriously* suggesting I go to bed with that disgusting old man for
money?

REED: You bloody little idiot! Ten grand! Tax free! Do
you realize what we can do with that sort of money?
We can go to Hollywood. We can have a holiday in
Florida. We can even buy a cottage in the country.
You better start cashing in on what you've got,
girl—doing plays at the Q for ten quid a week is
not going to make us rich in our old age.

JOAN: I won't do it, Max!

REED: One night, baby—that's all. One night with Abdul
and we can say "Fuck you" to all of 'em, be off to
Hollywood. What do you say, baby?

JOAN: Never! (Raising her voice) I will never, ever, ever
do that. Never in a million years, Max. Take your
sheik and go to hell, both of you! (She rushes out of
the club, leaving a stunned silence behind her.)

REED: Baby—

Next stop: home.

Joan faced her mother and father, but addressed her next
words to him exclusively: "You were right. I should have
listened to you."

And her father's answer was as unhappy as Joan's confession. "Why does this have to be the one time in my life that
I've been about to say, 'I told you so'?"

It was all over. Joan moved her things out of Reed's
apartment and rarely saw him even professionally after the
break. There was no divorce immediately. British law held
that a marriage had to be in effect at least three years before
one of the principals could file for divorce.

Joan lived at home—when she was in England. The rest

of the time she was traveling from place to place making movies.

There was one attempt at reconciliation, but nothing came of it.

Joe Collins once analyzed Joan's first marriage: "In retrospect, I am sure that during their relationship, Reed had his justifiable frustrations. His career began, inexplicably, to peter out just as Joan was becoming a real star. Joan, so young, having fallen in love with his film-star image and not the man himself, lacked the understanding and compassion vital to pull a marriage through a bad patch. She had no trust in her husband. When Reed became violent, Joan had only one instinct: self-preservation. She was frightened of him."

Chapter Four

The Hollywood Connection

lthough the breakup of her first marriage within months of its inception was a blow to Joan's ego, in many ways the change brought with it a breath of fresh air to her life. In effect, it underlined the different layers of her own existence: the personal life, and the professional one, or ones. From her early years, Joan had never really dreamed about being an ordinary housewife; she had dreamed of being an entertainment personality. If that kind of life meant bruised ego and battered persona, then that's the kind of life it would have to be.

It was time for making a long, hard choice—and her decision was not really a very hard one to make. She would be what she had always wanted to be: a professional woman. But in the matter of careers, she did have another option to exercise. Would she go on in film? Or would she opt for the stage?

She had loved the backstage life even at the Q Theater, far from the West End big time in London. "I loved the old drafty dressing rooms with the musty mothball smells of a

thousand ancient costumes and stage greasepaint. Our troupe
would sit for hours after the show in seedy pubs and even
seedier digs, talking about acting, about our lives and
aspirations—gossiping, drinking, playing cards, and judging
ourselves and each other."

But in film there was always the advantage of money—
perhaps not big money yet, but more money than on the
stage. In the end the decision was made for her when the
Rank Organization—with whom she and Bill Watts had been
negotiating now for some time—agreed to sell her contract
to Twentieth Century-Fox. This was largely due to the
machinations of Darryl F. Zanuck, who had become interested in her acting ability and thought she might have star
potential.

But before her Hollywood career was assured, Joan did
one last picture as a loan-out from the Rank Organization
to a Warner Brothers unit working in Rome. In a way,
this picture was really the turning point of her career.
Because of her work in it, Zanuck decided to take a flier
on her. The picture was one of those big dripping epics
about Egyptian history called *Land of the Pharoahs*. Joan
landed the really scrumptious part of Princess Nellifer—the
lead!

Pharoahs was a picture loaded with talent—although a lot
of it never really got up onto the screen. Jack Hawkins
headed the cast. Howard Hawks was the director. And the
script was written by Harry Kurnitz and—of all people!
—William Faulkner.

This was the early fifties, and Rome—in fact, most of
Italy—was in a state of postwar ecstasy and euphoria. Why
shouldn't Rome be happy? It had lost the war and was now
being revived by the victor's money! It was a matter of fun
and games from daybreak to sunset—and more fun and
games from sunset to daybreak again. It was, indeed, "the
sweet life."

Elsa Collins accompanied her daughter to Rome during
the shooting of the picture. She was, in effect, a sort of

chaperone over Joan during those days. But she was in no
way the strict duenna; besides, she and Joan had reached a
sort of understanding between them. Joan would keep things
in hand so that nothing bad would show. Elsa was practical
enough to know that if she put her foot down too hard, she
would be left with nothing to put her foot down *on*. But
perhaps, she hoped, Joan would be smart enough not to get
involved with another man so soon after the debacle with
Maxwell Reed.

Fond hope.

The vacuum left by the absence of Maxwell Reed—if it
might be called that—was soon filled by another actor, this
one playing opposite Joan in *Land of the Pharoahs*. He was
Sydney Chaplin, the second son of Charlie Chaplin, the
great film comedian, by Lita Grey. Named after his uncle,
Charlie Chaplin's brother, Syd Chaplin—also a great silent
picture comic actor—Sydney was a tall, dark, and handsome
young man in his late twenties.

What attracted Joan to him was his bouncy, intransigent
sense of humor—and his vocabulary. The early fifties was a
time of changing values, and one of the biggest changes was
occurring in literary and dramatic circles. The four-letter
words, which had branded one as a lowbrow and a loser up
to that period in history, suddenly became "in." Jet-setters,
beautiful people, all those everyone else looked up to—
abruptly adapted and spouted all the Anglo-Saxon words
from Elizabethan times that had been formerly used only by
ditch-diggers, poltroons, and other miscreants.

Young Chaplin was adept at using every basic scatalogical
and anatomical word he could think of, and then using it
again in a slightly different sense, and then once again in a
final and humorous sense. He larded his conversation with
all the unmentionables, at the same time composing his
sentences into laugh-provoking statements. He was a racon-
teur of enormous talent, a holder of center stage wherever
he was, a magnet of attention in any crowd of sophisticated
and upscale people.

Although Joan had sworn off sex for the time being to hone her dramatic skills and reestablish her career, and Elsa Collins was around to remind her of her promises to her art, it did not take Sydney Chaplin, the great kidder, very long to kid Joan into bed with him. One of his amusing lines that wowed Joan the most at the time was quoted in Joan's autobiography:

"Well," he told her, "I may not be much of a lover, but I'm a funny fuck!"

In Chaplin's Alfa-Romeo or his red Ferrari, he would squire Joan down to the various suburbs of Roma for parties, or to the beaches at Ostia—where the Tiber empties into the Tyrrhenian Sea—or Fregene, on the coast to the north, where the two of them would cavort on the sand or at the night spots or wherever there was gaiety and laughter.

"He's wonderful, handsome, talented, the very best in every way," Joan once described him. "Real cool," in the argot of the day.

But not the best in every way for her at that time. He was a go-getter who never let up, and at twenty-eight still vigorous and unputdownable. When Joan insisted on staying home and going to bed early in her room at the Hotel de la Ville, Sydney would laugh and go out with the gang anyway. And because he continued to go out with them, Joan decided she would accompany him and enjoy herself, too. Somehow she got around any obstacles put up by her mother.

Besides that, she was beginning to overeat for the first time in her life—especially pasta and all that starchy Italian fare. She began to put on some weight. But the weight was not the problem so much as the sudden evidence of Joan's navel.

Navel?

The costume designers had dreamed up an ensemble for her, with a low skirt and a gold bra—and nothing in between. Joan's navel showed in all its glory. At the time, of course, the Hays Office—then the arbiter of public taste— did not approve of the photographing and screening of the human navel.

"Cover it up!" ordered Howard Hawks.

According to Joan's recollection of the incident, it was she who suggested, tongue in cheek, covering it up with something like a Band-Aid—dyed skin-color.

The costume designer was ecstatic. "Not a Band-Aid, but a ruby!"

And so the scene was rehearsed with a genuine (stage) ruby, stuck in place with liquid adhesive. When it came to shooting the scene, however, Joan found herself self-consciously pulling in her stomach—and *that* caused the ruby to pop out!

Much laughter. Much reshooting. Much eventual stress.

Joan also got into trouble with Howard Hawks because of Sydney. He was playing Trenah, who falls in love with Princess Nellifer and declares his love for her in an impassioned scene. Because of Sydney's amusement at his own weird garb—he was wearing pointed slippers and a long skirt that hung down over his knees—he began to blow his lines with her, giggling uncontrollably.

With him going up in smoke at every utterance, Joan, too, got the heaves and began to break up. The takes went on and on. Finally even the crew began to roll around on the set. Hawks had to call off the scene and chew out his two young actors in front of everybody.

Chastened, they got on with the scene the following day.

However, it was not all fun and games in Rome. One day Joan looked up from the sand on the beach and was shocked to find Maxwell Reed, her ex, standing there gazing down at her with bemusement. She had heard he had been signed up for *Helen of Troy*, then being filmed in Rome across town.

Reed was not on a pleasure visit. He came at her in one of his typical but outrageous attacks. He had kept the nude Polaroid shots he had taken of her on their honeymoon. He told Joan that he had been offered a lot of money for the whole set by one of the Italian picture magazines that dealt in that kind of thing.

This was a squeeze that could hurt Joan. Her contract had the usual morals clause in it that forbade the publication of nude pictures of any kind. These were topless shots—not such a hot item today—but then dynamite in the strict moral climate of the time.

JOAN: What do you want for them?
REED: All the rings I gave you when we were married. Wedding, engagement, and the topaz.
JOAN: I'll have someone bring them to your hotel.
REED: And the check. Don't forget to sign it.

Reed was referring to a blank check he had sent to Joan from her personal account, requesting that she sign it for his convenience.

JOAN: I don't have much money. There's only a couple of hundred pounds in my account.
REED: The check and the rings at my hotel tomorrow night, or the magazine gets the pictures. *Ciao*, kid.

In the event, the exchange was never made. Joan fulfilled her end of the bargain, but Reed retained the pictures, substituting a number of publicity stills that the Rank Organization had in their files for promotional purposes. However, the pictures did not appear in print. It was obvious that Reed was holding onto them for bigger and better things in the future.

Joan was pretty much lost amidst all the big and small names in *Land of the Pharoahs,* but by the end of the picture, she was back in London with her agent wrapping up negotiations with Twentieth Century-Fox and Rank for a change of management. The tough part was working out her salary; it should be large enough for someone of her stature, accomplishments and nationality. The agreed-on figure was $1,250 dollars a month.

Now she became a client of Famous Artists Agency, represented by John Shepbridge, one of the agency's London officials. But it was really Charles K. Feldman, the top executive agent at Ashley Famous who had put in the good word with Zanuck at Fox, who was responsible for her successful negotiations.

At the age of twenty, Joan was making a fabulous salary, even for a movie actress.

In the interim, between her work in Rome and her next film in California, Joan and Sydney visited Charlie Chaplin in Vevey, Switzerland, where they stayed for three days. Then they went to London, where Joe Collins met Sydney for the first time.

"I was not impressed with Sydney Chaplin," he wrote later. "I do not care for young men who blame their parents for their shortcomings." As a matter of fact, Joe added, "He seemed to me to be a dissatisfied young man with a chip on his shoulder." No love was lost between them from the beginning. Elsa was simply resigned to the whole thing.

After London, the two lovers went to Paris.

Meanwhile, the negotiations between Rank and Fox were now concluded, and Shepbridge telephoned Joan in Paris with instructions to return to London for the trip to California where she would report for work at Fox.

Sydney had no idea at that time where he would be working next. The two lovers separated in Paris, with Joan feeling gloomily that she would never see him again, but looking forward to her new life in California.

The press did a human interest photo story of her in London, with the headline "Britain's Bad Girl Goes to Hollywood."

Actually, she flew to New York where she stayed for a token few days to absorb the atmosphere before flying on to the West Coast. It was there, as she later told a magazine writer, that she discovered "slot machines"—with which she was totally unfamiliar.

"Drop in a quarter," she said, "and zip! Out comes a

package of cigarettes. Put in a dime, push a thingamabob, and you get enough candy to make you sick."

She was particularly intrigued by the automats, which were then still functioning in the city. "A few dimes and quarters dropped into the right slots will get you a full meal!" she chortled. "I was never so delighted with anything in my life. Couldn't get past the machines, literally."

When she landed at Los Angeles International Airport, she didn't have a cent on her. "Had to borrow fifty dollars from a nice studio chap who met me."

Southern California fascinated her from the beginning—it was so totally different from New York and London. It was the spaciousness and the endless variety of the place that got to her. There were the posh areas—Beverly Hills, Bel Air, Westwood—and the seedy and tacky—Hollywood, East Los Angeles—and the ramshackle slums all around the core of the city, which really didn't have a center at all.

She found herself rooms in a transient residential hotel. As yet, she did not have the money to buy a car. But the problem of living in Los Angeles without transportation was brought to her attention forcibly on her very first days there.

The place she lived in did not have a coffee shop in it, nor was there one anywhere in sight. Joan started walking down the street in search of a place to eat. She walked and walked, but all she found were houses and more houses, and no place where food was sold—not even a deli.

And then the scene turned into a soap opera. Joan suddenly was aware that someone was walking behind her, step for step—a kind of stalking gait. It was a man, wearing a leather jacket and a hat pulled down over his eyes. It seemed that he was indeed following her.

"I walked faster and he walked faster. So I slowed down and all at once he was there beside me. He took hold of my arm and grinned."

MAN (grinning): Hello, baby. Out for a little stroll?
JOAN (pulling her arm free): What do you want?
MAN (laughing): How about taking a walk with me?

Joan began talking fast then. "I told him, of course, he was a gentleman and would understand that while I knew walking with him would be nice, it would be impossible because I must get home at once."

He stared at her. "All right, kid. Good night." Then, in a bit right out of a Bogart movie, he turned around as he walked away and tipped his slouch hat to her.

Wow! Did life ever imitate art in Los Angeles!

When Joan arrived at Twentieth Century-Fox, the days of the big studios and the studio system were just about on their way to total oblivion. Fox was a good studio, but it had certainly seen better days; box-office receipts were declining. Television was on the horizon and beginning to make all the studio heads nervous. The Golden Age seemed just a bit tarnished on the silver screen—which really wasn't all that silver anymore, with color coming on strong.

But the studio was still loaded with big, expensive talent, including Robert Wagner, Gene Tierney, Joanne Woodward, Clifton Webb, Susan Hayward, Debra Paget, and even Marilyn Monroe, although she was on her way down the tubes after a sensational career.

Joan's first assignment was a part in a creaky and almost unbelievable script based on Queen Elizabeth I's romance with Sir Walter Raleigh. Most of this was made up from scratch, of course. It had been twelve years since Bette Davis, who was fated to play Elizabeth, had made her huge hit with Errol Flynn, called *Elizabeth and Essex*. Richard Todd was cast as Sir Walter, and Joan was to play Elizabeth's innocent lady-in-waiting, Beth Throgmorton. It was her sad fate to fall in love with Raleigh and become pregnant by him. All the while, Raleigh was playing footsie with the queen and trying to retain his head. It was a reprise of Joan's roles in *Cosh Boy* and *I Believe in You*.

But the costumes were fantastic. Joan was all tarted up in laces and farthingales and petticoats and more petticoats. Even so, she managed to catch a few lashes of the famous Davis tongue. "She had a scathing wit and was not known for mincing words," Joan wrote. "I thought it best to keep a low profile around her."

The picture was released as a kind of oddity—a reminder, in a way, of the greatness of a Hollywood that was no longer in existence. There was Bette Davis, her face covered realistically with white rice-powder, as Good Queen Bess wore when she was beginning to mildew, and there was this old baggage making romantic passes at a much younger Richard Todd.

Even so, Joan was not lost entirely. Bosley Crowther, then doing the daily reviews for *The New York Times*, wrote: "As for Joan Collins as the court lady whom Raleigh secretly weds, she is pretty and mildly vivacious, adequate to the plot."

The wedding took place in the town of London, where Raleigh was imprisoned by Elizabeth after she discovered that her gallant courtier had gotten Beth Throgmorton pregnant.

What saved Joan during those gloomy weeks in which she was acclimating herself to the strange Hollywood social scene was the arrival of Sydney Chaplin. The two of them moved into a small apartment up in Beverly Glen, only five minutes from the Fox lot, where they resumed living together.

Life was not smiling on Sydney. He was unable to get work. The reason he had come to the West Coast was the fact that he had failed even to get picture work in Europe or London. Hollywood did not beckon, either. And so he was playing golf and cards and watching that new phenomenon, television.

Basically a European type, Chaplin loved to sit around at sidewalk cafés and shoot the breeze with the guys. He loved to party and to drink and to eat. He wanted the ambience of the big cities and the swash of the Riviera. Plus, he lived movie work. He loved the lights and the cameras and the girls and the directors and the camaraderie of the profession.

Chaplin and Joan were not left totally out in the cold in the weird social stratification of Hollywood. They were able to break into one level of the complex society. It was called the Gene Kelly set. Sydney was taken in with open arms; Joan with considerably less enthusiasm. However, she was always welcomed when she came in with Sydney, and she took what she could get.

It was in that group that she met Marilyn Monroe one night. Joan was unusually disconcerted to find the fabulous Monroe quite shy, quite diffident, and carelessly coiffed. She was cast to play the part of Evelyn Nesbit in an upcoming movie about the scandalous White-Thaw-Nesbit triangle that resulted in the melodramatic murder of architect Stanford White by playboy Harry K. Thaw in a public restaurant in New York City in 1906.

The problem was that not only was Monroe cutting up and playing coy with the studio heads, but she was thirty years old and Nesbit had been only seventeen or eighteen when she had precipitated the "murder of the century." The picture was to be titled *The Girl in the Red Velvet Swing*. It was only a matter of several months before Monroe was out of the cast and others were being tested for the role—including Joan Collins.

Joan won the role. Her second picture on the Fox lot would be *The Girl in the Red Velvet Swing*, and she would be playing the title role! She would work opposite Ray Milland as the famous architect White and Farley Granger as the dissolute playboy Thaw.

There was only one problem. Joan was a stranger to the American moviegoing public. Although she had appeared in several movies, no print publicity had appeared on her. In the public mind she was virtually a nonentity, and the studio flack was called in immediately to take care of that problem. A suitable bio was quickly assembled and stories were routinely scheduled for the movie fan magazines and even some of the big nationals.

"Cool, Crazy, and Jolly Exciting," was the title of a piece in *Photoplay*. Only two months later, the same magazine printed "The Lady Is Dangerous." In that second story, it even showed her in a still with Sydney Chaplin, with whom she was actually living at the time. The piece mentioned her "interest" in Chaplin, but went on to say that her interest had "reportedly ended." Her separation from Maxwell Reed, her legal husband, was glossed over with a statement about "plans" for a divorce:

"Asked if she had learned anything from marriage, she answered instantly, 'Yes, not to do it again.' " The divorce would be in the works, the same writer noted, "as soon as possible." Joan was described as a properly British young woman, endowed with "an English propriety." Proof of this was advanced by an anecdote about a publicity man in Rome during the filming of *Land of the Pharoahs* who had wanted to call her "The Kiss Girl."

"It was shocking really," Joan was quoted to have complained. "Complete strangers would ask me for a kiss. I had to be quite sharp with some of them."

All this did not sit well with Sydney Chaplin, who seemed to be surfacing in the public prints as some kind of sleazy playboy with whom Joan was "going" at the moment. One of the people with whom both Sydney and Joan got along very well at the time was Arthur Loew, Jr., a member of the elite Hollywood social set. His grandfather, Marcus Loew, was the founder of Metro-Goldwyn-Mayer Studios; another grandfather was Adolph Zukor, one of the big movers and shakers of the old studio system. Arthur was more or less a spoiled kid who wanted to be a playboy, and who dabbled in writing and producing feature films just for the heck of it.

One night when Sydney preferred to stay home watching television rather than go out to the first press screening of *The Virgin Queen*, he suggested that Joan call Loew and go with him. She did so, and when the two of them ended up at a joint on La Cienega after the show, they talked for hours and hours until it was early in the morning.

With Arthur in the wings, and with Sydney not necessarily center stage in her life, Joan came to decision time once again in her young life. It had to do with Sydney and with Arthur. Unable to accompany Chaplin one Friday to the Raquet Club in Palm Springs for the weekend, Joan loaned him her new car, suggesting he drive out to the airport in Palm Springs on Saturday afternoon to pick her up after she had flown to the desert resort.

When she finally got to Palm Springs, melting and cursing in the formidable desert heat, she found no Sydney, no messages, no car or taxi available to get into town. Storming about the place, she finally got on the phone and summoned a cab from Palm Springs proper, which arrived steaming hot and shuddering. It got her to the hotel, where she found Mr. Chaplin in the bar.

Her live-in lover was drinking there comfortably with Gene Kelly and several of his cronies, deep in the complicated ritual of swilling down lush concoctions dreamed up by the imaginative bartender. They were, according to Joan's account, drinking alphabetically, and had already passed through Amaretto to Drambuie, to—and were now on V for vodka.

The confrontation that followed was right out of one of the TV soaps that Sydney loved to watch. Joan, bored by television, did not realize she was playing such a scene as it progressed. But she was a natural. And she made up her own dialogue as she went along. So did Sydney.

JOAN: Sydney Chaplin, I let you borrow my car; I paid to fly on a bumpy two-engine plane to this godforsaken hole for aging tennis bums to meet you for a relaxing weekend, and you don't even *meet the plane!*

CHAPLIN (looking sheepish): Well, gee, Joan—— (He downs his Smirnoff in a gulp)

JOAN (losing her cool): Fuck you, Sydney! Fuck you.
    Fuck you. Fuck you. Fuck you!
CHAPLIN (staggering to his feet): Fuck you, too!
JOAN: Well, that will be the last time you will *ever*
    fuck me again, Sydney!

In the words of Joan's own life story:
"And it was."

Joan soon moved out of the Beverly Glen place she and
Chaplin had shared for such a short time, and rented an
apartment on Olive Drive. It was just off the Sunset Strip,
not far from Ciro's and the Mocambo, and perfect for her
intentions.

Almost as if by magic, Arthur Loew took over as a replace-
ment for Sydney Chaplin, and they would have their long
talks over drinks after parties and other types of Hollywood
bashes. It was during one of these parties—one at the Oscar
Levants' (friends of Loew's)—that Joan met the young actor
James Dean. Dean had just purchased a brand-new shiny
silver Porsche.

Joan wrote that she got to talking to Dean and dared him
to take her out in his new car. He drove her through the
streets of Los Angeles and Santa Monica, cutting in and
out of traffic, bragging to her about how "totally safe" the
Porsche was. Joan, who had been drinking somewhat more
heavily than usual, found herself sobering up fast at Dean's
wild driving. Somewhat shaken, she thanked him when it
was over, and vowed never again to do that little bit. Several
months later, Dean was dead, killed in an accident in his fast
little "totally safe" silver Porsche.

In Fox's buildup of Joan Collins, someone at the studio
maneuvered *Life* magazine into using a portrait of her in her
"red velvet swing" for a cover. There were a lot of other
articles in other levels of the print media, all giving the
public a view of the new sensation from Britain.

When the movie was finally released, the audience pre-
views were pretty good, but the film did not fare well with

the critics. Bosley Crowther at *The New York Times* did a rather long piece on the motion picture. It was an important production, one carefully scripted by Walter Reisch and Leigh Brackett (Brackett had been responsible for several successful Hollywood murder mysteries and many classic science-fiction stories).

What Crowther objected to was the treatment of the rather interesting and dramatic triangle of New York's famous architect, the Middle West's notorious playboy, and the beautiful girl caught in the middle. The picture that resulted was treacly, to say the least—in Crowther's view. He called it a "foray into the realm of soap-opera." This was the kiss of death on a film, especially when voiced in the medium of print.

Soaping up the very good and very true story of this crazy triangle succeeded only in vitiating its basic strengths. This was particularly true of the way the role of Evelyn Nesbit had been written. Instead of a tragic victim of the love-hate emotional tantrums of two public men, with her in the middle and ruined by the notoriety of the murder in public, the role was turned into that of a poor little female victim on the order of Charles Dickens's Little Nell.

"It is a piteous victim of love's injustice that is indicated in this film," Crowther noted, "and it is such an absurd, old-fashioned creature that a dewy-eyed Joan Collins plays. Miss Collins acts incredibly naïve. When she has to speak such lines as 'Look, Harry, you've been perfectly wonderful to me' or 'I'm sorry, I am not the girl you thought I was,' she manages to make the soapy clichés sound even more sudsy than they are."

The failure of the film was symptomatic of the films of that era. The studios did not really know that they had passed through the Golden Age, and that naïveté and sentimentality were no longer savored by the public or by the critics. The world had changed; the only thing that had not changed was the studio system itself.

Ray Milland and Farley Granger fared somewhat better,

but not much. Crowther finished his long piece with this
sardonic comment: "Outside of the brightly decorative and
rococo setting and costumes, there is practically nothing to
warrant attention to *The Girl in the Red Velvet Swing*."

Actually, from that point on, most of the pictures Joan
played in and the roles she played were not warmly praised
by any of the critics. She had apparently hit her peak in
films. She was now too old to play teen-age ingenues pursued by rapists and evil men; she was too young and inexpe-
rienced to play older shrews and ancient tarts. She was in a
position where it was impossible to find any roles for her.

Her affair with Sydney Chaplin was dead and buried. Her
film career was definitely on hold.

She was barely twenty-two years old.

But bad luck comes in threes. The third jolt was waiting
for her, right around the corner.

Chapter Five

Life with the Boys

For her next picture, Joan Collins was loaned out by Twentieth Century-Fox to MGM for a remake of one of its earlier triumphs: Clare Boothe Luce's *The Women*. Called *The Opposite Sex* now, the picture featured Joan in the role of the sex bitch Crystal—ironically, a very interesting name for its foreshadowing of the name of her rival (the non-sex bitch) in a television series by which she would become internationally renowned years later. Crystal was the role played by Joan Crawford in the original MGM film.

Crystal, in fact, *is* the kernel of Alexis Carrington—the TV role that later made Joan. Crystal is shrewd, bitchy, sexy, and conniving. And in the MGM picture, Joan was surrounded by a prestigious cast: June Allyson as the innocent victim of her machinations, Ann Sheridan as an over-the-hill chorine, Ann Miller, Dolores Gray, and Carolyn Jones.

It should have been a ball.

But, to paraphrase Adlai Stevenson's famous statement about the election he lost—"Something happened to me on

the way to the White House. . . ."—something happened to
Joan on the way to the studio.

Dining out one evening with Arthur Loew, Jr., Joan had
noticed a headline on a newspaper reading "Actor Sues
Actress for $1,250 Support per Month!" Wondering who the
poor woman was in this strange reverse-English lawsuit,
Joan picked up the paper and to her astonishment discovered that *she* was the victim. Maxwell Reed, the wife-barterer
and porno-purveyor, was suing her! He had beat her to the
punch!

The body of the story read:

> *Los Angeles, March 1.* Joan Collins's estranged husband
> today asked that the pert British actress pay him $1,250
> a month separate maintenance. English actor Maxwell
> Reed, 31, who charged cruelty and desertion in his
> Superior Court suit, said that he earned less than $1,000
> in the past year and was now unemployed.

Reed then went on to say that he had made his wife the
success she was. "I loved her," he said. "She left me to go to
Hollywood. Now I can't get a job."

Her eyes widening, Joan studied the story again. Its overall implication was that Joan had run out on her faithful,
hard-working mate. There was no indication that Reed's
problems were his own fault. As she knew, he had been
having trouble getting work even before he had met her.
Here he was, "practically destitute," with his wife making a
fortune in Hollywood. She had not been with him in nine
months. "I think she owes me something," Reed said.

Later on, Joan's mother and father sent her clippings from
the London papers about the lawsuit. One of them showed
Reed in a photograph, his eyes, as usual, heavily mascaraed,
dressed in a cashmere sweater, holding a picture of Joan to
his chest, and complaining about his love for her and her
desertion of him.

In these cleverly slanted stories, he alleged that he had

"discovered" her when she was a nobody. He had then taught her how to act and how to be a motion-picture actress. All the time he had loved her and had nurtured her in her career. And then, when her big break came, she had left him flat to go to Hollywood. Now she was a big star, thanks to Maxwell Reed's training. He had used all his energies to make her a success. Now he couldn't even get a job and was mired in poverty.

The night Joan saw the story in the paper, she and Arthur had a big dinner, during which they discussed strategy for fighting off Reed's claims on her. When they got home, Joan noticed for the first time that she had little hivelike bumps on her back and shoulders. She had never before been bothered by hives and dismissed it from her mind. She thought it might have been something she had eaten.

One of the first scenes to be filmed in *The Opposite Sex* was the "fight" scene between June Allyson, as the Injured Wife, and Joan Collins, as the Other Woman. There was a very good reason for this scheduling. It was that old devil publicity. Joan was a natural for a publicity buildup at MGM, where she was unknown. She had come off the Evelyn Nesbit role at Fox and made an impact, but still she needed more recognition from the public.

The publicity department at MGM remembered with glee the legendary feuds and battles on the set of the original production of *The Women*. The infighting and the slanders had made news for weeks during the filming of the picture. Now here was a whole new group of women, all with strong personalities; the possibilities for verbal and physical mayhem were endless.

Rubbing their hands in anticipation, members of the publicity department prowled the sets for days, looking for signs of feuding and fighting. Unfortunately, it turned out to everyone's surprise that all the new women *liked* one another! They would boost each other in private and praise each other on the set.

Nevertheless, there *was* hope. And that was in the fight scene. There was, in fact, a plot afoot.

On the day of the big fight, there was a huge crowd assembled to watch—much bigger than usual—including members of the print media. This would be a big one.

David Miller, the director, coached Joan carefully on the staging of the fight. In most pictures, there is always a standard way to deliver a "blow" to the face. The hitter simply aims his or her punch a little short of the hittee's face; and the hittee makes sure he or she has just slightly turned the head and drawn back a mite before the "blow" moves freely past. The sound of the "splat" that is really the key to the entire effort is usually dubbed in later; most of the impact the audience experiences comes from the *sound* of the blow.

"David came to me and coached me on how to dodge the blow," Joan recalled later, "and said June had instructions to pull her punch."

That was not exactly a true statement of fact. David had not yet instructed June Allyson on what to do, at the time he talked to Joan. When he did go to June, he told her frankly that they were going to use the first take, no matter what. To make it realistic, he instructed her to be sure to let Joan have it with all she could.

When it came to filming the shot, it was all very real. "I forgot to duck," Joan told a writer later. "June socked me so hard she gave me a black eye." Joan fell back, out cold.

June Allyson stared down at Joan on the floor and burst into tears. She raced for her dressing room. Finally the crew got Joan back in shape again. She had a bruised eye. It was sore.

"I was a long time coming to," Joan said. "Then *I* cried and cried."

Shortly after that, June approached her diffidently. Then the two of them sat down and cried *together*.

It was not a seemly way to stage a sequence for a motion picture.

As for the shots after that, Joan seemed to work into them all right. However, Miller seemed to want more heat and threat in her voice. What he felt he was getting was a very cool, sweet voice, that spoke without a trace of a British accent, yet did not sound sufficiently predatory or threatening for his taste.

"We'll loop her speeches until we get it right," he murmured at one point.

It was the famous bathtub sequence that really held up production. This scene was to be of Joan in a large bathtub, lying under a thickness of soap suds, chatting on the telephone, and lounging indolently. (Harbingers of her future—all those suds?)

For the scene, she was dressed in tight flesh-colored trunks and brassiere, making her look—if anyone could penetrate those glistening suds—naked! But the fact that the gook making up the suds might be troublesome was something no one had counted on.

When Joan got in the tub and sank down into the water, speaking her lines for three or four takes—she was actually chatting to a child actress nearby for the scene—there was suddenly a loud wail from her.

Joan came up out of the fake suds, her eyes red with weeping. She lifted her leg. It was bright red, slightly swollen. Her ankles were ballooning out, and so were her knees. It was immediately obvious that she was allergic to the concoction that made up the suds.

Several people wrapped her in a towel and a doctor was summoned. After a brief consultation, Joan was rushed to her dressing room. Operations were suspended temporarily.

After an hour, Miller ordered another try. This time Joan came out wearing rubber pants to protect her skin from the sudsy material. Almost immediately her skin turned red and blotchy and her ankles began to swell—sure signs that the allergy was working once again.

Another suspension of activities resulted. This time makeup rubbed Vaseline on her skin and applied bandages to portions of her legs. It was no go. Miller finally called it off for the day and proceeded to other setups.

That night the carpenter shop got busy. It fashioned a sheet of plywood with a hole cut in it to fit over Joan's body, letting the head and shoulders come through. This piece was laid in the tub to support the bubbles, arranged in such a manner that none of the gook touched her skin. Then, encased in bandages and grease, and wearing a pair of men's underwear, Joan sat under a sheet of rubber to keep out any errant bubbles that might get through the plywood.

In this clumsy fashion, the scene was shot to everybody's satisfaction.

It did not take a psychiatrist or doctor with an advanced degree to realize that the root of Joan's problems might well be worry over her situation with Maxwell Reed. Her symptoms were exactly the same as those that had appeared the night she had heard of the divorce proceedings: the same hives, the same nervous allergy, the same bright redness.

And then, to cap the climax, one day a process server appeared on the set and handed Joan a summons to court in Los Angeles. Reed was taking her to trial for the $1,250 a month he was demanding. Joan was forced to get a lawyer.

This was indeed a kind of landmark suit. In the 1950s it was almost unheard-of for a man to sue a woman for support. This was several years before the women's liberation movement had made some inroads into the rules of social and legal behavior. "Palimony" was unheard-of. Marriage was still a legal contract that was closely adhered to in the courtroom, usually heavily in the favor of the wife.

Therefore, when Joan's lawyer began to argue with her about fighting the suit and perhaps countering with a suit of her own, he was surprised to hear her telling him that she wanted out of her marriage with Reed no matter what the cost to her. Except, of course, she was in no way able to manage the amount of support money he wanted.

The case came to trial quite soon. A compromise of sorts was hammered out. In all it cost Joan $10,000 to get out of her marriage to Reed. Of that, $4,250 went to Reed. The rest went to legal fees for Joan's lawyer and for Reed's.

Although the experience was an unsettling one for Joan, she knew she had learned a lesson from her misfired marriage. "I've made one mistake and I would not want to get married again unless I decided it was for ever and ever and *ever*," she told columnist Earl Wilson. And then she added a comment that later would be considered an example of what *The New Yorker* used to call the "clouded crystal ball" statement: "I'd hate to be one of those girls with four or five husbands!"

The years between her divorce from Maxwell Reed and her second marriage in 1963 were turbulent ones for Joan Collins. She had married young against her parents' wishes and against the advice of many of her peers; when the marriage had turned sour, she had been unable to bail out in time and had been more or less unmercifully dumped.

Careerwise, she was not much luckier. Her big chance had been the role of Evelyn Nesbit in *The Girl in the Red Velvet Swing*—and the inevitable had failed to happen. She had not made a proper breakthrough in the picture. She was not a big star. She had not lost her confidence, but she had become embittered and frustrated over the fantasm of success that seemed to elude her.

In her personal life, this inner turmoil produced a series of liaisons with various men—some flaming affairs, others unsuccessful relationships of various kinds, and some hidden and longer-lasting love affairs. Her sex life was so active during those few years that it would be fatuous to make out a laundry list of the men in her life. A few of them have been discussed in her autobiography—some consummated, others unconsummated (according to the American edition of her story). Some confusion occurs because when her autobiography appeared in Great Britain in 1978, it contained a number of affairs that were deleted when she rewrote the book for American publication in 1982.

Generally speaking, most of the men in this interim appear

to have made up an apparently endless list of sometimes-casual, sometimes-intimate "dates":

Sydney Chaplin

Joan's short-lived but smoldering affair with Sydney Chaplin has already been discussed. It died when Joan finally walked out on him after confronting him in Palm Springs in that much-publicized (and not necessarily accurate) account from her life story. Chaplin returned to Broadway later on, and became a modest success on the stage. But Joan lost track of him then and there and made no attempt to pick up the pieces of their once-flaming affair.

Arthur Loew, Jr.

Joan continued to live with Arthur Loew, Jr., for some months after her divorce from Maxwell Reed. Ironically enough, Loew was the one man Joan was running around with in those days who made a good impression on her parents. Joe Collins was visiting America for the first time during this period, and he met Loew the night he arrived in Los Angeles.

"Arthur was the first man in Joan's life I positively liked," he wrote later. "Unlike her previous boyfriends, he was not particularly good-looking, but he was suave and smart."

"I hope you're being sensible this time," Joe told his daughter with uncharacteristic candor. "Don't treat sex as an aperitif."

Joan was too embarrassed to answer him. But Joe wasn't through.

"Now you've met someone nice, instead of wanting to run around all the time, it would do you good to stay in occasionally and watch television."

Joan gaped at her father. "Daddy! What are you talking about? Watch television! I hate the horrid thing."

More of the "clouded crystal ball" in Joan's life!

Unfortunately, from her father's standpoint, Joan soon tired of Arthur Loew much as she had tired of Chaplin—and for almost the same reasons. Why should Loew be able to find time to lounge around the house all day instead of working, while she had to go to the studio and put in a hard day in front of the cameras?

True, he did not have to work—he was the heir to the Loew fortune—but his idleness irked Joan. She walked out on her live-in lover after a verbal exchange that could have come out of any real-life soap opera (cleaned up for popular television consumption, of course).

"I did have another good exit line with him, now that you mention it," she told an interviewer once. "Arthur and I were dancing at a New Year's Eve party and were having a row, and he said, 'You are a fucking bore.' And I said, 'And you are a boring fuck!' And that was that. Pretty witty, huh? We broke up after that."

Harry Belafonte

When Joan made *Island in the Sun* on the island of Barbados in the Caribbean, she was seen occasionally with Harry Belafonte and with other high moguls of Hollywood like Darryl Zanuck.

Conscious that everybody was watching her to see how she would react to Belafonte's advances—which were legendary—Joan played it very cool, according to her account, and did not even touch him. Or he, her. But they did talk on the beach at midnight, she confessed, in a kind of soap-opera interlude.

Later, she saw him perform at the Coconut Grove in the pink-stuccoed Ambassador Hotel in Los Angeles, exchanged burning glances with him in his hotel suite at a big party later on, and exited from his life "regretting what might have been." At least, that was the way the story appeared in the cleaned-up American version of her book.

An interviewer, questioning Joan Collins about her relationship with Harry Belafonte later on, quoted a portion of the original British version of her life story, pointing out that she discussed him as the "King of Calypso," not mentioning him by name.

She shrugged. "It's all changed for America. Belafonte's not in it. It wasn't a very important part."

Nicky Hilton

Elizabeth Taylor's first husband, Nicky Hilton, son of the international hotel magnate Conrad Hilton, started taking out Joan shortly after her break with Arthur Loew. He had been wooing Natalie Wood, who later married Robert Wagner, but Hilton was not one to continue any relationship for long. Soon he was dividing his time between Natalie and Joan.

A rakish playboy, Hilton was a bit unstable; he used to fire pistol shots into the ceiling during the evening, resulting in police calls in the middle of the night.

Within a few years of the time he stopped dating Joan, Hilton was dead of an overdose of barbiturates.

Robert Wagner

Known then as "R. J." Wagner, Robert Wagner made a
picture on location with Joan in Tokyo, but at the time was
deeply enmeshed in a continuing—and eventually successful—
courtship of Natalie Wood leading to their first marriage.
Nothing but platonic friendship resulted from this relationship, according to Joan. In fact, the entire Japan interlude
was an enormous drag to her.

Wagner's second marriage to Natalie Wood turned out to
be one of the few happy-ending Hollywood marriages—only
to have it all end in a tragic way on a yacht off Santa
Catalina Island with Natalie Wood's death by drowning late
one night in November, 1981.

Darryl F. Zanuck

Joan was confronted by movie magnate Darryl F. Zanuck
in a stuffy room, where it was pointed out to her how her
film career might be advanced wildly beyond her dreams if
she would be nice to him.

"You've had nothing until you've had me," he told her. "I've
got the biggest and the best. I can go all night and all day."

She escaped.

Nothing came of it.

Rafael Trujillo

Son of the dictator of the Dominican Republic at the time,
Rafael Trujillo became interested in Joan and invited her

down to meet him in Palm Beach, Florida, for a fling. Finally weakening while in New York on a promotional tour, Joan agreed to jet down to see him.

And so it went.

Trujillo showered her with gifts, including an enormous diamond necklace valued at something like $10,000. This all came out in a congressional investigation that found that Trujillo had used American aid funds to buy this trinket, along with dozens of others presented to entertainers like Zsa Zsa Gabor and Kim Novak.

Marlon Brando

Joan was never really close with Marlon Brando, although he was seen out with her numerous times. According to the legend, he was acting as a "beard" for Joan's real lover of that same period, a man who stood head and shoulders above all the rest in this long laundry list as her favorite lover. The "beard" gimmick comes out of romantic fiction; it is interesting to note how closely Joan's life continued to parallel the fictional events linking the story lines of a typical soap-opera plot.

George Englund

According to Joan, George Englund was the man in her life during those tempestuous and unsettling years in California. Englund, born in 1926, and considered a pedestrian but professional director and producer of films, made *The Ugly American* in 1963, *Signpost to Murder* in 1964, *Zachariah* in 1971, and *Snow Job* in 1972.

At the time of Joan's involvement with him, he was still married to Cloris Leachman, the actress, and had three sons. He was the "lover" for whom Marlon Brando fronted in many public appearances with Joan at the time.

The problem with Englund was the same as Joan's problem with previous lovers. He could not really make up his mind what to do about her. On the verge of divorcing his wife for months, he never did file the papers.

But whenever he heard that Joan was running around with someone else, he would become insanely jealous and throw tantrums in front of her. At least, he did so in Joan's version of their stormy life together.

She wore the expensive diamond necklace Trujillo had given her on a date with Englund. "George got very upset the night I wore the necklace and he ripped it off at Romanoff's, throwing it across the floor in front of half of Hollywood," Joan told an interviewer. "A few months later, I was in New York and I saw a jewelry shop called Jolie Gabor, and one of its imitation necklaces looked terribly like mine. I bought it for a hundred and fifty dollars, and a week later, I was walking with George along the beach in Malibu on a very romantic moonlight night. I delved into my purse and pulled out this necklace."

Joan told him, "I've been thinking about what you said about the necklace, and because I love you so much, this is what I'm going to do with it."

And she threw the thing out into the ocean. He was, according to her, absolutely flabbergasted. He yelled at her in absolute dismay.

"You've just thrown fifteen thousand dollars away!"

Joan replied, "Yes, but I know how much it upset you, and I want you to know that your love means more to me."

Thinking about it later, Joan admitted: "It was a pretty good scene."

And right out of a soap opera plot.

Mr. Right?

Joan's peregrinations with men were coming to an interesting turn. A new man was on the horizon. Joan's previous interest had been in established stars, mature and hardened or born-rich males. Now suddenly the picture changed. Instead of using her own strength and willpower to manipulate stronger men into falling for her, this time she would use her strength and experience to make a younger and more callow youth fall for her.

It was in the months when her up-and-down, in-and-out affair with George Englund was coming to an end that she met the next man in her long line of conquests. And this one *was* different.

Her personal life was a shambles. The men were climbing all over themselves to get at her—but for nothing more than momentary satisfaction. Nothing permanent. She honestly *felt* that. Now . . .

She had a date one night with her friends Herbert and Barbara Viner, and the three of them went to a restaurant in Hollywood. In the lobby, waiting for the Viners to appear, Joan saw a young man looking at her curiously. He was sitting with a lovely suntanned woman, but he was *looking* at Joan intently. Joan recognized the woman: it was Jane Fonda, Henry Fonda's up-and-coming daughter.

When the Viners showed up, Joan took them aside and asked them who the man was. "That's Warren Beatty," whispered Barbara Viner.

At that time, the name Warren Beatty wouldn't have rung any bells anywhere.

"Who's he?" Joan wanted to know.

"He's Shirley Maclaine's younger brother."

It developed that when Shirley Maclaine had finally made it in the motion-picture business, she had changed her name, originally Shirley Maclaine Beaty, to Shirley Maclaine, taking her mother's maiden name as her last name. Her brother,

Warren Beaty, added a "t" to the name when he was starting out, since the single "t" looked too much like the English Beatles for him.

Joan immediately forgot about the young man's stare. He was pale and a bit callow looking. He was nobody. He even had a bad pimply complexion.

However, only a few days later, John Foreman took Joan to a party at the home of Debbie Power, the widow of Tyrone Power, who recently had died in Spain. Rumors were going around that she might marry Arthur Loew, Jr.! Thus the Hollywood merry-go-round continued to spin.

The moment Joan and her escort walked into the house—a huge place in Beverly Hills filled with people milling around everywhere—Joan spotted the same man she had seen at the restaurant seated at a piano, playing it with a free-and-easy manner. At his side stood a woman, obviously his date. It was not Jane Fonda.

This time Joan was interested. Beatty glanced up once at her, but made no sign that he had recognized her. Joan was annoyed, although she realized this might be Beatty's way of trying to intrigue her—by not putting a move on her.

When it came time for the party to break up, Beatty was still at the piano. Joan invited several of the people at the party to her place for coffee and whatever. Someone suggested she invite Beatty and his date.

"I really don't know him very well," Joan confessed. "But if you want to ask him—and the girl with him—that's all right with me."

"She's only a blind date."

And so Beatty was handed a piece of paper with Joan's address and telephone number.

Joan's party swung into the wee small hours of the morning and by two o'clock everybody was on their way home. Beatty never showed up. Joan went to bed, determined to forget all about him.

On her answering service next evening, when she got

home from a long Sunday at the beach, Joan found six
messages from him! She dialed him.

"I just got home from the beach and found your messages."

"Are you busy for dinner?" Beatty asked her in his slow
drawling voice.

"No."

He arrived in fifteen minutes and took her out to a Mexi-
can restaurant he had found on La Cienega. He was very
quiet and did not talk much. This gave Joan time to size him
up. She was fascinated by his blue eyes, but appalled at his
pale skin and rotten complexion.

Something was bothering Joan. "Why did you call me
today but didn't speak to me on Saturday?"

Beatty stared into space. "I was very depressed on
Saturday, and when they asked me to come over to your
apartment, I didn't want you to see me in such a blue
mood."

Joan didn't believe him.

He read her doubt. "I've been wanting to meet you since
I first came to Hollywood."

Joan blinked in surprise. Now she did believe him.

They began talking, and it was suddenly easy to converse.
They talked about books they liked, films they liked, California. She told him about her early years in England, her
student years at the Royal Academy of Dramatic Art in
London. About her father. About her sister, who was just
beginning to write stories and poems.

Beatty told her about his life: about his childhood in
Virginia, where his father was a college professor. About his
sister Shirley, with whom he used to fight over who would
have the car on weekends. He had won letters at sports in
football, basketball, track, and baseball. He had gone to
Northwestern University for a year on a football scholarship.
But he had dropped out and gone to New York to study
acting.

But so far nothing had happened. He was a newcomer.

Even with a successful sister in the wings—maybe because of her—he couldn't seem to get anywhere.

It was the beginning of a long affair. They were out night after night, talking, eating, drinking, laughing. And Joan's life suddenly seemed to smooth itself out.

"You know what?" she asked him one night. "I've changed since I've met you. I used to go into big, well-known restaurants. Now, I don't care about such things. Just as long as I'm with you. It's being with someone that brings happiness—not being somewhere. And you make me feel like a lady wherever I go."

There was only one niggling point in this romance that worried Joan. She was four years older than Warren Beatty. When she had married Maxwell Reed in 1952, he had been fourteen years older than she. That was a gap in years that was not good at all for the two of them; but it was a gap "on the right side." This gap of four years was a great deal smaller, but, unfortunately, it was "on the wrong side."

She could be accused of "robbing the cradle."

There was another problem. Joan Collins had missed being a star but she was a professional actress, already solidly committed to work in the industry. Warren Beatty had done nothing yet. All he had was a successful sister. He had never made it on the stage or in the movies.

It was an old cliché of fiction to play one's personal and emotional life against one's professional and intellectual life. In the case of the man in a relationship, the struggle is whether to choose love or a career. The strong man chooses love, and makes a career of his profession in spite of the choice. That is the usual way in fiction. The same is true of the woman with a choice between man and career. She chooses love, and succeeds at her career, too.

This time there was double trouble. Each member of this pair was involved in a personal struggle for happiness and a professional struggle for success. Their relationship with one another presented no problem at first. It was when their professional lives got in the way that the trouble began.

Towards the end of 1960, Beatty got his big break. He won the stage role of the lead in William's Inge's *A Loss of Roses*, playing opposite Carol Haney and Betty Field. It was a grand opportunity for him.

He immediately flew to New York to begin rehearsals. During this period, Joan finished the picture she was making at Fox and flew back to be with him. This was in November. The play opened on the road and now needed a lot of work. Nevertheless, on the strength of the reviews, Beatty was a success even if the play was not.

Joan brought with her the script of her next movie for Fox—an adaptation of D. H. Lawrence's *Sons and Lovers*. Beatty read the script. He thought it not quite right for her. Joan had a flair for comedy. This was going to be a serious and heavy role. Jerry Wald, the producer, promised to make Joan's role more fun and easier to take.

Meanwhile, the Inge play was preparing to open in New York. By the time it did open, the reviews were not good, although the players were all generally liked. For Beatty it was a good first review, in spite of the fact that the play closed after only three weeks.

The final rewrite of the *Sons and Lovers* script had not lightened Joan's role at all. Taking Beatty's advice, she turned it down, and it was given to someone else. The fact that Joan would have had to go to London to do the role may have had something to do with the reason Beatty did not want her to do the picture.

The two of them moved back to California, where, on the strength of his New York debut, Beatty was cast in another William Inge play—this one to be done on film for Elia Kazan. It was *Splendor in the Grass*, Beatty's debut in film.

Joan began tests for her next Fox film, *Big River, Big Man*. And quite suddenly, she discovered herself pregnant. The dialogue went something like this:

BEATTY: Pregnant? How did *that* happen?
JOAN: The butler did it—or maybe it's an immaculate
      conception.
BEATTY: This is terrible! Terrible!

Oh, fine, thought Joan.

Quite obviously the two careers were getting mixed up with the lives of the two individuals involved. The problem became one of proportion. Beatty was penniless, very ambitious, and it would do him no good at all to be hampered by a marriage now at his age. He was only twenty-two. No. Marriage was out.

Joan could not opt for what she could have opted for twenty years later: single parenthood. Having a baby would be definitely out; she would be fired from Fox on the basis of breaking the morals clause in the studio contract. Times were quite different then. One option remained: abortion.

It was performed in a grim structure in Newark, New Jersey, after Beatty got in touch with a "friend" in New York.

Joan was frightened and appalled at the whole thing.

Then, afterward, everything changed for the two of them. Beatty succeeded in *Splendor in the Grass*, even though it was *not* a hit, and Joan learned that *Sons and Lovers* had provided an Academy Award nomination for Mary Ure, who had been assigned to the part she had turned down.

"Warren has given me strength," Joan told a writer who was fascinated at their affair. "But then all lovers give each other strength, don't they? And the more we get to know each other, the greater our strength becomes. Our plans? Marriage, yes. But I don't think we should rush into it. If we take time now and get to know each other well, then I think we can face the ups and downs of marriage.

"Already, for instance, there are people who are casting little barbs at us. But I don't pay any attention to them. They say Warren's younger than I. He's only a year younger.

[That was what Joan told the writer.] Certainly, he's trying to get ahead, to find some security. He doesn't take me to smart places. He can't afford them.

"But all these things don't matter, somehow. Nothing matters when you're in love—except your deep-rooted belief in each other. That is what's enriching. We're not officially engaged yet. But that doesn't matter either. I trust our love."

But that fact was to be changed within weeks of the interview.

"Chopped liver was our favorite snack," Joan later recalled. "One day, Warren wanted me to get some chopped liver for him while he watched television. I got it and opened it up, and there was this ring—gold, studded with diamonds and pearls."

Joan stared at the meat and the jewelry. "What's this?" she asked him.

"It's for you," he said. "That's your engagement ring, fool."

JOAN: He had a certain throwaway way with a gift.

And so, engaged they were. But the love and the talk and the fun was all a smoke screen. By the time the engagement ring showed up in the chopped liver, the affair was already on its way to the graveyard to be buried.

Joan wrote that it all ended with finality after she was assigned to make an appearance in Norman Panama and Mel Frank's film, *The Road to Hong Kong*, opposite Bob Hope and Bing Crosby, and with Dorothy Lamour.

BEATTY (yelling): It's crap! Crap! (He throws the script on the floor.) Why do you need to do it?
JOAN (coolly): Two reasons. For the money. And to get away from you.

Two years of romance and fun were over. Beatty had grown up and was already on his way to becoming a star. Joan had simply marked time, sinking slowly as she failed to advance.

It was indeed time for a change.

Chapter Six

A Career in Crisis

Joan Collins's professional life was in no better shape than her personal one. The seeds of the trouble could be noted in Bosley Crowther's review of her performance in *The Girl in the Red Velvet Swing*, although a great deal of his criticism was actually aimed at the overall concept of the story. Nevertheless, he did remark on the fact that Joan acted "incredibly naïve," and made the "soapy clichés sound even more sudsy" than written.

She fared no better in the motion picture that followed *Swing*, the MGM remake of *The Women*. Again, *The New York Times* reviewer, identified only by the initials. "A.W." wrote:

"Joan Collins's performance as the two-timing chorus girl who snatches Miss Allyson's husband is eye-filling but hardly inspired." In that picture, retitled *The Opposite Sex*, it will be remembered that Joan played the part of the girl named "Crystal." Nevertheless, Steven H. Scheuer's 1972–73 *Reviews from Movies on TV* noted: "The supporting cast is very good, particularly Joan Collins, who plays the feminine menace 'Crystal' originally done by Joan Crawford."

Joan's next picture was *The Wayward Bus* for Fox. This was an adaptation of the John Steinbeck novel about a group of people trapped on a bus driven by a man determined to escape his humdrum existence and take the bus to the land of romance and make-believe. Originally written as a down-to-earth study of the difference between reality and fantasy, the motion picture adaptation by Ivan Moffat seemed to become a kind of *Grand Hotel* on wheels—the type of soapy treatment later popularized on television by "The Love Boat" and "Hotel."

Joan did not make out well in that picture, either, although she had the lead part playing Alice Chicoy, the wife of the wayward bus driver. This time it was Crowther who summed up her accomplishments:

"As for the acting of all and sundry—Rick Jason as the driver of the bus, Joan Collins as his moody helpmate, Jayne Mansfield as the stag-party girl, Dan Dailey as the traveling salesman, and maybe a half-dozen more—it looks as if it is being delivered by a stock company that might be traveling on this bus." Scheuer's *TV Reviews* noted: "Joan Collins and Rick Jason have some torrid love scenes."

As for *Island in the Sun,* a high-budget picture starring James Mason, Joan Fontaine, Harry Belafonte, Dorothy Dandridge, and Stephen Boyd, it too did not produce anywhere near the effect the original book by Alec Waugh had produced in print as a blockbuster best-selling novel.

Crowther more or less fobbed off the work of Joan Collins, who was actually listed fourth in the cast list as Jocelyn, the young woman who discovers in the course of the story that her grandmother was a black woman, meaning that she herself is a quadroon—one-quarter black. This discovery causes turmoil in her life; the book was a study of all kinds of miscegenation and various racial perplexities. At that time the story was quite controversial; that was the period ushering in the 1960s, in which most of these issues would become old hat.

"Joan Collins and Stephen Boyd play wanly with a vapid

upper-class love affair," Crowther wrote, spending most of his time analyzing the roles of Mason, Fontaine, and the rest of the cast of fourteen.

Sea Wife was a picture cast in a similar vein. It too was shot in the Caribbean and featured a strange relationship between a woman and three men. It had originally been conceived as a tour de force for the great Italian director Roberto Rossellini, who was still basking in the glory of his postwar epics, *Open City* and *Bicycle Thief*.

From the novel *Sea Wyf and Biscuit,* by Adrian Scott, the script involves a sinking at sea, with four people cast adrift in a lifeboat: one woman and three men. The woman is persistently provoked by the men. She later reveals that she is a nun. The script itself is turned around, with this "revelation" part of the original exposition.

Rossellini and Fox began to argue about the script, Rossellini maintaining that it was necessary for the woman to kiss the leading man—played by Richard Burton—in order to provide the story with any validity in its implications. Fox was afraid of the Hays Office. No Hays Office nuns kissed on screen. Eventually Fox took the easy way out; it fired Rossellini and handed the picture over to the unit man, Bob McNaught, to film.

"H. H. T." in *The New York Times* carped and sulked about the change in the story for script purposes before finally getting to the actors. "As for romance, there is Mr. Burton's gentlemanly pursuit of Miss Collins, who persistently spurns him."

On her next location film in Japan—*Stopover Tokyo*—Joan played Tina, in a loose adaptation of an earlier "Mr. Moto" novel by J. P. Marquand. Robert Wagner played opposite her, with Edmond O'Brien making up the third member of the cast.

The New York Times wrote: "Fox sent a unit, headed by Robert Wagner, Joan Collins and Edmond O'Brien to Japan to make this film. . . . The trip was not entirely wasted. They have found a dark-haired eight-year-old girl named Reiko

Oyawa, who portrays Koko . . . a joy to behold. All she has to do is smile and you forget you're watching satire triumph over skullduggery."

Not exactly accolades for the picture or its stars.

Rally Round the Flag, Boys! was a step up, this time because of Joan's costars: Paul Newman and Joanne Woodward. The picture itself, and the reviews, came off better than usual. Joan played one of the "other women" in the picture, a neighbor with "a dark and roving eye," according to *The New York Times* review. "The neighbor is played by Joan Collins, who also has a shape that is enhanced by the sort of clothes that plainly are right for a predaceous suburban type." At least Crowther was not anti-Joan Collins as he usually was.

Even today the falling-down-drunk scene with Paul Newman is a delight to see. Watch it on your VCR some night.

Seven Thieves was the last Fox film Joan made in the United States. It starred her with Rod Steiger, Eli Wallach, Edward G. Robinson, and Barry Kroeger. She was dismissed in one line in Bosley Crowther's review: "Joan Collins is a decorative 'shill.' " In Scheuer's *TV Reviews*, the note included the following: "High-gear suspense; fine performances. . . . Well above average."

Joan was shipped over to Italy to do a joint Fox-Italian venture titled *Esther and the King*, with Richard Egan, Denis O'Dea, and a big cast of Italians. The picture was shot half in English and half in Italian—with the English speaking English, to be answered by Italians in Italian. Joan was not even mentioned in the reviews.

When she refused to do *Sons and Lovers*, on Warren Beatty's advice, it was obvious that things were at a standstill in her relationship with the studio. She had already turned down two previous pictures, with the attendant problems of no money during the period of the filming of each title.

Her career was definitely fizzling out. No one knew it better than Joan.

"I'm afraid I'll be a has-been before I'm finished being

promising," she told a friendly magazine writer. "Right now, my career is in crisis. I can go up or I can go down. I can't stand still. I think, in a way, the times are against me. The days of star-building, as they used to be, are over. The real way to build a female star, the way it *was* done, is to put her in a succession of pictures with big names like William Holden or Greg Peck.

"Naturally, I don't consider myself a star, and I feel someone on the way to somewhere needs the moral support of a box-office male lead. That's why Grace Kelly—not that she wasn't wonderful—was so fantastically lucky. She rarely had to carry a picture alone."

Joan said that she felt the studio had placed her into too many different categories of roles, without finding a good niche to fit her into. She should be identified in the public mind as Joan Collins—person. But because she had been so many different things—a nun, a respectable English girl, a nymphomaniac, a Follies girl gone astray, a middle-aged alcoholic—the public was confused about her.

And then, in the wandering way her mind went, she continued to express her own ideas about herself and her life to come.

"I had marriage and fell on my face. I want to get married again—because I want to have children, but not for years and years and years. Maybe now I feel it's a kind of stagnancy—and I can't stagnate. Now it literally puts the fear of God in me, the thought of getting married again. Then, I get so frightened when I see other people's marriages and what's happening to them. My friends, too. Plus that when you get married, it's for life, or that's the theory, and say that at twenty-four I have another fifty years of living to do. It's an awfully long time to spend with one person. So I'd want to be very certain before I marry again, because when I do, I really want it to be forever."

The outcome of her "negotiations" with Fox—she was trying to work out a contract that would allow her more opportunity to do movies on her own—came to naught.

When her seven years ran out in 1960, they let her go. Since it was during her time with Warren Beatty, she was not too concerned. She had her wedding dress designed and ready for the day they would stand in front of the altar together.

That day never came.

When her agent got her the part in *The Road to Hong Kong* with Hope and Crosby, Joan left Los Angeles to make the picture in London. Beatty went to London later to make *The Roman Spring of Mrs. Stone* with Vivian Leigh, and after he was finished, he and Joan flew back to California—but it was a short-lived reunion.

The breakup occurred quickly.

Next stop: London.

Suddenly Joan was free of all entanglements and ready to move on ahead in her life. She was working on *The Road to Hong Kong* and living at home with her mother and father. Her mother had had several operations and was very ill, although the family members were trying hard to keep this fact from her. Joan's presence was good for her.

Ironically enough, back on the West Coast, Warren Beatty was beginning to run around with Natalie Wood, who had been fairly comfortable with Robert Wagner for some months—but that romance seemed to be withering on the vine, at least for the time being.

Now, Wagner was suddenly in London making a picture at the same time Joan was. One night he called her and told her he had some tickets for the hit of the season, a musical comedy called *Stop the World—I Want to Get Off*. It was a smash hit by a new and different type of Angry Young Man—this one a former child actor who had done the Artful Dodger in David Lean's highly competent film version of *Oliver Twist*.

The show itself enthralled Joan and impressed Wagner as well. But Joan was fascinated more by the man than by the work. Anthony Newley was a Renaissance man—he had composed the music, had written the book, and had starred in the show. In the composing of the music and the writing of the book he had been aided by his coauthor, Leslie Bricusse.

Backstage, Joan and Wagner introduced themselves to Newley, and he took the two of them to dinner at something called "the Trat"—a new Italian restaurant, Trattoria Terrazza, across the street from the theater.

Joan was impressed. "Tony was bright, amusing, and attractive, intelligent and likable."

And after that night he came back for more. A friend of Joan's warned her. "He fancies you like mad," she told her. After that, she continued to talk about Newley. And Joan learned that Newley was a living example of his own song, "What Kind of Fool Am I?" that purports to be the love song of a man who has never been in love.

Nevertheless Newley was married, of course, to a woman named Ann Lynne—but the marriage had turned sour.

JOAN: Very interesting. Is that where the song comes from at the end? You know, the fool song?

FRIEND: Those lyrics are *exactly* the story of his life.

JOAN: Oh, save us from *that*! I'm *not* interested in making him change his ways.

Of course not. But that didn't prevent her from going out to lunch with him a few days later. Nor did it stop her from beginning to date him with a regularity that presaged only one thing.

But Joan was unhappy in her vaunted freedom. There was no doubt about it—her mother was terminally ill. It was simply a matter of time. At least Joan's sister Jackie had made her mother happy by having a child, named Tracy Austin, just a few months before.

In a way, Joan felt a stabbing pain now and then wondering what kind of baby she might have had by Warren Beatty. But she resolutely thrust that kind of thought out of her mind. Spilt milk and all that.

To Jackie, Elsa Collins would sometimes murmur: "If only Joan would get married and settle down."

Meanwhile things were heating up between Joan and Newley. Joe Collins, who had known Newley for some time and had booked him for a variety tour a few years previously, was stunned. "Knowing his unsociable ways, the total opposite of my gregarious Joan, I would never have thought him her type of man, and I told her so."

"Daddy," Joan responded, "you're wrong about Tony. When he's with me, he isn't morose at all. I make him laugh. You *must* see his show. He's a genius." Joe did see the show, was impressed, but still thought he was wrong for his daughter.

Nevertheless, in spite of her father's opinion, Joan and Newley were soon sharing bed and board in a casual way. This state of affairs was not lost on Joan's mother and father. In fact, Joan was seen enough with Newley in London circles to cause a few eyebrows to raise.

Only a few days before Elsa died, she and Joan had a rather remarkable conversation—remarkable in that Joan listened for a change and *participated* in the thoughts exchanged. The exchange went something like this:

ELSA: What are you going to do with your life? It's time you settled down. You're not going to be young and beautiful forever, you know.
JOAN: Tony and I will probably get married—when he gets his divorce.
ELSA: He seems good for you. He's stopped you from gadding about. (pause) You'd be a marvelous mother, darling. I hope you have a baby one day. I hope you have one soon.

"I went to my room and sobbed for hours," Joan wrote. "I then made a resolution. If I did nothing else, I was going to try to do something to please her and make her happy."

Newley was an authentic genius. Even *Life* magazine in the United States called him an "all-purpose Cockney." He had begun his film career playing the sleazy antihero of *The*

Small World of Sammy Lee. Born in 1931 in Hackney, a blue-collar section of London, he was brought up by his mother after his father vanished from sight. He attended Mandeville Street School for Boys in London, but his schooling was interrupted by the bombings, and he was evacuated to the countryside. In Brighton he stayed with a retired music-hall performer named George Pescud, from whom he got his theatrical aspirations.

After serving a brief stint as a copy boy in Fleet Street, Newley went to an acting school where he was "discovered" by Geoffrey de Barkus, an English film director, for *The Adventures of Dusty Bates*. After the Artful Dodger, he played in *Winds of Heaven* at the Colchester Repertory Theatre. After a number of roles, he was cast as a rock'n'roll singer in *Idle on Parade*, for which he wrote and sang "I've Waited So Long." It went to the top of the Hit Parade. This created a new image for Newley, and soon afterward he began to work on the autobiographical story with Leslie Bricusse that later became *Stop the World*.

Even though the musical did not get marvelous reviews in London, it became established as a solid hit, and it did not take the moguls of Broadway long to realize the potential of the young Cockney genius. Soon enough, David Merrick made arrangements to open the show in New York, with Newley in the leading part. At this point, Newley and Bricusse were working on a new show.

Several years later the two of them were to collaborate with John Barry (who wrote the music) on the title song for the James Bond motion picture *Goldfinger*, sung by Shirley Bassey, and probably one of the biggest hits ever generated by a title song for an action movie.

Merrick's offer to the writing team proved irresistible, and Newley and the Bricusses left London for New York. By now Joan Collins had become inextricably linked with Newley. She went back to the states with them. Rehearsals took up most of Newley's time, and Joan spent her hours with her new acquaintances the Bricusses, with whom she got along

famously. Finally the *Stop the World* company was ready to
open out-of-town in Philadelphia.

Newley suddenly began having an affair with one of the
young women in the cast of the show. Joan and the Bricusses
had gone to the Caribbean for a few days, but Joan discovered Newley's philandering on her return. She was so angry
at him that she flew out to California to look up her agent for
a film deal. The Bricusses, acting as matchmakers, insisted
that Newley still loved her, but Joan did not want to hear
that kind of talk. She promised only that she would be
present at the opening of the Newley-Bricusse show on
Broadway.

The New York opening was an unmitigated disaster. Bosley
Crowther hated it. Howard Taubman noted: "Starting as a
brave attempt to be fantasy with satirical overtones, [it]
ends by being commonplace and repetitious." Walter Kerr,
then working for the *Herald Tribune* also loathed it. It was
no good; it would fail.

It was all over. Joan was ready to telephone the Coast and
agreed to do one of the films that her agent had lined up for
her. But then—quite suddenly—the sun broke out of the
clouds. In spite of the kiss of death put on the show by the
critics, the word-of-mouth around Manhattan was great. In a
few days crowds were lined up around the block, waiting to
buy tickets for the show. It had become an instant hit in
spite of Crowther and Kerr.

Joan was still angry at Newley and his cavortings with
certain cast members. She had met Terence Stamp, an extremely handsome British actor. He had just scored a huge
success in the film *The Collector*, playing opposite Samantha
Eggar, and had finished *Billy Budd* for Peter Ustinov.

Stamp was also a Cockney, a friend of Michael Caine, both
of whom were penniless a few years before, but were now
beginning to make it big in the movie world. And of course,
as Joan had hoped, Newley found out about *her* gorgeous
new boyfriend.

Newley and Joan met in Central Park, according to her

story. It was there that she laid it on the line for him. Either he drop the woman she knew he was playing around with, get a divorce from his wife, and marry her—or she was taking the next plane for Rome to make a movie.

It worked.

Within seven days they were in a penthouse apartment on the East Side. Newley filed for divorce. Joan became pregnant. On October 12, 1963, Tara Cynara Newley was born in New York.

Not to belabor the point of Newley's inconstancy too much, but it is interesting to speculate on the middle name Tara was given. "Cynara" was originally a queen in one of Horace's odes: "I am not the man I was under the reign of the good Cynara."

Toward the turn of the last century, Ernest Dowson, entranced by the sound of the name, turned it into something much more significant in a poem titled "Non Sum Qualis Eram Bonae Sub Regno Cynarae (I am not what I was in kind Cynara's day)". Dowson chose to write about his lost love, Cynara, but in a tongue-in-cheek manner reminiscent of the bittersweet aftertaste of a lost but ever-remembered love.

Each verse in the poem winds up with this one key line:

"I have been faithful to thee, Cynara! in my fashion."

If Tara's father was indeed the one responsible for her middle name, the act is certainly indicative of his own perception of his inconstant view of love—a sardonic parallel to his thoughts expressed in the "Fool" song.

(Incidentally, the title of Margaret Mitchell's book *Gone with the Wind* comes from the first line of the third stanza of Dowson's poem:

"I have forgot much, Cynara! gone with the wind . . .")

Joan had insisted on bearing her first child by natural

childbirth. She even chose to nurse the little girl herself, in line with current practices of the back-to-nature 1960s.

Although nursing the baby had its traumatic moments, the final outcome of the exercise was to put Joan into the category of a fully satisfied mother—physically, physiologically, and psychologically. From that moment on, for a number of years, Joan Collins was not Joan Collins, Actress, but Joan Collins, Mother.

Her friends were stunned.

It was as if the old Joan Collins had vanished to be replaced by a strange new traditional Joan Collins.

SUE MENGERS (observing JOAN suckling her infant):
     Joanie, I just can't watch this—it's *too* disgusting!

Newley was interested in his wife and child, but not completely enthralled with the life he was now leading. It had little to do with either Joan or Tara. It had much to do with Newley's feelings about the United States. Frankly, he did not like New York as well as he liked London. He did not get along very well with Americans. He was becoming soured on the whole scene. England was where it was at, Newley felt—and quite rightly so. The American imitation of the Beatles movements—the flower children, the drug scene, the communes—had all originated in England. Newley felt that the British were there first and doing it all better.

On November 22, 1963, President John F. Kennedy was assassinated in Dallas. That was all Newley needed.

NEWLEY: Shit! Let's get out of here, Flower. I want to
     go back to England.

And so it was that the Newleys—Tony, Tara, and Joan—waited out the end of the American run of *Stop the World* and in February 1964 flew to Paris to set up quarters. The stopover in France was a necessary one; the Inland Revenue System of Britain, similar to the United States' Internal

Revenue Service, had decreed that the tax year for all British citizens begins on April 6. Thus a British citizen who has been working out of the country the previous year to avoid British taxes cannot enter the country before that date unless he or she pays taxes for the entire year involved.

Because of that wrinkle in the law, hundreds and thousands of British citizens—always the more affluent and successful—set up tiny enclaves all over the world to huddle forlornly until April 6, upon which date the airports are heavy with arriving exiles.

At this point, Joan told her Los Angeles agent that she would be out of the country indefinitely and would be unavailable for any film offers from Hollywood. One had come in the spring of 1963, and Joan had turned it down because of her pregnancy. This disquieting note had distressed her agent but had alerted him to what he might expect from Joan's changing persona. It was as if Joan had indeed drawn the curtain down upon her movie career.

Paris was marvelous. Paris was infused with energy. Paris was enchanting. Paris was . . .

It is a soap-opera cliché that all glamour must be overlaid or underpinned with tragedy, melodrama, or out-and-out schlock.

Case in point:

The Newleys were ensconced in the Hotel Grand Point on the Champs-Élysées, with Joan in complete charge of Tara. "She was my baby and I was going to do right by her," she said later in explaining the curious fact that she did not have a nanny for her daughter—even in Paris.

One night the three of them were awakened by a commotion outside in the street. Hastening to the window, Newley discovered that the street was filled with people looking up at the hotel. Above him smoke was pouring out into the sky.

Joan rushed for Tara, grabbed her, and blundered about in the suite, which was now rapidly filling with black smoke and unbreathable air. Their room was on the seventh floor. Picking up as much of Tara's bottles and equipment as she

could, Joan arrived at the window with her baby to await
rescue.

By whom?

A few bemused citizens were wandering about in the
street below, where firemen were trying "lackadaisically" in
Joan's words to fasten a hose to a water pump nearby. Fed
up with this, Newley grabbed Joan and they jumped out
onto the fire escape where they tried to signal for help.

Signal whom?

Sparks were now shooting into the air and descending on
them from above. Newley, never an athletic type, managed
enough adrenaline to climb from one balcony to another to
try to find a way to get out of the smoke and heat. Face black
with soot, he returned after a few minutes shaking his head.

The bad news was that the fire was in the elevator shaft,
and was burning out of control on the eleventh floor, moving
downward, fast. The good news? Well——

They were trapped. It was a scene right out of a ridiculous
stage melodrama. Too young to die! Joan thought. Too young
to die!

Exactly the way it happens in a B movie, the door to the
suite burst open and two firemen jumped into the room,
wearing gas masks and heavy asbestos gloves. They gabbled
at the Newleys in French.

Translation was not needed. One fireman took Tara and
rushed out, the other gestured to Joan and her husband to
crawl along the floor down the corridor with dampened
towels on their heads.

"The floor was burning now, and acrid smoke filled my
lungs even with the wet towels," Joan recalled. The ceiling
looked as if it might burst into flame at any moment, and
plaster showered the floor around them. There were screams
and the sound of glass breaking.

Finally they got to the stairs and started down. The stairs
were next to the elevator shaft. Once Joan made the mistake
of looking up into the shaft and saw the top of it going up in
huge orange flames.

Saved in the nick of time!

The next day they left for St. Moritz, another fashionable watering hole for British tax evaders waiting out the last several months of the tax year before returning to London.

On April 7, 1964, the Newleys were back in London, with Newley hard at work on a new show, *The Roar of the Greasepaint, the Smell of the Crowd*. Newley and his collaborator, Leslie Bricusse, plunged into the work, leaving Joan to Tara's upbringing.

In August Joan was signed to make a motion picture in Italy—*La Congiuntura* (Conjuncture, Crisis)—with Vittorio Gassman. The picture turned out to be a hit in Italy, where it was number eight at the box office for the following year. It was one of the best things Joan feels she has done. She was still working on the picture when *Greasepaint* opened in London; she was not on hand to see the cataclysm unfold.

Everything that *Stop the World* was, *Greasepaint* was not—at least according to the critics (who had been tepid on *Stop the World* in the first place anyway). The play was doomed. However, David Merrick wanted to open it in New York in spite of the bad reviews and lukewarm reception in London. There was one proviso: that Newley play the lead, Mr. Thin, in the New York version. He had kept himself out of the cast in the London opening.

One other consideration arose. Because of his income, Newley found that he could not stay in England without paying 90 percent of his income to the government. That meant the move to the United States was inevitable. And so it was that the Newleys were back in New York in the same apartment that they had left two years before. And it was there that the birth of Joan's second child, a boy, Alexander Anthony Newley, occurred, as if by rote, on September 8, 1965. It was just a little over two years after the birth of his older sister. The boy was always known as Sacha.

Greasepaint did much better in New York, with Cyril Ritchard playing opposite Anthony Newley. Joan was beginning to relax a little in the role of mother. She had finally hired a nanny to help her take care of her pair of rambunctious youngsters.

Newley's next project was an appearance in a big musical comedy for Joan's old studio, Twentieth Century-Fox. It was *Dr. Dolittle*, adapted from a children's book (and series of books) by Hugh Lofting. Newley's collaborator, Leslie Bricusse, was doing the book and lyrics. Rex Harrison would be playing Dr. Dolittle.

Joan's return to the Fox lot was somewhat disenchanting for her. Everything had changed. To liquidate a bit of their holdings, the studio moguls had sold off a huge hunk of the big lot, which was now being built into Century City. Joan, who had been a familiar face on the lot in the old days, was now glanced at and ignored. She was—Joan Who?

And a kind of depression was starting to settle onto her once again. This time it was not the lack of children and a stable home, but the fact that she had everything she wanted—and yet she must be wanting something more!

What?

She had no idea.

But there was always a way to overcome depression. For Joan, it was to become excited about something, involved with something, invested into something.

This time, as usual, it was another man.

His name?

Ryan O' Neal.

Chapter Seven

Off Again, On Again

Born in Los Angeles in 1941, Ryan O'Neal was a typically Californian macho male—well, maybe not macho, but certainly good-looking in a wind-blown, totally blond way. Casual and as laid-back as the typical Californian of the postwar era, he yawned his way through school and his teens until finally he was more or less forced to seek a job to support himself.

The son of novelist and scriptwriter Charles "Blackie" O'Neal and actress Patricia Callaghan, he fell into show business naturally by joining the stunt crew on Kirk Douglas's *Tales of the Vikings*, on which his mother and father were working. After doing more stunt work he eventually drifted into television parts as an actor and was even under contract at one point to Universal Studios, which hoped to mold him into a young Doug McClure!

His breakthrough came with a role in the television Western series "Empire," starring Richard Egan. O'Neal played the younger son of the wealthy ranch owner (oddly enough, Anne Seymour!). And so, as Anne Seymour's offspring, he

111

became a noticed actor. The next step was the starring role in ABC-TV's evening soap-opera series "Peyton Place," which was made at Twentieth Century-Fox. His name in the series was Rodney Harrington; with slight alterations, soap operas have a way of repeating names year after year. Carrington?

Although working on a weekly hour-long show is probably one of the toughest of all acting chores, O'Neal was resilient and tough enough to allow himself to be seen around town at all the right places—including discotheques and restaurants where all the "in" people of Hollywood congregated after hours.

It was there that Joan Collins first saw him—at one of the meccas of the rich and famous called The Daisy. She saw him, but paid little attention. She was brooding and moody over her own life at the time. The emptiness of it was showing. Sure, Anthony Newley was working on a new project—was up to his ears in it, as usual—but all Joan had was the kids and the kitchen.

O'Neal came over and asked her to dance. As they danced, it developed that he did know who she was—or who she had been—and that he was a regular at the place. It was obvious that he and she were alike. He was divorced now, with two children, Tatum and Griffin, who were just about the same ages as Tara and Sacha. They were soul mates, after a fashion.

Nothing happened between them until Joan attended a party thrown by the producer of *Dr. Dolittle*, the motion picture Newley was acting in. Newley begged off going out that night, pleading that he was beat to the socks from work. "I'm exhausted, luv," he protested. "You go."

The party was the usual, and when it was over, Joan took herself over to the disco—and to Ryan O'Neal. They danced. They talked. They drank. O'Neal took her home in his sports car.

Nothing more—at that point.

Joan had been working an occasional gig here and there. The big roles were out for her. But television had a voracious appetite and devoured material—and actors and actresses to make the material come alive. She would get small roles in the big series of the time: "The Bing Crosby Special," "Mission Impossible." She even played opposite her old classmate David McCallum from RADA in a "Man from U.N.C.L.E." episode.

And she did a "Star Trek." The segment, titled "City on the Edge of Forever," later became a cult classic. Every Trekkie knows it and remembers it. The story gimmick is strictly a sci-fi time-warp wrinkle, with the *Enterprise*'s Dr. McCoy—"Bones"—swept up into another time and another world, and Captain Kirk and Spock tracking him down. McCoy has wound up, sick and incapacitated, in a mission for poor souls during the Great Depression in New York. Joan is a female mission worker fascinated with the charms and the utter charisma of none other than Adolph Hitler! She's quite probably a Nazi plant. Kirk falls in love with her and seems to be swallowing her Nazi philosophy. Spock warns Kirk that Hitler nearly ruined the world in the years following. When an out-of-control truck threatens to kill Collins, Shatner at first leaps to the rescue, but, recalling Spock's warning, lets fate take its course and allows her to be killed, keeping the world from being destroyed by the monster of Berlin— through her proselytizing, presumably.

Meanwhile, Newley was deeply enmeshed in *Dolittle,* at this point working in New York, and Joan was all alone at the house. She was startled one night to get a phone call from none other than her laid-back Californian discotheque associate Ryan O'Neal. It was Joan's birthday, and although Newley had promised to be there with her, he had been unable to break away from his work.

O'NEAL: Happy birthday! Where's your husband taking you tonight?

JOAN: He's stuck in the Big Apple.

O'NEAL: Well, uh, we wouldn't want you to be alone on your birthday, would we?

JOAN: No. We wouldn't.

In Joan's autobiography she describes the scene, and caps it off with these lines:

"I suddenly decided what I wanted for my birthday present. A girl should get what she deserves on her birthday. And she did."

In spite of the precarious situation that Joan's affair with Ryan O'Neal presented, she never let it get out of hand or even surface to a degree that her husband was forced to do something about it. There were plenty of rumors. There were even mysterious little notes in the newspapers. But Newley was busy and, if he knew, he managed to keep his own reactions under control.

To put it on an even stranger level, Joan would invite O'Neal and his two kids over to the Newley house to swim in the pool with her own two kids. In a manner of speaking, this forced Newley to mend his own ways. He became the more-or-less loving husband his marriage vows had promised he would be.

This state of affairs continued unevenly for some time.

In 1968 Joan and her husband formed a partnership with a number of other actors including Paul Newman, Sammy Davis, Peter Lawford—along with some businessmen—and opened an English-style discotheque in Hollywood. They had found an old factory that had been abandoned on Robertson Boulevard up near the foothills where Robertson intersects Santa Monica Boulevard. The disco became known as The Factory.

It became an instant sensation, with a rock group playing between the usual records, sweating under the strobe lights of all colors that kept bouncing back from the huge stained-glass windows in the high walls. It was very sleazy, very glitzy, and very unbelievable. It cost $350 to join the disco—and people were lined up to surrender their money!

The overnight success of the disco was as unbelievable as its overnight demise after being in business for only about a year. It obviously did not have the staying power of Arthur's in New York, or of London discos.

Newley now embarked on an even more daring venture: to write, produce, direct, *and* act in his own motion picture. Its title was typical of the nutty extravagances of the sixties: *Can Hieronymus Merkin Ever Forget Mercy Humppe and Find True Happiness?*

To make this picture, the Newley family packed up and moved to England. It was impossible for Newley to do the film in Hollywood at the time. Besides, he still had his doubts about America, and preferred England.

The plot concerns the usual triangle, with Newley in the middle trying to make up his mind between his two children, his Cockney mother, and his wife—and a young luscious blonde, Mercy Humppe, obviously his "dream ideal" that he has been searching for all his life.

Joan played herself. The wife. A young actress named Connie Kreski, who had been a centerfold in *Playboy*, played Mercy Humppe. As usual, Newley and the young ingenue became very close as shooting progressed on the movie.

The film was made on the island of Malta in the Mediterranean. The result of it was that Newley was pretty much involved with his new friend, and Joan was pretty well aware of what was going on. She might have been in Hollywood and at least able to see Ryan O'Neal, but no—here she was stuck in Malta, too!

After shooting, the Newleys returned to London, where he became involved in the cutting and editing of the film. And it was there that still another man came in to fill the vacuum in Joan's life.

Ronald S. Kass was cut from a different bolt of cloth than any of the other men in Joan Collins's life. He was not a *creative* type. Most of her men were actors, writers, musicians, and others who existed in the entertainment business as principal players—not as members of that enormous world out there where men counted their dollars at the end of the day to see whether or not they were successes or failures.

Ron Kass was *involved* in the entertainment industry—he was an extremely successful entrepreneur—but he was essentially a producer and manager, not an actor, writer, or performer.

He was an American, typical of the 1960s businessmen and executives who knew how to make other people do things to make money for them and their enterprises. Born in Philadelphia, he grew up in Chicago and Los Angeles, where he graduated from the prestigious UCLA Business School with a degree in Business Administration in the 1950s.

At one time in his youth, he had been a professional trombone player, working with Herb Albert's famous Tijuana Brass. But performing was just a passing phase. Business was his field; Kass knew music, so he concentrated on that area of operations.

In the early 1960s he moved to Lugano, Switzerland, to become European head of Riverside Records. Soon he went to Britain, where he served as European vice-president of Liberty Records. It was while he was working for Liberty Records that he came to the notice of Paul McCartney, one of the most famous four singers in the world: the Beatles.

McCartney hired him to head the Beatles' new Apple Records label. That was Ron Kass's big breakthrough. His American know-how and entrepreneurial pizzazz made the Beatles' enterprise a whopping success after they had decided to corner as much of their loot as they could, rather than getting only the skim and handing the rest to the government or someone else standing in line.

Soon, however, Kass's reign was cut short. American hotshot Allen Klein had become the manager of the Beatles, and in order to make himself look good, he began purging people inside the Beatles' organization. One of the first to take the fall was Ron Kass.

But Kass was too good to vanish into limbo. He was immediately snapped up by MGM Records to become its head in London, where he became interested in Joan Collins. His own marriage was already a shambles.

Joan's father had known about Kass through his show-business contacts, but when he met him through his daugh-

ter, he saw him as "the archetypal American executive"—
"good-looking, fair-haired, clean-cut and immaculately tailored." Even his manner was "affable and easy." Joe thought
of him as "a reliable sort of chap, with nothing fly-by-night
about him."

At the time Joan and Ron Kass met he was a mature
thirty-three years old. Unlike Joan's usual lovers, Kass had
both feet on the ground, knew the value of solid professionalism as opposed to self-indulgent narcissism, and was not a
guy you could push around. He had been married, had sired
three children, but had separated from his wife several years
prior to meeting Joan. His wife and children were living in
Lugano while Kass worked in London and wherever else his
business took him.

Joan was instantly attracted to him, as he was to her.
They would meet sporadically at the "in" restaurants and
discos in London. Although the swinging sixties were about
over now and the era was really beginning to lose its appeal,
things were not dead in London—and in the company of
Michael Caine, Dudley Moore, Susan Hampshire, and Roman Polanski, Joan and Ron Kass began and continued a
friendly relationship even as Tony Newley stood by and
watched, not approvingly but not necessarily disapprovingly.

Joan Collins was considerably more mature and self-
confident now than she had ever been before. Kass fascinated her. She knew in her bones that her marriage to
Newley was foundering. The kids were both away in school
—growing up, really. It was time for something to happen.
And now Joan knew that if she wanted Ron Kass—and she
did want him—she would have to play the game a little
more smoothly than she had played it before.

"I didn't want to injure our blossoming friendship and love
by jumping instantly into bed," she wrote. And she did not.
In fact, she wangled a role in an Italian movie and flew to
Trieste for the shooting as part of her plan. The idea seemed
to be to make herself more desirable in her absence.

The picture was called *State of Siege*, the director, Romano

Scavolini, a "dedicated Communist" who would not allow any of the actors to smile on camera, considering the smile as a lowdown Hollywood capitalist plot to exploit the working masses. Communist or not, he believed in exploiting *his* workers—and Joan played her first nude love scene for him.

The scene itself was a hilarious affair, according to Joan's account. But she and Mathieu Carrière, a man much younger than Joan, playing opposite her, were almost frozen to death in the brutal cold of the set, and to keep warm, consumed a bottle of brandy between them before shooting—the brandy helpfully supplied by their Marxist director who considered comfort and warmth the epitome of bourgeois decadence.

Although the scene was a serious part of a rather light plot, filming it was something else again. The two frozen performers began the scene, with Joan trying to simulate lust in a huge frozen bed. At this point Scavolini got into the act, too, beginning to shout instructions to the two "lovers" in fractured English and Italian.

> SCAVOLINI: OK. OK. *Azione! Kees*—beeg beeg kees. . . . More *sexy*! You *woman*, he *boy*. Ees veree veree beeg *thrill* for you!

Trying to keep from breaking up into laughter, Joan continued to wrestle with the young actor, feeling, as she put it, about "as passionate as a cat on a cold tin roof."

> SCAVOLINI (finally): Cut! We will shoot the rest of the scene tomorrow—when you 'ave both *sobered up*!

The picture never made the big time, but it was basically an "artsy" film, and not a total failure in Italy. However, it led to nothing. Joan was soon back in London, where Newley was preparing his movie for release. But when it opened, it was another bomb. The reviews were disheartening. The movie was a disaster. It helped neither Newley nor Joan nor their waning relationship. If anything, its general tone—the plot, the story line, the attitude—persuaded Joan that it was all over between the two of them, if there had indeed ever been anything between them in the first place other than an easygoing, sometimes companionable marriage of—"convenience"?

That fact itself was disturbing. There were the two children to think about. They would be badly scarred by a separation, badly traumatized by a divorce. What to do?

The best thing was to attempt a trial separation, which they did by living in the same house but going their separate ways. Joan had told Newley about her interest in Ron Kass; Newley knew about it anyway. And so the separation was "amicable," in the ridiculous argot of the law. And now Joan began to work on Kass. He was agreeable.

The messy business of the divorce began. Joan had let her professional career languish for so long to bring up the children that Newley agreed to help support them, even though Joan would be responsible for their upbringing. Kass would have to support his own three sons, but he was a good businessman and would be able to do so without strain.

In 1970 Joan and Kass moved to London to live. Kass was president of MGM Records and Robins Fiest and Miller Music Publishing Company. Joan had been away from the big time too long, and she knew it would be hard getting back into the swing of it—not because she would have trouble getting into shape herself, but because others in the business would have forgotten who she was.

Just before moving to London, Joan had made a movie on location in New Mexico—a comedy called *Three in the Cellar*. She worked with Larry Hagman, whom she had met years before when she was at the Royal Academy. Hagman, who was Mary Martin's son, was dancing in the chorus of *South Pacific* at the time, while his mother sang out front.

Of course, neither of them was aware that some twenty-odd years later they would both be household names in America as the most villainous of television villains.

Joan's days of playing the ingenue teen-ager pursued by

the mad rapist and her days of playing beautiful and panting young leads in big films were over forever. In fact, the entire motion-picture business was in a state of flux. With adults spending time watching television in the home, it was the kids who had really became the arbiters of public taste in movies. And that taste was almost predictable: teen-age love and doomsday and horror flicks.

And so for the next five years Joan played roles that were there to be played. At first she was able to get a few regulation dramas, but the list soon shifted to the genre of horror and terror. After making *Quest for Love* in 1971, she was forced into the horror genre with *Revenge*—released in the United States as *Inn of the Frightened People* or *Terror from Under the House*—and *Fear in the Night*, with Judy Geeson, Ralph Bates, and Peter Cushing.

The next few years were strictly on the dark side: *Tales from the Crypt* in 1972, *Dark Places* and *Tales That Witness Madness* in 1973. These were not quite so cheap or gaudy as they might sound. The latter featured a cast of Kim Novak, Jack Hawkins, Donald Pleasence—now becoming quite a successful prototype of the mad-and-glad man-monster—and Georgia Brown, among other notables. *Dark Places* featured Christopher Lee, another notable horror performer, Herbert Lom, and Jean Marsh. *Tales from the Crypt* included Ralph Richardson, Nigel Patrick, and Peter Cushing in the cast.

Joan was fast becoming the Queen of the Horror Flicks. But what the hell—it paid the bills!

In 1973 she was offered a change of pace in Italy to make *L'Arbitro*, released later in the United States as *The Referee*, and in 1974 she made *Alfie Darling* (in the United States *Oh! Alfie!*) with Jill Townsend and Alan Price. In 1975 she was in Spain making *Call of the Wolf* with Jack Palance, which later appeared in the United States as *The Great Adventure*.

Then Joan was back in London making *The Bawdy Adventures of Tom Jones*, a remake of the original *Tom Jones* with some additions, featuring a cast of Trevor Howard, Georgia

Brown, Madeline Smith, Terry-Thomas, and others. Joan played Black Bess in this production, and was even noticed by *The New York Times* critic Richard Eder: "Joan Collins makes a waspish highwayman." She also made another British thriller titled *I Don't Want to be Born* (released in the United States as *The Devil Within Her*), along with Donald Pleasence and Ralph Bates.

It was obvious that Joan was not moving forward in her career at all during this period. In fact, she was still subordinating her career to her job of homemaking. In 1972, on June 20, she gave birth to her third child, this one by Ron Kass, named Katyana. Even so, she continued to make an occasional movie, and even appeared in an NBC production for Hallmark Hall of Fame of *The Man Who Came to Dinner*, the marvelous comedy about Alexander Woollcott written by George S. Kaufman and Moss Hart. Woollcott—called Sheridan Whiteside in the play—was played by Orson Welles.

Once again, the cast was excellent. Joan was Lorraine Sheldon, the character whom the playwrights had selected to represent Gertrude Lawrence. Lee Remick was Maggie, Sheridan Whiteside's loyal secretary. Marty Feldman was Banjo, the nutty caricature of the prototypical gofer, and Don Knotts was the family doctor, Dr. Bradley. Peter Haskell played Bert Jefferson, the newspaperman.

The plot is a long extended joke. Whiteside, the Woollcott character, visits a family for dinner, falls, breaks his leg, and must ensconce himself in the household for weeks. There he carries on his eccentric business, with all his mad friends appearing one by one.

Apart from Orson Welles, whom she detested, Joan got along well with everyone in the cast. It was Welles, according to Joan, who upstaged everyone, robbed all the scenes of reaction shots, and doomed the play from the start. It was a bomb when it was broadcast on NBC—and earned very low ratings.

Joan also made *Fallen Angels*, the Noel Coward show that had debuted in New York in 1927 with Tallulah Bankhead and Edna Best in the leading roles. The plot concerns two women who are married to wimps and who inadvertently share an affair with a smooth and swinging Frenchman. Joan shared casting with Susannah York, and Sacha Distel, as Maurice, the Frenchman. That one got good ratings on British television.

These were the best years of Joan's life up to now. In that period she had borne three children to two different men. In spite of the fact that her career was not what she would have liked it to be, she was still able to pull off an occasional good role. But her children were the focal point of her existence.

Ron Kass was now president of Warner Brothers Records in Britain, and making a great deal of money—as was Joan through her acting efforts. But there was trouble in the wings. Finally it appeared onstage in the form of the Chancellor of the Exchequer of Great Britain.

In Britain, the Chancellor of the Exchequer resembles the Treasurer of the United States. It is he who manages the taxation of income for the citizens of the country. And it was decided in early 1970s that the rich in Britain had been cheating the government for long enough by living outside the country, by engaging in business other than British business, and by not paying their proper dues to be British citizens.

The familiar cry of "soak the rich" was heard again in the land. This time the crier was Denis Healey, the chancellor himself. The laws were quickly skewed around to squeeze the prosperous; tax enforcement was intensified. The rich and famous quickly heard the cry and vanished to the four corners of the earth.

Ron Kass, who had worked and made a great deal of money in Britain in the past ten years, was a special target for the officials of the Inland Revenue System. Kass knew immediately that he must leave the country to escape the clutches of the government. Joan herself discovered that her own possessions—the house in England, her furniture, her Mercedes, her extensive collection of jewelry and a lot of paintings and Art Deco objects she had collected—would be taxed heavily under the newly established "wealth tax" not once, but continuously—*each year*.

This was a disaster of major proportions. In fact, the totality of the disaster was not recognizable at that time. Nevertheless, Joan knew in her bones that this was not going to be a good move. Like her husband, she preferred living in England to living in America—even though her sister Jackie was now a happy resident of Beverly Hills, California.

Something told her not to go to the United States.

But they simply had to go. The serious loss of income would be too much to bear. Both Joan and Kass were accustomed to living the good life and to working for money to support that good life. To change their life-style now would be silly, and probably impossible anyway.

But Kass must give up his lucrative and prestigious job as head of Warner Brothers Records in London. What would he do in America? A friend, Edgar Bronfman, the principal heir to the Seagram whisky fortune, came to his rescue by putting him in charge of a new film company called Sagittarius. Its offices would be on the Sunset Strip.

Bronfman had a history of interest in the entertainment business. For a short time he had been chairman of the board at MGM in the early 1970s—but then, almost anyone had been head of that company for a while in its period of rapidly changing heads. Bronfman had been actively engaged in several film productions in England, where he had met Ron Kass.

Incredibly wealthy and full of the joy of life, Bronfman loved to put his energies and his money into projects of all kinds related to show business. Married for over twenty years, with five children, he was a stable person, even though terribly stingy—as many of the very rich tend to be. He hated to think people wanted to be with him only to milk him for his money—another typical syndrome of heirs to great wealth.

Edgar Bronfman was the godfather of Katy Kass, who was,

significantly enough, born on his birthday! But even with
the support of Bronfman nearby at all times in California, it
was with a great deal of trepidation and apprehension that
Joan Collins and Ron Kass packed up their belongings, gathered their three children, and took the plane to the United
States in 1975.

Bronfman's aid helped get Joan and Kass through the next
two rather trying years. Joan rolled up her sleeves immediately, and got the kids into good schools, continuing to
supervise the nanny who was bringing up Katy. It was Joan
who searched out and bought the house in which they lived,
and it was Joan who decorated and renovated it.

At the same time, she was out of the house to do an occasional television stint in spite of her continued reservations about the medium, which she felt was far inferior to
film.

She did episodes of "Future Cop," "Switch," "Police-
woman," "Space 1999," "Baretta," and a "Batman and Robin,"
in which she played "The Siren," whose falsetto voice is
enough to halt her enemies and even freeze Batman into a
statue. These jobs helped pay the mounting pile of bills.

The truth of the matter was that while Ron Kass had been
doing very well in London, he was not doing very well in
Southern California. Sagittarius was not getting off the ground.
He had been into film ventures before, the first a coproduc-
tion with David Puttnam of *Melody*. And he had made *The
Optimist*. For television he had done *Jane Eyre* and *Fallen
Angels*, the latter with Joan as the lead. Somehow he could
not seem to get things going now on Sunset Strip.

Of course, with Bronfman at the helm, there was plenty of
money. But for some reason Kass had lost his creativity or
his pizzazz—or that spark of something that made him go.
Joan could see the warning signs in their own relationship.
The old spontaneity was missing. If it had not been for the
children, she might have done what she always did when her
interest in a husband waned. But this time she did not go
her usual route. She plunged into the work of the normal

housewife and used her television roles to bring in the money needed to supplement her husband's rather faltering income.

Even with the $1,250 arriving from Newley each month in support of Tara and Sacha, there wasn't enough to live on comfortably. Hopefully, Sagittarius would soon hit it big and take off, but . . .

Suddenly even that hope was dashed.

"Ron walked with a heavy tread into our green-and-white bedroom, slightly overdecorated with bowers of palm-tree wallpaper," Joan recalled in her memoirs.

The rest was soap-opera purple:

KASS: Edgar's fired me.
JOAN: I can't believe it!

It was true.

What had been a bad situation was now impossible.

What to do?

Should Joan walk out on Kass? Impossible. What about the children? One of them was his!

Help Kass find a job? Not feasible.

Work in television? She was already doing that, off and on. She would have to get a big role somewhere.

But that was simply a dream.

There was one practical possibility.

It was a long shot—but it just might work.

Chapter Eight

Reinventing Joan Collins

Jacqueline Jill Collins, Joan's younger sister—whose name seems like something out of a nursery rhyme—was born when Joan was five years old. For that reason, in their early years, they were hardly sibling rivals or even companions. It was not until much later in life that they began to understand each other and to socialize as equals.

"Jackie and I were not that close as children, because of the age difference," Joan explained once. "I was always really interested in writing off to film stars."

On the other hand, Jackie found herself writing little pieces about what she was doing or what she might want to do, or even making up sketches about some of the people who frequented the Collins residence in London—all those vaudevillians with their loud laughter and their hair-raising anecdotes. Like Joan, Jackie could handle all the four-letter words from the Anglo-Saxon lexicon with skill from a very early age.

Because she was so much younger than her older sister,

Jackie followed her in all her pursuits, lending some support to them and managing to spin some of her sister's glamour off onto herself as much as she could.

"Joan quite liked the idea of designing fashions," Jackie said once. "She used to sketch things." In fact, Jackie sensed from the beginning that she would never be able to be the clotheshorse her sister was, not particularly because of the lack of a figure, but because she was simply not interested in clothes per se the same way Joan was.

To Jackie, Joan *was* interested in anything she could put on her back.

"Those are lovely," Jackie would say to some of her sister's sketches of dream gowns. "Can I have them?"

"But of course," Joan would say, and hand them over, going on to draw even more glamorous clothing. Meanwhile Jackie would take the drawings and create characters.

"I would cut out all those little doll-like drawings, and she would stick them in a book and write stories about them," Joan explained.

And Jackie would write tales that would have sent the smoke out of the ears of either of her parents. As a matter of fact, later on, she would incorporate the more steamy of her story ideas into her own diary, writing down the fantasy dreams as they occurred to her—the wilder the better. Quite soon her diary was discovered by a girlfriend, not entirely by accident.

Annoyed at having her secrecy breached, Jackie soon got a bright idea. If her girlfriend seemed so interested, why not——?

Soon she was charging her girlfriends a fee to take a peek at her updated diary. And of course the fantasies got crazier and crazier. "I knew that sex sold at an early age," she said. And, of course, "fictional" sex sold even better than the real thing.

Because her dreams were uninhibited, her action soon followed suit. Joan had kept within the proprieties of her social world, but Jackie was not quite so restrained. She

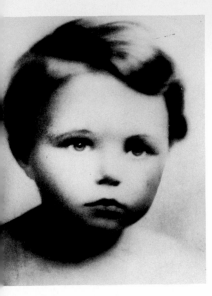

Joan Collins aged sixteen months.

ittle did the world know that this allur-
g fifteen-year-old would become "Dy-
sty's" bitchy Alexis.

Joan as a precocious youngster in 1958, soon to become Britain's answer to
Gardner.

Joan with Maxwell Reed, her first husband, in the early days of their romance.

Anthony Newley, the Hollywood singer, actor and producer, was Joan's second husband. They are seen here in 1968 at the marriage of Roman Polanski and Sharon Tate, who was later cruelly murdered by Charles Manson.

Warren Beatty, one of Hollywood's great lovers, seen here with Joan at a party in 1968.

Members of the "Dynasty" family grouped around the love triangle that forms the core of the famous soap opera.

Joan with third husband Ron Kass at a function in Hollywood in 1975.

Joan has no qualms in shedding her modesty for the TV film "The Moneychangers" in 1976.

The two famous sisters. Jackie helped launch Joan to stardom with the publication of her novel *The Stud* in 1978.

Joan in an extravagant sex-symbol pose in ''The Bitch'' (1979).

Joan goes to meet her children Sacha (left) and Tara at London's Heathrow Airport after they flew in from a holiday with their father Anthony Newley.

Jon Erik Hexum was co-star with Joan in a TV series. He later shot himself accidentally during a rehearsal.

Joan with daughter Katy after the child's tragic accident.

Joan with daughter Tara who was twenty years old in this 1984 photo.

Joan's elevation to the time-honored institution Madame Taussaud's in London.

(opposite page) A shot of Joan in the TV mini-series ''Sins.''

The fourth husband, Peter Holm, is in good humor here with Joan at a party held to announce the second edition of *A Night of 100 Stars*.

At a 1986 film première in London.

Joan with "Bungalow" Bill Wiggins, her first boyfriend after divorcing Peter Holm.

began smoking when all her peers smoked, and because of it was kicked out of school at the age of fifteen. Joan was better at keeping her indiscretions under cover. Jackie didn't particularly care.

"I led a very wild childhood," she said. "I was expelled from school in England for smoking and for waving at the resident flasher who used to stand there as all us kids went to play tennis in the park."

Jackie would yell across the way to him: "Hey, cold day today, isn't it?"

Like her sister, Jackie seemed to have developed a kind of feistiness and a contempt for the restrictions of the traditional moral codes as a reaction to her mother's lack of gumption and independence.

About Elsa, Joan used to say, "She was a mother who was totally caught up in the business of being a mother. There were no outside interests at all. I think that is one of the reasons why Jackie and I are both so independent."

Whatever caused this unmanageability in the two daughters, Jackie was pretty much an ungovernable teen-ager— even more so than Joan had been. Of course, she was growing up in the wild and woolly 1950s, just before the sixties broke on the world. London was coming apart at the seams. Having survived the war, it had decided to dump all the restrictions and live it up a bit. It was even rougher than what it had been during Joan's crucial teen-age years.

"I guess I was really a juvenile delinquent," Jackie said. "I would pad my bed at night with pillows and be out the window. My parents were constantly threatening juvenile hall. Joan wasn't like me at all. She just went off and became a star."

It was at about this time that Joan became somewhat concerned with her sister's antics—largely because of their mother's worry about the two of them—and decided to act as a sort of in-house policeman over her younger sister. She would try to stop Jackie from sneaking out, from smoking, from doing anything that wasn't within the rules.

And Jackie retaliated in the usual fashion. In fact, since she knew her sister's most vulnerable point, she attacked her there, right on target.

"I used to go to her wardrobe and ruin her dresses," Jackie confessed. "Really bitchy stuff. Looking back, I think she was just trying to protect me, because when Joan went to America and I followed some time later, she was really marvelous to me, and we became the best of friends." But that was later.

It was during the period when Joan went to Hollywood to work for Twentieth Century-Fox that Jackie got the Hollywood bug as well. This happened at the time of her expulsion from school. When Joan heard what had happened to her sister, she sent for Jackie and Jackie immediately flew out to the West Coast to join her older sister.

"She met me at the airport," Jackie recalled, "gave me the keys to her apartment, and told me she had to go off for a month," Jackie said. "I couldn't believe it! I had a real ball, and Joan helped me tremendously."

She moved in with Joan and watched with fascination as the motion-picture world played out its scenes of opulent luxury and seamy decadence all around her.

And while Jackie was living there with her sister in a seedy little apartment complex, she absorbed background information and ideas for upcoming stories she might write in her diary. This was in the 1950s, and of course Jackie was still a teen-ager—but with rather advanced ideas about life and love.

Fascinated by the swinging movieland set, she seemed able to stay on the fringes without being totally immersed in the *dolce vita* atmosphere. She became what most writers are automatically: an interested observer.

"Having a sister who was a movie star was sensational," Jackie said later. "To have entrée into meeting more or less anybody, because she knew *everybody!*"

Jackie returned to England to finish school, but she soon rejoined her sister in the States. Joan's career may not have been shooting toward the stars, but it was at least still going full blast. And so were Joan's affairs with various men.

"I remember coming to visit [Joan] once," Jackie recalled. "She had a suite at the Chateau Marmont—a great glamorous suite."

Jackie looked around and told Joan, "Oh, this is lovely, great!"

And Joan came right back at her. "Yes. You won't actually be sleeping *here*. There is a little room at the top of the hotel where you will be sleeping."

Somewhat chastened, Jackie discovered that during the sleeping hours the suite was more-or-less occupied by a more-or-less struggling actor and Joan Collins. "He would sleep in the suite, and I would be in his little attic room."

The little attic room belonged to a young man named Warren Beatty.

But there were all kinds of perks in being Joan's sister.

"Like everybody else," Jackie admitted, "I got propositioned by Warren, too. But since I turned his proposition down, [Joan and I] never shared a boyfriend. The possibility was there—let's put it that way. But Warren would proposition a chair if it looked at him sideways."

There were other men who took an active interest in Jackie, who actually shared a great deal of her sister's amazing beauty. It was her verve and her ability to turn a line and make life a game of fun and chance that served her well. Men flocked around her the way they flocked around her older sister.

Jackie was only eighteen years old when she married a businessman named Wallace Austin. He was twelve years older than she.

"He was a fabulous, dynamic man," Jackie said. "And he was also a manic depressive." They had one child, Tracy Austin, and within four years of their marriage, her husband was dead. During those four years, Jackie had finally had it with the problems of living with a manic depressive, and had gotten a divorce from him.

"It was a very unfortunate first marriage." Jackie noted later. "Wallace was a drug addict, and he ultimately killed himself with an overdose. I divorced him because I knew he was going to do it. I figured four years was enough to wait for someone to kill himself."

Austin was only thirty-four when he died. At that point, Jackie, hardly knowing where to turn with her life, tried a brief career in acting, appearing in a handful of movies and television shows like "The Avengers" and "The Saint"—first as "Lynn Curtis" and then as "Jackie Douglas." Perhaps she thought some of her sister's magic had rubbed off on her. If she thought so, she was wrong. She never seemed to get into the big time the way her sister had—even with its limitations—and finally Jackie backed away from acting.

Marriage appealed to her—its ancillary delights even more so. As a widow at twenty-two, Jackie managed a series of flings that might have come out of one of the books she was to write later on.

"I led a very wild life before I got married the second time," she admitted.

During that time, she moved about a great deal—from place to place, from friend to friend, and from man to man. And at the same time she began writing in a more professionally serious vein—stories and finally books. Like her sister, she was not one to inhibit herself either in language or in action.

In a sense, Jackie was a creature of her times. The sixties opened up the concepts of morality until the original concept itself was not much more than a shattered shell. The concepts of speech and behavior were likewise shattered, so that nothing remained of them.

Like her sister, Jackie loved to talk about people—gossip about things that happened, about who was going with whom, and who was leaving whom. She learned to put it all down in her stories.

Three years after the death of her first husband, Jackie met and fell in love with American businessman Oscar

Lerman. A second daughter, Tiffany, was born a year or so later, and a boy, Rory, two years after that.

Once her family was established, Jackie began turning once more to her old love—fantasies and writing about them. Five years after her marriage to Lerman, Jackie sold her first novel, a book with the unwieldy title *The World Is Full of Married Men*. She took the phrase from the often-heard lament of all her women friends who were on the prowl for single men. Good men.

It was a sophisticated story about women on the prowl for men with whom to celebrate affairs—either adulterous or nonadulterous. The action consisted mostly of bedroom scenes and steamy seduction sequences. But it was the dialogue that made the thing a good read for the uninhibited. Like her sister Joan, Jackie was exceptionally skilled at the use of all the four-letter words that spice up the language. She used them all. Coming from the mouths of the women in her book—exactly as coming from the mouth of her beautiful actress sister Joan—the four-letter words had a most exceptional life and vitality of their own.

For the ordinary middle-class woman, unused to hearing the words that Jackie and Joan had heard all their lives among the show-business people they knew, the book was a zinger that would not let them put it down.

The critics were appalled. The book was published in Britain, where many of the ancient taboos had not been broken by the wide-open sixties culture. The general reaction was stunned disbelief, and then total disapproval. One reviewer called the book "the most disgusting book ever written." Tom Driberg, of *The Guardian*, opined that "he had never read a nastier novel." Whatever, the novel quickly shot up to the top. Within a week of its publication date in 1968, it was the number-one best-seller in England.

Now the Collins sisters were household names in Britain. Joan had been the up-and-coming movie star, then the Hollywood starlet, and finally the Queen of the Schlocks. In fact, many of their countrymen were seeing the Collins sisters as "liberators" in the full sense of the word as it was used in the sixties by feminists.

Jackie, as well as Joan, was confronting the double standards that kept women down even in the enlightened days of the twentieth century. The very title of her first book was a statement in itself.

"Joan has always said, 'Fuck convention. I'm going to do what I want,'" Jackie pointed out. The attitudes of the sisters about convention and about the "double standard" prevailing in male-female relationships are similar, although couched in different terms.

For example, Jackie has said that she is definitely against this so-called "double standard." "I think there should be a better balance between the sexes, and maybe in my own teeny way, I might help. I was once being interviewed by a very good journalist in New York, and I gave all my views on the double standard. And I got up to leave, and he pinches me on the ass! I thought, This is exactly what I am talking about!"

As for Joan: "I think Jackie felt for a time that men are takers and women are used. I don't feel that way. I feel that sexual relationships are equal, and that women are entitled to have as free a sexual life as men. Absolutely. I'm not the sort of woman who can say, 'All I need is my career, my children, my family.' I very much need to love somebody and to be loved."

In the long run, of course, the two sisters turned out quite differently. Jackie once frankly admitted: "I'm the watcher. I like to observe, and [Joan] very much likes to participate. She likes to be center stage, and I like to sit in the background."

In a way, Jackie's own characters in her first book reflected her sister Joan's attitude, although Jackie was always careful to say that she did not *ever* model a character after her sister.

As for personal habits, Jackie liked to lounge around in blue jeans and shirts. And Joan would never be seen anywhere but in a drop-dead ensemble that cost half a million.

Nevertheless when Jackie's second book appeared in 1969, there were many hints that one of the characters—the central one, in fact (other than "The Stud" who was really the antagonist against the female protagonist)—was none other than her sister. In fact, the very name of the woman around whom the book's story revolved was a dead giveaway. "Fontaine" calls up the natural linkage with "Joan" in "Joan Fontaine." As so if Fontaine is not Joan, she is a look-alike: a woman who dominates the men in her life and manipulates them to within an inch of their lives.

In fact, when the book was published—it had almost as blazing a career as her first best-seller—Jackie herself remarked to her sister, "You'd be perfect as Fontaine."

And that was the kernel of the idea that lodged itself in Joan Collins's mind in 1969 and 1970, when her marriage and her career were not exactly revving up to top speed. Jackie was exactly right, Joan decided. She approached her sister one day in 1970 and told her as much.

"I've decided if an actress is to get anywhere today, she has to get properties for herself. May I have *The Stud*?"

Later Jackie said; "How can you possibly say no to your sister?"

And so the idea was born. Joan took copies of the book around with her and visited all the studio heads and independent producers she could think of. Not one of them was interested. The trouble was that Joan was not a hot property anymore. She had had her day, the word was; if not exactly over the hill, she was definitely on the wane.

It was no go.

With *The Stud* relegated to the background, Joan continued to play series segments on television, while beginning to rue the day she had decided to go back to films. It was not the same. Her clout was not as great as it had been—if it ever had been great. And once her husband was fired from the job that had been holding the family together, it became evident that it was up to Joan to bring in enough money to feed the hungry mouths.

In her autobiography Joan detailed the unbelievable sequence of events that took place when she was hired to do a segment of "Starsky and Hutch" filmed in Hawaii. While it sounded like a welcome vacation from Hollywood, it turned out to be a determining factor in Joan's future life. The problem was not in the principals, but in the way the entire segment was put together and worked out.

While amenities are not exactly expected on location film shooting, there are requisites in Equity contracts with studios and producers that necessarily get the best out of actors and actresses hired. In a lively review of the episode, Joan pointed out that even the normal lines of demarcation between the various levels of acting roles had become blurred beyond recognition—so that bit players were confused with speaking roles—and the entire production a shambles from one end to the other.

When a bit player dumped all her makeup and costumes on Joan's things in a tiny dressing-room area, Joan had had it with working in this type of environment. Besides that, the stars on the show were doing their own stunts when they should not have been doing them—and all sorts of miserable things happened.

Once Joan had made up her mind to bow out, she realized that she had painted herself into a corner. She must get work—her family's survival depended on it. But film jobs were few and far between. She was getting desperate. When Samantha Eggar suggested that she collect unemployment insurance—something Joan had never tried before, but which was a fact of life with most actors and actresses in television— she disguised herself in dark glasses and a pulled-down hat and stood in line with the usual group of Hispanics and laborers.

This did not sit well with her, and when she finally did get up to ask for her money, she became an object of excited attention when the woman taking the forms recognized her from the "Starsky and Hutch" sequence that had apparently just been aired.

"It's Joan Collins!" And so on.

Forced to flee almost for her life, Joan vowed never again to try to collect any unemployment money. It was too humiliating for her. Besides, it turned out that she was not able to collect the money for two weeks while the bureaucrats tried to determine whether she had tried hard enough to get another job!

Joan's reaction belongs to the soap-opera business; indeed she was becoming more and more carved into that kind of figure by everything that was happening to her. Compare her reaction to the unemployment line with the reaction of another soap-opera heroine:

JOAN COLLINS: I made a vow. I would never get myself in this situation again. I *must* work. If I couldn't cut it as an actor, then I would write or do interior decoration. I couldn't abide the humiliation of receiving a handout. . . . I had to succeed now by myself. . . . It was all up to *me*.

SCARLETT O'HARA: I'm going to live through this, and when it's over, I'm never going to be hungry again. No, nor any of my folks. If I have to steal or kill—as God is my witness, I'm never going to be hungry again.

No matter how hard Joan determined to get it, money was not forthcoming. Besides, it was necessary to liquidate some of the family's belongings to pay the bills that were piling up. The house had to go, too, and in its sale, Ron Kass's first wife managed to get a large portion of the money and refused to share it.

By 1975, Joan was becoming desperate. Somehow she had to get money to keep things going. Her husband seemed unable to get anything to do—at least anything that would pay the bills. Well, there was always *The Stud* that Joan

138   Jay David

might be able to do. By now Jackie had produced *Lovehead* in 1974, *The Hollywood Zoo* and *The World Is Full of Divorced Women*, a sequel to her first novel, both in 1975.

But there was still no luck with *The Stud*.

Joan had an idea. She went to Jackie again. "Write the screenplay for *The Stud*."

Jackie was cold to the idea. Besides, she was getting good advances now on her books. To plunge into a whole new world of writing seemed pretty silly. "Oh, I've never written a screenplay."

"We can't afford to hire a good screenwriter," Joan pointed out. "Write the screenplay!"

In spite of all her other commitments, Jackie did turn her hand to doing a version of *The Stud* for the screen. It followed the story line of the book rather closely.

"Joan can be extremely persuasive," Jackie said. "I wrote the screenplay in six weeks."

When Joan read it and studied its possible effect on her career as well as on the audiences used to the type of thing she had been doing, she was somewhat concerned. What bothered her was the fact that she seemed to be doing exactly what she disliked other actors and actresses for doing. In her heart and soul, she felt that an actor or actress was doing his professional best when he or she *played* a character created by a dramatist.

If Joan were to play Fontaine in Jackie's screenplay, she would not really be *playing* Fontaine at all. What she would be playing would be an exaggerated and glamourized version of Joan Collins—as seen through the sometimes slightly jaundiced and at other times somewhat rose-colored glasses of her sister.

And then it occurred to her that there was really nothing *bad* about this idea of exploiting the fact that she was Joan Collins and the fact that Joan Collins lived in a fashion that resembled the way the woman in her sister's book lived.

Why not reinvent herself? Why not *become* Fontaine? But at the same time she would be Joan Collins—maybe even more so than the Joan Collins that already existed. The old Hollywood studio system invented life stories for their young contract players; she would simply reinvent herself for a new and wider public.

In short, she would become a commodity rather than an actress playing a role. Yes. She would blatantly exploit herself as an entertainment property—in short, a commodity in itself. She would re-create herself in the image of herself as seen by the public.

Then and only then would she be able to play the part her sister had written in *The Stud*—and make it stick. First she must work on her own image. And she knew the way to do it.

For some years now, the publishing industry both in Britain and in the United States had been floundering about trying to find its way amidst a morass of trashy paperback novels, cult books, and particularly bios—usually the life stories of individuals who were "celebrities," which term included statesmen, politicians, millionaires, singers, sports figures, and anybody on the acting or sports end of the entertainment business.

The guru of the entertainment publishing world was the agent "Swifty" Lazar. With his help, Joan felt that she could write a story about Joan Collins that would be as exciting and as riveting as any role she had played on the screen or stage.

Lazar was not so sanguine about her possibilities. When he pointed out that perhaps she might be able to publish a book about her life in England—since she was better known there than in the United States—Joan knew that she was facing an uphill battle.

But, with the help of her sister, who did know the publishing business firsthand, Joan finally secured a contract to write a book about her life for the English firm of W. H. Allen and Company—the same firm that had printed Jackie's first book.

Joan went about her work very seriously, spending many hours on getting everything in the book as interesting and as exciting as she could. It was hard work—but not quite so humiliating as doing "Starsky and Hutch" or as standing in line at the unemployment bureau.

At least when Lazar heard about her work, he promised her that if the book was a success in England, he could probably work out a deal for her with a U.S. publisher.

In the book, Joan concentrated on her liaisons with men— paying particular attention to the way her sister handled that theme in her books. So much had happened to Joan that the story line of her life read the same way the story line of a soap opera would read—and that was all to the good. At least it was readable.

In the midst of her work on the book, and her unsuccessful agent work in trying to sell *The Stud*, Joan did manage to secure a job in a science-fiction/horror movie—a thing called *Empire of the Ants*. In her book she wrote up the experience as a horror story in its own right—not as the science-fiction story that H. G. Wells had written earlier. In fact, she billed it as "an H. G. Wells classic (so they said)," implying that it was not.

Actually, the *Ants* version she worked in was based only loosely on the Wells classic—which indeed has always been considered a classic of the genre. Wells had envisioned a battle to the death between man and insect, this particular confrontation between a group of men and hordes of ants. In the short story, the protagonist and his friends are cut off by mountainous waves of ants in the billions coming at them to eat them alive. It was the *waves* of ants that Wells visualized and portrayed in his story; the waves were the menace.

Visually, the makers of *Empire of the Ants* worked on a different theory—imagining that each ant was a magnified version of the actual ant, with the menace in the *size* of each ant rather than in its *numbers*. For the camera, of course, waves of ants would be indistinguishable from waves of anything else—carrots, or broccoli—and not half so menacing as the sight of a huge tottering, devouring ant the size of a human being.

The Wells story was shifted to an island in the Florida Everglades, with the cast menaced by these six-foot beasties. Shooting conditions were formidable, with immersion in the stinking swamp water, accidents on the set; Joan even sustained a bad cut over her eye and a black eye when a door was slammed shut by the wind.

When the stuntmen and stuntwomen were delayed en route, Joan was forced to perform her own dunking in the swamp from a canoe. Once immersed in the water, she suddenly found her legs swelling up with cuts from the roots of swamp plants. She was immediately cleaned off with eyedrops, eardrops, nosedrops, and throat spray. Even so, it was two days before her legs got back to normal. And there went Thanksgiving and Christmas!

In all, *Ants* was the worst movie that she had ever made.

Actually, within the genre, the film is not all that bad. It continues to be rerun on television from time to time. Whatever, it was money for Joan at a time when there was no other money coming in. And it led to a trip to Cannes to promote the movie.

In Cannes, in May 1977, Joan did get a nibble on the project that was foremost in her mind: *The Stud*.

It was there, during her promotion tour, that she met George Walker, an English former boxer who was the head of Brent-Walker, a film production company that specialized in making B movies. Joan launched into her by-now-familiar sales pitch for *The Stud*, and was stunned when at the end of the spiel, Walker smiled at her and said, "As a matter of fact, I would." He went on to say that he had been looking for just such a project. He asked her if she had a script—and of course she did have Jackie's!

After reading it, Walker agreed to finance the movie. He also agreed later to hiring Ron Kass and Oscar Lerman, Jackie's husband, as coproducers. Joan would star in the script as written by Jackie—with one slight change. Walker wanted a nudie scene to hype up the exploitation value of the film.

Joan had already done a nudie scene in that Italian movie—
and they were all the rage at the time. She agreed.

Shooting began almost immediately. Ron Kass created a
gigantic publicity campaign that centered on the key words:
"Over forty and she takes her clothes off!"

It was the double whammy. Coincidentally, Joan's autobiography *and* the picture *The Stud* appeared in England
within the year. The timing of the book and the motion
picture could not have been better.

The book itself was a sizzler and an eyebrow raiser—and,
in conjunction with the movie—caused Joan Collins to become the sensation of the moment.

Without the book, *The Stud* would have been a success at
any rate, but in conjunction *with* the book, it caused Joan to
become a true "personality"—a "celebrity"—all on her own.
The fact that her persona as seen in *The Stud* could be
backed up by the words in a book she herself had written
made her seem more *real* than before!

In fact, she was established as Joan Collins now, whereas
before, she had simply been that actress Joan something or
other—oh, yeah—Collins. There was no one in Britain now
who did not know who Joan Collins was.

The movie was one of the most successful of the season. It
made money—plenty of money. The money all went to
Brent-Walker, but it established Joan Collins as a formidable
actress in that particular genre. Not forever the Queen of the
Horror films. Now Joan Collins *lived*!

As Jackie Collins herself said; "I was so pleased that in
later years I could repay Joan's kindness and thoughtfulness
by writing a book that put her back on the screen. Now
we're great friends."

To reprise the success of *The Stud*, Brent-Walker ordered
another script in the same vein from Jackie Collins. This one
was titled *The Bitch* and was later published by Pan, the
paperback house in Britain, as a novel.

Joan portrayed *The Bitch* with the same zest and fervor
she had displayed in playing Fontaine in *The Stud*, but when

it was all over, she did not like this spin-off—it was a sequel to the first—of the original story as much as she had liked the first.

"I hate, hate, hate that film!" Joan exploded once to a *Playboy* magazine interviewer. "It was just a cheap imitation of *The Stud*. I didn't like the script, I didn't like the director [Gerry O'Hara]." Even though the script was also written by Jackie, Joan felt that it was not nearly so good as *The Stud*. "It was just an utter rip-off. It didn't have the rawness and the kind of modern vulgarity that *The Stud* had. And I hated, loathed, and detested the title with such a passion that I practically went down on my knees begging the producers not to use it. They wanted the ads to say:

JOAN COLLINS IS THE BITCH

I wanted them to be:

JOAN COLLINS AS THE BITCH

"I remember I was in the south of France when one of those planes flew by at the Cannes Film Festival with a banner that read JOAN COLLINS IS THE BITCH. I thought then, I'm in trouble here; this is going to stick. And it did. It's one thing to play a part, but it's another for it to become your nickname."

But it was largely on the strength of the popularity of and the revenue from those two pictures that Joan was able to secure the lead role in a Liverpool version of *The Last of Mrs. Cheyney*, opposite the actor Simon Williams, of *Upstairs, Downstairs* fame.

Joan now had high hopes that she might quit the film business forever—with its skin-flick overtones—to make a success on the legitimate stage. She had always wanted to be a dramatic star.

It was during preparation for the staging of the play in the West End in London after its successful Liverpool opening—

while Joan and Ron Kass were in Paris together—that the news came to Joan that her daughter Katy had been hurt in an automobile crash and was in a coma.

And that, of course, was quite another story—a story that put an end to Joan's appearances in film, on television, or on the stage for some time to come.

When she resumed her career, it was to be one of quite a different kind. Nevertheless, its underpinnings were firmly in place because of the rather notorious success of *The Stud* and *The Bitch.*

Without the family togetherness and teamwork that made those two movies, what awaited her—the brightest and most spectacular part of her theatrical career—would never have happened.

Chapter Nine

The Genesis of Alexis

Great literature is full of lines of dialogue that forever keynote and epitomize a fictional character. Charles Dickens knew the trick. "Barkis is willin' " is an unforgettable character line, from *David Copperfield*. William Shakespeare knew the trick, too. "Oh, what a rogue and peasant slave am I!" sums up the self-analytical, introverted character of Hamlet.

Even Margaret Mitchell understood the art, compressing Scarlett O'Hara's character into one short and memorable line: "I'll think about it tomorrow."

The writing team of Richard and Esther Shapiro, who had met at a UCLA writing class in the 1950s and were married sometime later, became scriptwriters for various television shows like "Bonanza" and "Route 66." Finally they hit the financial jackpot when they were hired to do a daytime soap opera called "Love of Life" at $3,000 a week. It was a rough go, turning out all that dialogue, and after surviving several seasons, they quit. Eventually Esther Shapiro became ABC vice-president for miniseries and produced "Masada," "Inside the Third Reich," and other miniseries.

In 1979, ABC executive producer Aaron Spelling, whose "Love Boat" and "Charlie's Angels" had become solid hits, got in touch with the Shapiros and ordered a nighttime soap opera in the style of the unbelievably successful "Dallas"—to put ABC in competition with CBS. In the way of competitors, Spelling wanted something different from "Dallas"—but not *too* different. You know, a sort of—well—rip-off.

The Shapiros came up with a kind of action piece with overtones of money in their story "Oil," a tale of the Carrington family—rich, rich, rich. There was an oil billionaire, Carrington, and his lovely new wife, and his son and daughter by a previous marriage. The soap elements were strewn throughout the story. One of Carrington's main foes was another oil baron who was trying to do him in on the fields; his new wife's past lover was working for his main competitor; his son was a homosexual; his spoiled daughter was an incipient nymphomaniac who jumped into bed with everyone available.

Renamed "Dynasty" to give a kind of wide-range serenity and grandeur to the project, the show was approved and cast, with John Forsythe (the voice in "Charlie's Angels") playing the lead, and Linda Evans as his new wife. To get the ponderous thing moving, the first episodes were heavy with outdoor action: tricks at the oil well, fights in the rigging, smoky scenes between Linda and Bo Hopkins as her former lover, the daughter's affair with the family chauffeur. And so on.

By the end of the first year, it was obvious to Spelling that the thing wasn't breaking through the stratosphere as he had hoped it would. But the Shapiros weren't to be daunted. They had an idea. The idea was to inject the story with a character who might rival "Dallas" 's J. R. Ewing, the baddy with the big grin.

Who to get?

By now the writing was being done by a fairly large group of people, among them a man named Ed De Blasio who handled most of the surface dialogue superimposed after each scene had been blocked out. By now the first season was ending and the cliff-hanger for the summer was written and in the works. Blake Carrington was on trial for man-slaughter. His son and daughter were present. And his ex-wife was suddenly called on to testify against him.

A model was hired to dress up in white with a thick veil and big hat to cover her face. The point was: what kind of woman was she? Could she be made into a female counter-part of J. R. Ewing?

> DE BLASIO: I was sitting there thinking, Okay I've got to give her a line; what do I write?

His mind continued to wander. What would a woman say who had not seen her son or daughter for a number of years even though she was their actual mother?

> DE BLASIO: I found myself writing: "Hello, Fallon. I'm glad to see your father had your teeth fixed, if not your tongue."

And so another keynote line was invented. This one per-sonified the character of the woman who would now be known as Alexis Carrington. Though the line had bite to it, it revealed only a bit of Alexis' character. From there, the writers and character could move out and cover many more angles.

The line was the theme of Alexis.

"Hey, that's a good line. Give her another like it," De Blasio was told. And from that moment on, Alexis, too, had trouble controlling her tongue—to the delight of millions of viewers who became fast fans of Alexis.

She was a solid, waspish addition. But who was to play the role?

Sophia Loren was actually in the running, along with Raquel Welch. But Esther Shapiro held out for someone she felt would be better than those two. "The truth is, I hired an actress for the day and put her in a white suit, a hat, and a veil so I would have more time to persuade everyone to get Joan Collins." Perhaps she had gotten the idea of hiring Joan Collins after she had seen *The Stud*. She once described the Collins role in the movie in this manner:

"The role happened to be a man-eating nymphomaniac, so a lot of people think, 'Hey, she must really be like that.' Well, it isn't so." She admitted, "Joan was older [than Welch] and the reaction was strong against her. People felt her accent would not be understood and they thought she was over the hill. But I thought she was the only person for the role. She has humor, and I felt the part could not work without humor. And Alexis had to be—and Joan is—a great beauty. And you had to see something other than a monster. I realized when I started this show that if you could make them fascinating enough, you could write unsympathetic characters."

Could they get Joan for the part? There were rumors of her troubles with her daughter Katy. There were rumors she was out of show business for good. There were rumors she was washed up with Ron Kass.

When Joan first heard about the part of Alexis Carrington she was in Europe on vacation with her husband. Later, she put it this way for a *TV Guide* story:

"I'm no dope. I could see the possibilities of Alexis. She's an evil, conniving bitch. She's larger than life and that's what I like about her."

It seemed that the transition from her role in *The Stud* to Alexis in "Dynasty" would be an easy crossover. The characters are both written as connivers who are larger than life. In spite of the fact that Joan understood the possibilities of Alexis, she was hesitant about playing Alexis; she had never heard of the show before. She was vacationing in Marbella, Spain, after the long siege with her daughter Katy, when Tom Korman, her agent in Los Angeles, called to tell her the "Dynasty" people wanted her to try out for a juicy role.

JOAN: What's "Dynasty"?

KORMAN: It's a series—sort of a soap opera. A bit like "Dallas." It's been on for thirteen weeks so far. Could become very successful, although it's about number forty-five in the ratings right now. They want you for it.

JOAN: Oh, no way.

KORMAN: You've *got* to do it. Aaron [Spelling] loves you, so do the Shapiros and the Pollacks [the head writers]. They want you badly. It starts shooting at Fox next week. Can you do it?

JOAN: (silence)

KORMAN: It's a great role. Her name's Alexis. She's a bitch but witty and clever and she has some great dialogue. It could make you a very big star again. Think about it.

JOAN: Okay. I'll think about it, Tom.

Hardly the reaction of an actress thrilled to death at the chance of playing the part that was to be the making of her. Joan Collins had known Spelling since her work on *The Opposite Sex* so many years ago at Fox. At that time he had been an aspiring actor.

When Joan finally agreed to do "Dynasty," she actually supposed that it would be a short-lived job at best. When she arrived in Century City, she rented an apartment for only six months, figuring her job would be finished at the end of that period—if not sooner.

When she viewed the thirteen episodes on the lot, Joan found the show extremely boring. "In any case, I wasn't a lover of soap operas, particularly ones with a lot of action in the oil fields. But a buck was a buck was a buck, so I was back at Fox again."

Another factor in her decision to do "Dynasty" was her daughter Katy, who was recuperating from her car accident. Joan felt the California sunshine would do her a world of good.

Joan still had not made up her mind on her future. "I was going to concentrate on the theater," she told a writer for *McCall's.* "My agent called and mentioned "Dynasty," and I had never heard of it. Then he read me some of the script, and I thought it would be nice for a six- or seven-month gig. We could spend the summer in California; it would be good for Katy, who was still recovering from her accident."

She also told *McCall's*: "I was certain I'd be back in England in a year or so, since "Dynasty" was number thirty-eight at the end of its first season. I didn't expect much for it—hardly that my presence in it would turn it around. But, in actual fact, I suppose that's what I did. First, I decided I would do something distinctive with my costumes. At that time, all the women on TV were rather boringly dressed . . . all sorts of silk shirts and trousers and the occasional cocktail dress. I wanted to dress much more haute couture—hats and gloves and nipped-in waists."

Joan was right. Her attention to dress revolutionized the soap-opera industry. She was able to say later:

"*Now* the look is proliferating all over television. I look at women and think, My God! She looks like me!"

Joan's move from London to Hollywood was not all sweetness and light. There was one ugly problem that had to be solved before she could even *leave* Europe. At the time she signed the contract to do "Dynasty" she was still under contract to Triumph Productions, Duncan Weldon, and Louis Michaels to perform *Murder in Mind*, a stage play, in the English provinces. This commitment had come about largely as a result of her four-month appearance in *The Last of Mrs. Cheyney* in the fall of 1980 in the West End, when it had been determined finally that Katy was out of danger.

The contract to do *Murder in Mind* was nowhere as important as *Mrs. Cheyney*, but Joan had taken on the job anyway since things were pretty thin at that point. After thinking it over, however, she decided she wanted out of it because the commitment contained no guarantee of a West End run in London. But Triumph was adamant.

Her confrontation with Louis Michaels went like this:

MICHAELS: The only way we will *not* see you appear in
    our theaters is if we have your *death certificate* in
    our hands, Joanie dear—I've got that in writing in
    a telegram.

Joan was outraged. She could not believe her ears. "Death
certificate?" What was this—the English Mafia?

Ron Kass was in a panic. He had helped Joan negotiate
the contract and did not want her to pull the rug out from
under him. He would look like an idiot as well as a liar. Joan
and he arrived back in London to fight the battle of the
contracts and Ron immediately called Joan's father, who was
experienced in theatrical matters.

"This is terrible!" he cried to Joe. He explained that Joan
had signed a contract with the "Dynasty" people—and was
now responsible for being in two places and for doing two
projects at the same time. "She can't take it! She's contracted to tour in that play for Triumph Productions. They
won't agree to release her."

Joe Collins unloaded his scorn on his son-in-law by simply
stating the truth in these scorching words: "Do you want
Joan to go round the provinces in some bloody stinking play
that may not even draw audiences when she could be seen
all over the world on television? You must be off your head!"
Joe Collins talked that way.

"But don't you understand? The situation is impossible!"
Ron continued. "Joan has offered to do two plays for Triumph
as soon as the work on "Dynasty" ends, but they won't hear of
it. We've even offered them money to let her go. Yet they're
still threatening to sue us if she takes up the television offer."

Joe told Ron to get Joan on the line, and he told her in no
uncertain terms: "You get over to my place and we'll thrash
this thing out. I know all about the situation you're in and I
know how to deal with it! You *are* going into "Dynasty,"
understand that!"

"All right, Daddy. We'll come over right now."

Joe was a skilled bargainer of the old school, and even though he did not know if he could help at all, he knew that arbitration would probably settle for Joan inasmuch as the "Dynasty" contract was worth so much more than the Triumph contract. Also, there was the matter of Katy; it could be proved that she would be better off in the salubrious California climate. All in all, it looked to him as if Joan would win. He counseled her and his son-in-law this way:

"Forget about being barred or banned or placating people. Just do what I say. Take Katy, get on a plane, fly out to America, and start work on "Dynasty." Katy will be better off in California, so you take her there—just go! Let the rest take its course."

It wasn't quite so simple as Joe had hoped it might be. One of the ironic things he had not even told Joan was the fact that he himself had been one of the original owners of Triumph! In the event, Triumph threatened to get at Joan through Equity, declaring that Equity must forbid Joan Collins from working in America and England if she opted for "Dynasty" over *Murder in Mind*.

In turn, Equity contacted the Screen Actors Guild. Lawyers issued threats and counterthreats. Talk of lawsuits flew hot and heavy. Joan, going by the advice of her hard-nosed father, stood firm amidst the fracas.

In the end, however, Joan and Ron did bend a little and make an out-of-court financial settlement concerning the broken contract for the *Murder in Mind* tour. "I still think that had the case gone to arbitration, this would not have been necessary," Joe wrote.

When Joan finally made her appearance in Hollywood, the producers of "Dynasty" were delighted. They had wanted a sultry brunette beauty to play the role of Alexis, and they had got her in the form of Joan Collins. Lynn Loring, a vice-president at Spelling Productions, described her feelings about the selection of Joan for the role:

"Joan is not only an excellent actress, but one of the most

professional I have ever worked with. She's never late. She does not have a temper. She gives an enormous amount to the other actors. She's straight, gutsy—a terrific broad in the best sense of the word."

Joan Collins seemed the perfect Alexis almost from the very beginning. At times she seemed wicked and bitchy; at other times she could heat up the stage with her smoldering sexuality underlined by her generous pouty lips and smoky eyes. Her face and her full figure could drive men crazy with desire until they found out that Alexis was a snake in the grass, with a mind constantly hatching plots to manipulate everyone in sight so that she could be sure to get what she wanted no matter who or what stood in her way.

From the beginning, Alexis—it was simply a matter of osmosis that Joan Collins should almost immediately *become* Alexis Carrington even in her own mind—could strut onto the set, challenging every man watching her with the swing of her body. Pretending always to be unaware of her effect on the male libido, she would nonchalantly light a cigarillo and act as if she owned the world and everyone in it. She was a sex kitten, a tigress, and a man-eater—all at the same time.

It is interesting to see in retrospect how easily Joan Collins fitted her own persona to that of Alexis Carrington. In fact, Alexis' life in almost no way directly compared to the life of Joan Collins. Yet both seem indistinguishable today. For the record, here is a sketch of "Dynasty" 's Alexis Carrington from the "authorized biography" of "Dynasty":

Rich, sophisticated, sensual, Alexis has the best of everything in clothes and houses. [So does Joan.] She is completely in charge of her life and does anything she wants, knowing that she is always the center of attention no matter where she goes. [Not true of Joan.]

Alexis is an intelligent jet-setter with political and social connections, contacts she uses whenever she wants something that is hard to get. As well as being a skilled painter, she knows ballet, art, and the theater. Besides English she speaks three languages fluently: French, Italian, and Spanish. She has her finger in every pot and leaves her imprimatur wherever she goes. [Half-true.]

She conquers rich and powerful men from all nations at the drop of a hat. Her beauty and eroticism are irresistible to men, who cannot get enough of her. She knows how to manipulate men (with her striking looks and figure) and feels no guilt about trading on her beauty to attain any desired object. [Joan could, all right.]

Doggedly persistent, she never gives up once she sets her sights on something or someone. She has a taste for men who play hard to get, which she inherited from her mother. [Joan has a habit of going after men she finds attractive; she has a willpower that is indomitable—witness her work with Katy.]

Alexis Morell was born in England during World War II. She enrolled in a Swiss boarding school, from which she was expelled, and worked as a model for artists in Brussels. [Joan was a model, too.] Alexis studied at the Royal Academy of Dramatic Art. [So did Joan.]

At the age of seventeen, she married wealthy oil tycoon Blake Carrington, who was in the process of consolidating his economic and social positions in Denver and international circles.

After their marriage Alexis felt spurned because Blake spent so much of his time away on business. In 1955 they had their first baby, Adam. [Joan's Tara was born in 1963.] Bored with being a mother and nothing else, Alexis initiated an affair with her husband's best friend, Cecil Colby. Racked by guilt afterwards, she swore to herself that she would be a faithful wife. She bore her second child, Fallon, in 1956. [Joan's Sacha was born in 1965.]

Misery followed quickly on the heels of Fallon's birth. In 1957 somebody kidnapped Adam. At loose ends, Alexis moved into her new mansion and bore another son, Steven, in 1958. At this point she withdrew from the world, reared her offspring, and took up her painting with renewed diligence. [Joan's third child, Katy, was born in 1972. Indeed, during the period of her childbearing years, Joan did more or less withdraw from the big time, although she managed to keep her hand in the world of show business.]

While helping estate manager Roger Grimes build an art studio on her property she engaged in an affair with him. When Alexis wants a man, she gets him, come hell or high water.

As luck would have it, Blake discovered Grimes in bed with Alexis in 1965. She barely survived the horrible scene that ensued. Terrified, she watched Blake beat Grimes to within an inch of his life. It was a new experience for her. Jet-setter though she was, she had never known fear before.

Consumed by guilt once more, Alexis agreed with Blake's accusation that she was unfit to be a mother. At his behest she left their home and retreated into seclusion.

Living in exile in ritzy Acapulco, she enjoyed herself with beachboys, bellhops, and loaded playboys. Even with all these new bed partners, she could not overcome the pain she felt at the loss of her babies. The only thing that ameliorated her pain was travel. So she traveled: to exotic playgrounds like Cannes, Capri, and Portofino.

Alexis' first appearance on the "Dynasty" series occurred as she returned from her travels and attended the Blake Carrington manslaughter trial in Denver in 1981. Her unexpected testimony about Blake's propensity for violence jolted the spectators in the courtroom.

She had come to hate Blake, but on seeing him after so many years away from him, she began to find herself in love with him more than ever. She wanted him now because of his strength of character: he was the only man she had ever met who was as willful and strong as she.

Now she demanded to have Blake back. She determined to take him away from Krystle. Blake rejected Alexis' advances. Humiliated and defiant, Alexis burned for revenge.

Alexis thought she could get the better of Krystle because she saw Krystle as a softie, but she was wrong; she had sold

Krystle short. Krystle had a tough inner core and would fight
Alexis tooth and nail.

Hoping to get back at Blake, Alexis married his arch-
rival, his erstwhile friend Cecil Colby. The ceremony took
place in a hospital where Colby was recuperating from a
heart attack induced by his passionate lovemaking with
Alexis. After the marriage Colby suffered another heart attack
and died.

Because of his intense loathing of Blake Carrington, Colby
left instructions in his will to Alexis to use the millions of
dollars inherited from him against the Carrington empire.
Alexis was now one of the richest women in the world.

Alexis needed no encouragement from Colby. She was
already bent on destroying Blake and his company, Denver-
Carrington. She contrived to take over his company, and by
so doing, take over control of him.

Her children resented her schemes of revenge and could
not get along with her. Fallon's and Steven's enmity upset
Alexis no end. She remained determined to destroy Blake.

As chairman of the board of Colbyco, Alexis was the first
woman to enter the predominantly male oil business. Her
skillful leadership guided the international oil company to
the upper reaches of the business world. Her enemies grudg-
ingly admired her even though they despised her for her
ruthlessness in business dealings.

Tough on the outside, Alexis has become vulnerable beneath the surface. For example, she loves her children
unstintingly. [This could be a keynote character element in
the real Joan Collins.]

Since Alexis has schemed at every turn, many people have
targeted her for destruction. Joseph Anders, the majordomo
of the Carrington mansion, tried to burn her up by setting
fire to Steven's cabin while he knew she was in it—1983. If
that wasn't enough, he tried again to smother her with a
pillow when she was in the hospital.

But Alexis wreaked revenge on Anders. Did he really
think he could get away with trying to kill her? In typical

Alexis fashion, she drove him to suicide by threatening to reveal his wife's nefarious past in public.

Alexis' character is not one of a totally evil person. She does not attack everybody in sight. She can be quite kind to some. Once she employed her former lover, Mark Jennings, as her bodyguard. Ironically, she was arrested for his murder in 1984. But she was not convicted.

Joan Collins once discussed the character of Alexis Carrington with her sister. Jackie thought she could perceive the original source or sources of Alexis' genesis within Joan Collins, as exemplified in her autobiography and in one other place: "I can even see touches of Fontaine from *The Stud* in Alexis," she said. "I think it's a natural progression."

"The funny thing is that people don't hate [Alexis]," Joan pointed out. "They can somehow relate to her. And that goes for the men fans as well as the women."

Joan had positive thoughts about Alexis as well. "I admire Alexis' ambition and her determination. She's not frightened by anyone. She does things other women would love to do, yet don't have the courage to do. Alexis is a winner! Oh yes, she may be a bitch at times, but she loves her children."

That key character element has been discussed before. Oddly enough, it is a key character element in both the character Joan Collins plays and Joan Collins herself.

"Viewers can identify with that aspect of her personality," Joan pointed out. "If Alexis were a man, she would not be called a bitch. She would be admired as a tough businessman."

And she elaborated on the bitch element briefly. "Alexis Carrington *might* be a bitch, but Joan Collins isn't. I honestly can't think of anyone who really knows me who would suggest that I was."

Jackie Collins concurred with her sister's remarks about the "double standard" for men and women in a *Redbook* article she wrote recently: "Isn't it a shame that TV still equates *strong* women with *bad* women?"

Even though she admired and had certain traits in common with Alexis, Joan repeatedly claimed that she was unlike Alexis the Bitch and could not understand why the press maintained the opposite attitude toward her.

"I've had a huge amount of disapproval in the press," she told one magazine writer. "I always wonder why they are so hard on me when I'm not really a bitch at all—just very straightforward." She also said that she was very much like her father Joe in this respect. "He lacked tact and diplomacy, too."

Of course, it was great sport for the magazine and newspaper writers to compare Alexis and Joan—it was what the publicity people at "Dynasty" wanted them to do, wasn't it? Besides, it made good copy. And for every statement made pointing out how closely Joan resembled Alexis, another would come out—usually by Joan—pointing out how far apart they were.

"I can't stand people who become big-headed, whether they are successful or not," Joan told one writer. "I find it a distinctly revolting quality. But that doesn't mean that you have to be a humble little miss, which I am not!

"Sometimes I'll say things that don't win me any popularity contests. But I, unlike Alexis, don't try to manipulate things. Alexis will move in devious ways to get what she wants. I will come right out and say what I want.

"If I don't like a certain dress that I have to wear on the show, I'll say it. If I don't like the way a certain scene is being shot, I will say it. If I don't like it that I'm working too late, I will say so!

"This is construed as the wrong way by a lot of people, possibly because I'm a woman, and women aren't supposed to speak up. I refuse to conform to the way things are 'supposed' to be. I've always spoken my mind."

Indeed she has! She was suggesting that because she was a woman, she was entitled to say whatever she felt; the fact that women were discriminated against in modern society gave her free rein to let off steam at any time.

This is a convenient if fallacious argument. It bears out what some writers have noted as a "spoiled little girl" image that occasionally surfaces in Joan Collins. What Joanie wants, Joanie gets.

"Alexis is a character I've played for years—she is not me. If I were like Alexis, I would have been a star twenty-five years ago, believe me, because I would have slept my way to the top. And that [would have been] very easy to do, because I have been asked by some of the most important men in this business, who promised me the best roles and all sorts of goodies if I did. Had I been as clever as Alexis, there's no question that that's what would have happened."

She has claimed that she is the way she is because she has such *joie de vivre*. Therefore "I tend to live my life very much in the fast lane. Because I work hard, I believe I deserve to play very hard. Which I *do*. I *adore* partying. I *love* traveling. I *adore* meeting new people. The men that I've loved? Very strong, all of them. Sure of themselves. With marvelous senses of humor. That matters most.

"I'm funny, too—*sometimes*. I'm strong. I'm ambitious. I'm gregarious. But I am *not* Alexis."

She went on: "The public got my TV character and myself rather muddled up. Because, you see, I am also very sensitive. And I'm a good mother. And I've got a very strong sense of responsibility. I know I've got this wicked-lady image, but there's a part of me that's just, you know, good old Joan."

If the public happened to think Joan Collins was a bitch in real life like Alexis Carrington, that was their problem. Joan knew what she was really like. A close relative of Joan's put it this way a few years ago, backing up Joan's attitude about her image:

"We're British, don't forget. Joan's highly emotional—but very guarded. Despite her clipped words and her 'hard' image, she's tremendously vulnerable. Yet she's *such* a survivor that she makes the puzzling out of who she really is the *other* person's problem."

None of this seemed to bother her rapidly increasing number of television fans. About 1982, a car full of ten-year-old boys and girls drove up to her once while she was going down the street. Recognizing her, they waved at her. Delighted, Joan smiled and waved back.

"The little darlings," Joan thought to herself. "Ah, the benefits of being a television star."

As they passed one another, she could hear them chanting loudly: "Alexis, Alexis, we *hate* you, we *hate* you."

Nonplussed, Joan Collins could hardly believe her ears! However, she really didn't mind. Why should she mind? After a year and a half on "Dynasty" she was making around $45,000 per episode. In addition, she received most of her clothes within the show's $15,000 budget.

Once Alexis had appeared in "Dynasty," the name Alexis, up to that point a rare name for little girl babies, suddenly skyrocketed in popularity from the low nineties to the top twenty as a name for newborns.

After appearing in only three "Dynasty" episodes, Joan Collins was swamped by fan letters. She had been an actress for almost thirty years. Now, out of the blue, fans recognized her everywhere she went. She had never received so much attention when she was doing films.

The odd thing was that in her case, most of the letters came in addressed personally to Joan Collins, the actress, not Alexis Carrington, the character in the soap opera. In the case of most television personalities appearing in series offerings, the letters usually came to "Thomas Magnum," not "Tom Selleck," or to "J. R. Ewing," not "Larry Hagman." It showed the strong impact the deliberately reinvented Joan Collins *as* Joan Collins had made on the electronic medium.

By the time she had done half a dozen "Dynasty" episodes, she could not even shop at the supermarket anymore except in disguise. Other shoppers would besiege her with questions about "Dynasty," and it would take her twice as long to do her shopping.

"I'm so sick of humping in the office or on the sofa or in the living room. Next season, I get a bedroom, and I'm so happy!"

Once again the personal life of Joan Collins was beginning to resemble the plot wrinkles that the scriptwriters dreamed up to keep "Dynasty" moving.

For some years now—except those years spent in trying to bring Katy back to life from her coma—Joan and Ron Kass had not been getting on at all well. The fight for Katy's life had caused a truce to descend over their marital battlefield.

But now, with Katy much better, and with Joan in the saddle with an international career that knew no bounds, it was time for some kind of showdown in her personal life. It was too much to expect her to continue the way she had been going. Kass was definitely not the same man she had married. He was not the same man as the one who had been a successful entrepreneur.

Something was wrong.

A decision was coming up that would have to be faced. A hard decision.

Chapter Ten

Joan Who?

As Joan Collins's professional life rocketed to its zenith, her personal life, ironically, sank to its nadir. Her marriage to Ron Kass was on the rocks even though she was making every effort publicly to save it for the sake of her daughter Katy, who was still recuperating from her near-fatal car accident.

Katy was doing reasonably well in school, but her traumatized memory had not returned completely to normal. She spoke slowly, dragged her left foot when she walked, and suffered an occasional shaky left hand.

Poor Katy! She did not want her mother to divorce her father. Joan wanted to oblige her daughter, but her faltering marriage was taking its toll on her nerves, even though she constantly wore a happy mask on the "Dynasty" set pretending all was right with the world.

Her marriage counselor had advised her not to tell Katy that her family was coming apart at the seams and might self-destruct in the near future. Joan and her husband thus played a game with each other, and continued to lie to the media that their marriage was fine.

163

Joan hated herself for being such a hypocrite, but most of all she hated herself for having to put up a phony façade of happiness behind which to hide. Her self-deception was slowly but surely affecting her emotionally.

Joan did receive *some* good news during the early part of the 1980s. In 1982 she was asked to be mistress to ceremonies at a benefit concert at the Royal Albert Hall in London, largely as a result of her international success as Alexis in "Dynasty." The concert by the Royal Philharmonic Orchestra would feature music of the Beatles. Her Royal Majesty Queen Elizabeth II and His Royal Highness Prince Philip were both to attend. The profits would go to the charity called The Royal Society for the Protection of Birds.

Following swiftly on the heels of that good news was very bad news. Joan discovered that a parcel of unpaid bills had piled up at her London home. Her husband had simply not been paying any of the household bills. The British press had a Roman holiday when it got wind of the news.

In fact, as she arrived at Albert Hall for the concert, she was presented with a writ by the London Electricity Board, the city's power utility, for nonpayment of her electricity bills. In addition to that, they cut the power at the apartment.

The headlines were typical:

ROYAL STAR JOAN GETS WRIT!
A WRIT ON JOAN'S BIG NIGHT!
THEY'VE CUT OFF JOAN'S ELECTRICITY!
BIG ROW, JOAN BLOWS A FUSE!

Joan was humiliated for her own sake as well as for the Queen's sake. Her nerves were stretched to the point of snapping. She kept blaming all her problems on her foundering marriage.

Inevitably her nerves did give way. After the concert she returned to Hollywood and continued work on the "Dynasty" set. Linda Evans and she were scheduled to shoot their first season's crucial fight scene—the climax of all the hostility between Krystle and Alexis. After weeks of scrapping for Blake Carrington's affections, the two of them were called on to stage a big, brawling, motion-picture type of fight—a physical and emotional contest with no holds barred.

"This scene was to be a high point," Joan recalled. "A knockdown, drag-out cat fight. . . . Scratching, biting, and feathers flying. Claws out. The cat fight to end all cat fights. ABC was gleefully anticipating huge ratings."

As Joan watched the stunt double for her and Linda Evans rehearsing, she suddenly felt a searing pain shooting through her body. In excruciating agony, she doubled over. In jig time she was rushed to the nurse's office on the lot. They examined her and sent her immediately to Cedars Sinai Hospital for treatment.

"After a thorough examination in the emergency room, punctuated by beefy policemen barging in and reporting that there was 'a cadaver' in the corridor, I lay bare from the waist up, electrodes attached to my chest, trying to cover that up as well as my by-now famous face," Joan wrote.

Finally Dr. Al Sellers diagnosed her trouble as routine gastroenteritis, exacerbated by tension, nerves, and extreme exhaustion. Released from the hospital a few hours later, Joan returned to her apartment and tried to wake up Ron Kass to tell him what had happened to her. She informed him that she was sick and had to go to bed. He ignored her and turned over to go back to sleep. It was at that moment that Joan had had it. She determined to obtain a divorce, no matter what happened.

The two of them were separated for several months before the divorce eventually came through in 1983. It was a very bad time for Katy, but she survived.

And with the bad, there was some good. During her career, Joan had received few awards for her work. In 1956 she had been voted "Star of Tomorrow" and "Most Promising Young Actress." In 1957 she had been voted "Most Outstanding Young Actress."

Finally, in 1977, she got a best actress award for her work

in *Empire of the Ants*, a movie she loathed intensely because
of the insect-infested Florida swamps where it was shot. In
point of fact, the swamps enhanced her natural beauty by
counterpointing it, as did the giant ugly plastic ants that
menaced her. Hate the film though she might, she looked
luscious in it and you could not blame the ants for wanting to
grab her.

And so it was a complete surprise in 1982, when Joan
found herself nominated for the Hollywood Foreign Press
Association's Golden Globe Award for Best Actress in a TV
Drama Series. As expected, she did not win.

In 1983 she was again nominated for her role as Alexis—
and this time, to her astonishment, she *did* win. Joan described her elation on hearing the results of the votes:

"Stunned, I stood there for a second, then dashed onstage
to raise my arm in a victorious gesture and hear my green
chiffon Nolan Miller dress rip under the arms. I had no
speech prepared—just 'I would like to thank Sophia Loren
for turning down the part, and everyone on "Dynasty" from
Aaron Spelling on *up!*'"

She was delighted, but nothing could dull the pain of her
destroyed marriage.

It was soon quite evident that the "Dynasty" scripts were
aping Joan Collins's personal life. Whether or not the writers
deliberately set out to pattern Alexis after Joan is beside the
point. Both the real person and the fictional person had
several failed marriages.

Another striking similarity was the fact that both Alexis
and Joan had sisters who were writers—although the television audience did not find this out right away. Joan's sister
Jackie was a well-known, best-selling novelist of steamy ro-
mances; Alexis's sister "Caress" was a writer of dirty books,
namely one about Alexis. (Obviously, no one was supposed
to recall the importance of Jackie Collins's *The Stud* in the
eventual hiring of Joan Collins for her star part in "Dynasty.")

Caress hated Alexis, the story line went. Because of her
unmitigated loathing of Alexis, Caress wrote a book about

her detailing her dastardly and sleazy actions. Caress found a publisher for the book, but when Alexis discovered who it was, she bought out the publisher and suppressed publication of the book. Caress held Alexis to blame for the time she had to spend languishing behind bars in a South American jail—this all part of the hairy story line invented for the prime-time soap.

Kate O'Mara, who played Caress, was surprised by the reaction people had to her character. She told a reporter, "I was surprised, too, that they thought I *deserved* anything I got at the hands of Alexis. Even though she's a swindler, and worse, they side with *her!*"

Blake Carrington's brother Ben was sickened by Caress's scheming, according to the plot line; he had her drugged and consigned to the South American jail whence she had come.

It was no coincidence that Kate O'Mara physically resembled Jackie Collins. The "Dynasty" producers chose her for the role *because* of her facial bone structure that made her look like Jackie Collins (and Joan Collins as well!).

O'Mara once spoke of her role as Caress: "I knew from the first that Caress was to be a challenger but probably a loser. I mean, if Caress won over Alexis, then it would be her show, and I don't think they're ready to let me take over the show. So, you see, if you just think about it, you can figure out these plots from the billing and casting more than from the script itself."

O'Mara, a British actress, was no stranger to Joan Collins. They had met before in England. "I had bumped into Joan several times through the years," she said. "She was a very well-known movie star in England; but then of course, I was primarily on the stage. I was offered a role in *The Stud*, a movie she made, but I didn't do it. She's right up front and honest. She's a terrific entertainment value for any viewer."

O'Mara also denied that she had feuded with Joan Collins on the "Dynasty" set. She put it this way:

"I'm a professional actress, and a professional doesn't deal in that type of nonsense. Everyone was very kind to me. There was no chance for fights or feuds because everyone has a job to do and very little time to do it. The show is done at a breakneck speed."

About Caress, O'Mara once said: "There's a lot of anger in Caress. She's been in jail for five years for murder, and her sister's made no attempt to get her out." And, archly, "Caress tries to publish a book about her sister's past. It's a bloody nasty thing to do. I certainly wouldn't want my private life splattered over the vulgar press."

One interesting parallel between Caress's supposed book about Alexis and Joan Collins's book about herself was that although Joan published the book in England, she later suppressed that edition even after it had been sold to an American publisher, opting to rewrite the entire book, expunging parts that were considered too steamy by her British audience, and effectively censoring her own life. It's all part of the soap-opera life of the real Joan Collins.

A firm believer in astrology, Joan has said: "I'm a Gemini, and I believe in astrology. I know I've got two, three, four, even five sides. I therefore have a wardrobe that's extremely eclectic. Everything from funky sports clothes to jeans to outrageous things in very high chic to over-the-top glitzy glamour. If you saw my wardrobe, you'd say its very hard to know what the woman who has this closet is like."

In 1984, photographer Raul Vega wanted to snap Joan in a black leather motorcycle jacket, black leather boots, black leather miniskirt, and heavy chains. Joan was disgusted. She picked up a nearby chain and sniffed, "That isn't *my* image at all." She went on, "Evening. Elegant. Sexy. *That's* my image. And that's Alexis' image."

Joan Collins knew how Alexis would dress. She ought to; she was playing Alexis even before Alexis was invented. She admitted that they even have similar tastes in food. They both like baked potatoes with caviar and sour cream.

James Wolcott wrote in *New York* magazine: "[Joan] Collins is the sort of woman who seems born to swing from chandeliers as geysers of freshly popped champagne flare in tribute."

Joan responded to this description with: "I don't know. I don't really spend a lot of time sitting around analyzing myself. But I can tell you one thing: I spent too much of my career thinking everyone knew better than I did. These days, I realize I know a lot more than anybody else."

As her success continued to grow, Joan found it interesting that people really believed she *was* Alexis. During the show's second year, she said: "It's interesting to see how people see you. It's not the way I see myself, but I can see how people see that. Because I'm not a retiring violet. I make no secret of the fact that I go out with men. And I'm not going to stop.

"But I accept that people see me as notorious. I'm very . . . outgoing, and I love to dress up to the nines. I know I get a lot of attention. It's like this: I love to work, but I also love to play. I go out to dinner at least twice a week, and I go to parties at least that often as well. I work two or three days a week, all day long, and after that, I will not go home and sign checks."

Dean Martin held a roast for her, where ribald anti-Collins jokes were the order of the day (or evening). For example, Phyllis Diller said, "Joan Collins has whitecaps in her water bed."

The same actress who once had been known as the "British bombshell" had become an international sex symbol—but being one wasn't her goal in life.

"You know, I didn't set out to be any of this. I didn't set out to be an over-forty sex symbol. But I've always had a very good inner voice, and I also believe that the person who has never made a mistake never accomplishes much."

Joan had once stated her belief in positive thinking: "I have a very thick skin. I think you can basically do anything you want to do. That came to me with Katy. I refused to allow myself to see how bad the situation was. And she is a miracle. She recovered, and that is a bloody miracle."

Getting sick was all in a person's mind. "I just don't want negativity in my life. For instance, I don't believe in getting sick. I never have a cold. Diseases occur when people think in a negative way. I just believe I'm not going to get a cold. I can be around people who are sneezing and have the flu, and I won't get sick because I think, 'I'm not going to get a cold.' "

Apparently gastroenteritis was immune to Joan's positive thinking, but then again, negative thoughts about her marriage to Ron Kass were going through her mind at that time. In any case, most of the time Joan Collins was as healthy as an ox and looked much better than one.

Joan never let the photographers push her around. They might make suggestions, but then she would either reject or accept them. In her *Wild Ones* black-leather-jacket outfit, she refused to pose for certain shots, such as reclining limp over a chair.

"I don't want to do any kinky weirdness. You have your fun with your models, and forget me."

The photographers suggested that she wear a skin-tight camisole with a filmy petticoat as she paddled around the shallow part of her swimming pool at home, causing the skirt to float about her.

"I've never had *any* photographer have so much trouble taking a picture of me," she snapped. "It's bad enough that I have to *wear* this outfit!"

Clothes have always been a big part of "Dynasty" because clothes are such an important part of Alexis' character.

"I have to work with the clothes, which is a big part of my character," Joan once said. "It isn't the Yellow Brick Road, but it beats working in a factory."

"Dynasty" had become the linchpin of the Joan Collins career. She devoted most of her energy to working on the series.

"Everything comes back to 'Dynasty,' but it's secondary to me right now. Unfortunately, I can delegate errands, fan mail, and housekeeping, but I cannot delegate the role of

Alexis. I must read the script, think about the dialogue, and work with the writers if there are changes."

"Dynasty" needed high ratings to justify the amount of money spent on each episode—$1,000,000 on average to produce it, a figure that sometimes ran up to $1,500,000. The average hour-long television show done at the same time cost around $85,000 to make. The "Dynasty" wardrobe alone amounted to about $25,000 a week; sometimes it could reach $100,000 for just one show.

To detail some of the unusual expenses: a fourteen-ounce "pound" of caviar that was wolfed by Alexis in a scene cost about $350 because Alexis eats nothing but the best—in this case, Petrossian beluga.

Executive producer Doug Cramer once explained to *Cosmopolitan* the reason so much money was spent on details on the "Dynasty" set:

"Aaron [Spelling] and I both have always cared a great deal about the *look* of a film. I know a lot of producers in this town who never think about what the background of a room is and what the actresses are going to wear. We *worry* about that—about the jewelry matching, about the ladies contrasting, about the colors of clothes matching the mood."

Appearances are of the highest importance on the show.

When Alexis lies on a bed, she never lies on just sheets per se; she lies on Pratesi sheets that sell for $1,000 a set! Twice that amount is spent on *flowers* each week. Yow!

On one Yuletide episode, Spelling was dismayed that a Christmas tree for the Carringtons cost a mere $200. He had the show shell out more than $2,500 for a new tree.

"My God, that's not the way the Carringtons would have Christmas!" he had yelped. "You wouldn't expect the Carringtons not to have the most beautiful ornaments on their tree. It had to be *special*. That's the way *they'd* have Christmas."

Alexis' character must also be correct down to the very last detail. The newspaper that adorns her breakfast tray must be the real *Women's Wear Daily;* nothing less will do.

Each morsel of food that Alexis eats is carefully selected. Fans are so fascinated with what she eats that the newspapers once ran a contest to guess what type of food she would put into her mouth next.

Cramer has described Alexis with ecstasy:

"She handles food beautifully. The vengeance with which the lady can attack a piece of celery—or oysters, drumsticks, or frog's legs—is remarkable."

In one episode Alexis decided she wanted to have baby pheasant flown in where she was lunching with Amanda. An actual pheasant was indeed brought to the set from a Los Angeles trattoria specializing in game.

Alexis relishes cold lobster. She used to consume it by the pound until Joan Collins finally could not stand even the smell of it any longer. Alexis also used to like shellfish, but not after the actress developed an allergy to it.

Tom Trimble, "Dynasty"'s art director, once pointed out that attention to detail in designing and dressing the sets makes the actors "feel good" in their roles. "By keeping the standards in every area at a certain level, the product turns out better, because everyone picks up on this ambience and responds to it."

It was, in fact, the arrival and presence of Joan Collins as Alexis that led to a gradual change in the "look" of the Carrington mansion. Art director Trimble put it this way:

"[The 'Dynasty' mansion] has a grand look to it. It's very opulent. The way it turned out exemplifies Alexis' presence. Alexis has a very dramatic flair. The style [of the setting] is reminiscent of the glamour period of the nineteen-forties. It has somewhat of an Art Deco look—light coloring, that chic look popular in the nineteen-thirties and -forties. You'll see it in the coloring, unusual shapes in furniture, the art work [such as contemporary Japanese paintings] and sculptures."

The entire entryway of the mansion slowly shifted in design, too, dating from the arrival of Alexis. Whereas the staircase down which Linda Evans and Joan Collins tread so stunningly was once seemingly the *center* of the house—an obvious architectural absurdity—it soon moved closer to the front door. A conservatory—greenhouse, actually—was added to the setting, where the grand piano used to be. A solarium was added just under the staircase. The idea of all this shifting about was to provide a more interesting playing area in which the actors could stage their scenes.

Nolan Miller, the wardrobe designer for "Dynasty," is another stickler for details. He makes sure Alexis dresses right and looks right. He has described his haute couture dressing of Alexis in this manner:

"The whole world knows what a bitch Alexis is, so we just do everything as dramatic and flamboyant as we can. This is a woman who's obsessed with power and wealth, so she wants everything that shows it up. When Alexis is home by herself, drinking champagne and waiting for a phone call, she's in satin pajamas and eating caviar. There's no fooling around with her. When you see her walk in and throw her furs on the sofa and open her gold cigarette case with diamonds on it and she's wearing a beautifully tailored suit and a hat—you just know that *My God, is she rich!*"

He said of Joan: "She has an incredible flair. Joan never just puts something on and stands there looking at it. She's dipping and sweeping and turning and sitting—she's all over the place. She *wears* it. I don't care if I brought in a cardboard box; she'd figure out something to do with it."

After an outfit is worn once on the show, it is never used again on "Dynasty." The actresses can wear the clothes off the set, but must eventually return them to the studio wardrobe. The clothes then appear on other Spelling productions such as "Hollywood Wives," "Hotel," or "The Love Boat."

Miller has said, "When you watch 'Hotel,' you might see three ladies walk through the lobby, all wearing Alexis castoffs."

"Dynasty" directors have always loved Joan for her rare ability to match prop movements with spoken lines. That, in turn, makes cutting and editing much easier and more effective. One of her directors, Irving Moore, once said of her after take ten:

"She's no ordinary TV actress; she never missed it in ten times. She gets every prop perfect!"

On a typical day, Joan Collins's work on "Dynasty" starts at the studio at 7:30 A.M. She drives up to the lobby connecting the two stages—3 and 4—in her bronze Rolls-Royce. Although she used to have her own vanity license plates marked JOAN WHO?, she finally dispensed with them. She goes to her dressing room.

Her assistant, Judy Bryer, arrives, carrying an appointment book with Joan's schedule written out. Joan met Bryer while she was married to Anthony Newley. Since that time, Bryer has become her right hand.

At about 9:00 Nolan Miller arrives with Joan's newest outfit. One day it might consist of a regal purple evening suit skirted with long fur sleeves dyed in the same color. Another day it might be—almost *anything*!

On one memorable morning, Joan Collins had a love scene with Michael Nader, the actor who played Dex Dexter on the show. During their kissing scene, the only sound that could be heard was that of the heavy breathing of the actor and actress. Afterwards, noticing the faces of the crew around her, Joan quirked up her eyebrows and remarked, "You ladies getting hot?"

She later commandeered a cigarette, laughed, and said, "They say we're the only two who kiss believably. Nobody else makes noise!"

After the bedroom scene Joan cried out that Nader had bitten her lip. Consequently, Nader fell all over himself apologizing. The hazards of show business!

As of May 1985, Joan Collins was making $10,000 less per episode than costar John Forsythe was making. In fact, she rarely if ever discusses her salary.

Once, she did say, "I know it seems that we [stars] make a lot of money, but we're highly taxed and expenses are high.

I have a glamorous image and can't really wear the same dress more than once, nor can I buy a little outfit off the rack at Macy's."

Obviously, Joan felt no regrets about raking in piles of money. Nor did she especially like to give interviews.

"When it comes to interviews, I much prefer to do television. That way I can say what I feel and come across the way I am, rather than talking and then seeing it look different when it's written down in cold print. I suppose, sometimes, my mouth's my own worst enemy."

At the end of her work day, Joan always visits a gym to exercise, and then returns to her home. The house in Coldwater Canyon is decorated in Art Deco, her favorite style—aped by the set designers on "Dynasty." Silver wallpaper was used to set off black, gray, and cream furniture in her living room, before she redid the room in white. Beneath the arch to the apricot-painted dining room, stands a silver palm tree. Her bedroom is painted peach.

Inside the bar-cum-family room, over a hundred magazine covers with Joan Collins's face grace an entire wall. The magazines come from all over the world, some dating back to thirty years ago. On an opposite wall, photographs of other celebrities plaster the surface. One of John and Robert Kennedy was autographed by Robert.

Various awards and statuettes decorate the room. One wall-shelf holds some dozen books written about or by Joan Collins. A huge stack of "Dynasty" videotapes lies near the projection TV.

When not at home, Joan Collins enjoys meeting her fans. Speaking on one of her regular tours, she told a reporter: "Eddie in New York sends cookies and scarves and handbags. When I was there for the 'Night of a Hundred Stars' we finally met." Joan Collins laughed at the recollection. "He wears more eye makeup than I do!"

One of the most memorable episodes of the first "Dynasty" years was the one in which Alexis fired a shotgun into the air, causing Krystle, riding a horse, to lose her unborn baby in a fall from her mount. This was a new low for the evil Alexis.

Joan actually argued against the scene, objecting to the producers that Alexis would not stoop quite so low as to commit such a heinous act. She lost the argument.

The first time she rehearsed that scene at the ranch in Hidden Valley, she fired the shotgun, whose round penetrated a scrim surrounding an arc lamp, blowing the lamp apart.

Naturally they had to reshoot the scene, which was written in this way:

ALEXIS: You must remember, Steven [her son], that a Carrington does *everything* well. We swim well, ride well, play tennis well, and skeet-shoot well.

"Thrilled that I had said the entire line without a fluff," she related, "I was about to raise my gun with studied nonchalance when the butt of the gun caught in my hanging plaid scarf and I inadvertently pulled the trigger, shooting myself in the foot! Luckily the gun was loaded only with blanks, but it still stung madly and I hopped around on one foot cursing wildly."

ALF KJELLIN (the director): Okay, that's a print. Now let's move over to the tree and have Joan shoot Linda.

"Disheveled, sweaty, limping, and humiliated, I put on my most evil Alexis look, and with angora fluff and insects floating like an aura around me, I raised the shotgun and shot the two blasts that caused Krystle's horse to bolt, throwing her to the ground and causing her to lose the baby. For which she and thousands of viewers never forgave me!"

Joan has admitted: "There is a bit of Alexis in me—the resilience, strength, and ambition are certainly there now. I wish I had more of her shrewdness and cleverness in dealing with business, but I am learning from her.

"I have given up bemoaning 'but I'm *not like* Alexis.' Like it or not, the bitch-goddess label will probably stick with me forever. As long as I, and my family and close friends, know me as I am, that is all that matters to me."

But the scriptwriters never rested. Soon they concocted an Alexis scheme in which she clandestinely arranged a loan to Blake Carrington to the tune of a billion dollars. Then she called in the loan, knowing that Blake had no way of paying it off, and bankrupted him. This allowed her to move into the Carrington mansion and kick him and Krystle out.

What a damned bitch!

Jackie Collins once discussed Alexis' evil qualities in a magazine article: "One of the appealing aspects of watching TV's bad girls is that they give one a strong feeling of moral superiority, a feeling of 'Sure, she's rich, but just look at what she had to do to get that way.'"

According to Jackie, women love to hate Alexis. "And there lies the secret. For far too long, women have been brought up to abide by the rules—to be polite, unthreatening, docile creatures. Now Alexis and all TV's other wicked women throw the rules out the window and go for it. They're bold, bad, and beautiful—and we *love* 'em.

"Long live the women we love to hate!"

But guard your back if you're Blake Carrington. Alexis could be sharpening a knife to plunge into it this very moment.

As Alexis, from her first appearance in court, Joan Collins always wore heaps of makeup. As any viewer could see, Alexis even wore her makeup to bed. Joan herself would never do this. Without makeup, people could not recognize her as Alexis.

"People can't really believe it's me [without makeup] because they're so used to seeing how I look on 'Dynasty.' I mean, Alexis even wears false eyelashes to bed! But I'm a creature of extremes. With cosmetics, I either do nothing or go whole hog. With clothes, too, I wear very dressy outfits or sweatsuits. There's no middle-of-the-road."

Though she uses tons of makeup, Joan Collins would

never consider the use of plastic surgery to keep her image ageless. "Absolutely not," she once said. "It erases all the character—the natural beauty. Skin may look smoother, but the whole appearance is artificial."

In one interview, Joan Collins attributed the success of her Alexis characterization to—believe it or not!—her innate shyness. "I have a certain amount of shyness. I think most actors do. I was very shy when I was a child. I think that could again be one of the reasons why the character I play on 'Dynasty' is popular. Although she's painted as a dare devil, she has a side that is quite warm and vulnerable—and, I think, quite witty in a way."

Joan then laughed and groped for a cigarette.

"It's called acting," she chuckled. "I based the character on a very good friend of mine who unfortunately died. She was a jet-setter. Very amusing, very interested in men and power, but very likable by both men and women. The part of Alexis I don't like particularly is the part the writers like. They're always writing in those nasty things for her to do, and saying how terrible she is. Four years ago, she blew up a gun at Krystle, who shouldn't have been riding a horse anyway when she was pregnant."

Joan Collins shy? With a face and figure like hers? Alexis shy?

Like a crocodile.

Alexis dresses pretty much as Joan does. "I felt very strongly about the character when I came into it. I wanted her to look like those women I know who live in Rio or New York or Paris or Rome, who do spend a huge amount of money at couture houses and do dress up a lot. It's right for the character."

About Alexis' character, Joan once said, "I'd be bored to distraction if I had to play a little goody-two-shoes. I like playing fairly normal, nice people, but on an ongoing program, week after week, year in and year out, I think it's fun to have a character you can embellish. I feel that I know how Alexis would react to any given situation."

Joan Collins really never did have Alexis' acid tongue, but she always knew instinctively how to deliver one of Alexis' bitchy punch lines—like the one she uttered when she spotted "Dynasty" character Ashley talking to Dex at La Mirage.

ALEXIS: I've never had to pay for mine, Ashley, have you?

As all "Dynasty" fans knew, Alexis was referring to her favorite indoor sport: sex.

"There are parts of me that are like Alexis," Joan Collins has said, "but I don't think in general I'm like her. The strong desire not to be taken advantage of by people, that's similar—not allowing people to manipulate me and being assertive in certain areas. But I don't have Alexis' double-dealing, Machiavellian out-and-out bitchiness, because I don't have any need for that."

Nor did Joan ever pretend to be as wealthy as Alexis.

"I don't have that kind of wealth by any means. I live in a house, not a mansion. I do walk around nibbling on caviar and sipping champagne, but not in a negligee. I also nibble on tuna fish and Ritz crackers. It depends. I like caviar and I like champagne and I like living well. I always have."

Heather Locklear, who played Sammy Jo, compared her character as a wandering troublemaker to that of Alexis in this manner:

"Alexis is nasty and gets what she wants, whereas Sammy Jo is nasty and doesn't get what she wants. She goes about it all the wrong way."

Somehow, there seems to be a *rightness* about Alexis' *wrongness*.

Chapter Eleven

Alexis-Joan on Joan-Alexis

I f Joan Collins had listened to what she was told when she was seventeen years old, she would have given up acting before starting out on her career. She was advised then to make as much money as she possibly could before she reached her mid-twenties, because at that age she would be over the hill as an actress.

"That's the way it was then," she said to a reporter in 1986. "I guess I've proved them wrong."

Joan had proved that a woman in her fifties could still be sexy and successful as an actress. She had also proved something else: that a woman in her fifties could attract and hold a man in real life who was at least fourteen years her junior!

For during the years she had been putting all her professional energies into "Dynasty" and into making Alexis-Joan an international celebrity, she had been working almost as energetically on her personal life.

Once Joan had divorced Ron Kass and tried to pick up the shattered pieces of her life, she had begun going around with Peter Holm, a man she had met in England at a "pool party" during the beginning months of her "Dynasty" phase. He had followed her to Hollywood and was around to give her a shoulder to weep on as her marriage collapsed.

Holm was thirty-eight in 1985, when the two of them were married. His real name was Peter Gustaf Sjoholm, and he had been born in Sweden. True to her habitual life-style, Joan had not really left the man in her life—Ron Kass— before she had spotted another who might take over for him.

Such a man was Holm. A former rock singer, Holm had made something of a name for himself in rock circles, and was at loose ends in England when he had met Joan and begun to squire her around. His rock career had disintegrated and he was fooling around with photography, trying to get into that rather unstable business.

Holm later described his feelings on meeting Joan. "I was attracted to Joan for all the obvious reasons. And I was a bit shy, so I stayed in the pool, jumping and playing around. We started talking, and later she said casually, 'If you ever come to Los Angeles, look me up.' I thought that would be great fun to do, and I called her to say I was coming for business. That was obviously an excuse. I planned to come for a week—but I stayed a lot longer, went back to London for a few days, and then came back to stay."

And at the same time he began organizing her business details for her.

It was a surprise to Holm, he later said, that Joan was so lackadaisical and disorganized about her affairs.

"In the beginning, based on her reputation, I thought that she would be extremely well-organized, especially when you judge her from [her characterization of] Alexis. I was quite surprised when I discovered that she wasn't organized at all, and I gradually got into helping her."

Soon he was involved in every aspect of her life—not just the business side of it. And her friends objected. "Sure," Holm said, "people can obviously knock something from the outside. Anyone can knock this son-of-a-gun from Sweden, but that doesn't affect me at all."

In spite of his jaunty attitude, it *did* affect him. It affected him even more so when details of his past began to surface in the United States—becoming obvious enough finally to reach the ears of Joan Collins.

In 1976 he had been accused by Swedish officials of smuggling diamonds. Sweden issued an arrest warrant "in his absence" when he failed to show up at a court hearing to face the charges against him. These charges maintained that he and twelve other people had smuggled at least $2,000,000 worth of gems into Sweden.

Although he did not show up in court, he denied the accusations nevertheless.

Later, in 1987, he said, "Ten years ago I bought some diamonds and took them into Sweden without paying the import tax. One could say that is smuggling, I guess. I don't want to plead innocent. The fine was three hundred dollars, and I paid it." He said that his "exotic" reputation was "quite flattering."

By 1983, when Joan and Ron Kass had split up, Holm had moved into Joan's Beverly Hills mansion. At the time he was busying himself in her affairs, but was also running a business in England cryptically called "Glaze Trade." This was a system that transferred photographs to dinner plates. By then he had also purchased a small computer business in America; this was before Silicon Valley went into its economic tailspin.

Nevertheless, when Joan's friends heard about the diamond-smuggling caper, they warned her that he might well be taking advantage of her—or be about to take advantage of her.

"He seems to care very much about her, but now everyone is wondering if there are any other skeletons in his closet," declared one friend.

Whatever Joan thought about it, she did not kick him out of the house. She was reported to have argued with him about the charge, suggesting that he do everything he could to clear up this cloud on his name. Apparently nothing convinced him that he should do so.

But Joan was forewarned. And she did something about *that*. While there was some informal talk about a marriage, she refused to marry him until he signed a prenuptial agreement that prevented him from splitting Joan's fortune in the case of a marriage breakup. At first he tried to talk her out of it, but she was firm; she was learning about finances from Alexis. They were together at least two-and-a-half years in a nonwedded state before the marriage finally took place.

But that's getting ahead of the story.

She believed that, "Peter and I make a great combination, in all aspects. . . . We're able to work together, something a lot of couples can't do. He handles the financial side of things, while I tend to the creative end."

Joan was not entirely fooled by the effortlessness of the relationship, however. She was aware of the age difference—on the "wrong side" of the line. "I don't fool myself in thinking the double standard doesn't exist. It does. It's always been quite acceptable for an older man to have a relationship with a much younger woman. Not so when it's the other way around."

But Joan was sanguine about her own "old age." She felt that forty should not be a cut-off point in anybody's life. A person should continue seeking out new opportunities, she said.

"Age can be a big obstacle. I'm proud of my accomplishments, and those of women like Jane Fonda, Linda Evans, and Sophia Loren. If we can set a good example of what life after forty can bring, and if that can change societal attitudes, it's all for the better."

Even in her fifties, Joan was successful because she had learned that "there's a certain attitude that I have in certain things that a lot of women admire. I think I have a sort of fighting spirit."

She had frequently been called a "scrapper."

"Not a scrapper in that way. I don't like scraps. But in terms of having an innate belief in myself, which can't be negated by other people's opinions of me, so that that innate belief in what I can do and my potential has nurtured me through the years in which I was not particularly successful."

When actresses got older, they had a tough time getting work.

"Actresses over forty are considered, you know, phhhht. Put in the slag heap. I felt very strongly that wasn't right. I consciously wanted to make a point for myself. Then I realized I was also perhaps making a point for other women, not just actresses."

She was successful, she felt, because—for one thing—she had succeeded in staying away from drugs throughout her long career.

"I'm much too smart to take dope. I think I have a very good grounding in life. I had a solid upbringing, a very strict father and a very loving mother. I didn't come into this business all wide-eyed, thinking it was going to be fairyland. I knew it was going to be tough. It happens that I got to be very successful when I was very young, had my success, then sort of wavered for a while. But it was good because I had time to have children and then I was lucky to be able to come back—even though I had to deal with rejection a lot, and a lot of difficulty."

Joan had her feet firmly planted on the ground all the time. She didn't let her publicity swell her head, and likewise didn't let her critics get under her skin—even those who were carping about her life with Peter Holm.

"I'm the last person to believe my own publicity," she told a magazine writer. "Better you don't believe all the superlatives—and all the negatives—that people have a tendency to throw at you. Then nothing can get to you. I'll tell you, what really made me realize what a hit I've become was getting 'Sins' [a TV miniseries] together."

More about "Sins" later.

She refused to let her age depress her.

"What I think is very sad about the way people talk about age is that everybody is going to get old, and, if not, they're going to die young. It's wonderful to be young, but young,

really young, is a very short time in your life. And then
responsibilities come on, and people have another fifty years
or so when they are not young. I've certainly come to terms
with getting older."

Joan also elaborated on her idea of the double standard in
marriage. She was talking about her marriage to Peter Holm—
which occurred finally on November 6, 1985, in Las Vegas at
the Little White Wedding Chapel. Joan was fifty-two, Holm
thirty-eight.

"It makes no difference to me. People talk about this
'huge age difference,' but it's only fourteen years. Michael
Caine is the same age I am, and his wife is the same age as
Peter, but I've never read anything about *that* age difference."

In addition, "Gene Kelly plays one of my husbands in
'Sins.' And he is quite a bit older than I am—like about
twenty-one years. Someone wrote about a supposed May-
December romance between us. For once, I was on the side
of May!"

When Joan married Peter Holm, she was not setting out
to find a younger man to take the place of her divorced
husband.

"It just happened. I wasn't consciously looking for anybody of that particular age. It just happens that he's younger. I think of myself as being in my prime—I have an
outlook that's very lively."

Marriage still terrified her, even with her fourth husband.
"I married because I wanted to introduce him as my hus-
band and not as my boyfriend. The thing I like best about
Peter is his forthrightness. He's more forthright than I am.
He has tremendous strength of character and is also very
much his own man. He couldn't be manipulated by the
President of the United States."

Well, possibly, he could manipulate *her*, but she liked
him because he had a very good sense of humor.

"He has also achieved a lot in this town [Hollywood] in the
past two years. I know there are a lot of people who say,
'Yes, he has, but it's because of Joan.' I didn't push him at

all. Without contacts it would have been much more difficult. You can't do anything in this town without contacts
—nothing!

"But there is no question that Peter has helped me, too,
and enormously. He has helped me sort out my whole
financial situation. He does all of the things that one would
pay a business or personal manager to do. We just bought a
house in St. Tropez for example. I was talking about buying
a house in London a year ago, and he told me I couldn't
afford it. But the house in France is a very good investment,
and I hope to spend time there.

"I suppose Peter has also taught me to be more calm
about things I can't change. He's very stoic—so stoic I think
he comes from another planet. If he's stuck in a traffic jam or
a plane is late, he's completely calm. I think it's a very good
attitude to have."

Holm in fact resembled the bartender Wes Money in
Jackie Collins's sex-drenched potboiler *Hollywood Husbands*,
and Joan Collins sounded quite like Silver Anderson, the
middle-aged sexpot actress. The two got married in the book
despite the fact that Money was much younger than Anderson.

Jackie Collins had this to say about Silver Anderson:
"A lot of people . . . thought Silver was a bitch. Nora
[Carvell] saw another side of her. She saw a successful woman
alone in the world with no real friends. She saw an ambitious
woman who had been hurt and used by men. She saw a
woman who had alienated her family, yet needed them
desperately."

Could Jackie Collins have been talking about her sister
Joan? In any case, it was clear that Joan Collins's life resembled a soap opera enough to make her a natural character in
any soap-opera story line. Her life could certainly be developed into an interesting motion picture. There was enough
double-dealing and infidelity in it to fill many episodes of a
series like "Dynasty." Perhaps there was too much sadism in
her life for the likes of television—especially her time with
Maxwell Reed.

Joan felt that it was better to get married at an older age than at an age too young to know better. "If I can get older and more productive and intelligent and be able to contribute to my family and friends, I'll be happy. My major mistake was getting married at the age of eighteen, which I think is wrong. It's so hard. I feel more strongly about this, as somebody who was married in my teens and then married again in my twenties, with both marriages not working. One should wait until the late twenties or early thirties to marry. If you're going to try to spend the rest of your life with this one person, it's pretty hard to predict at twenty-two or twenty-three what you're going to think like at thirty-four or forty-four. My first marriage was a mistake. "

Even though Joan grew older, she apparently did not get any wiser vis-à-vis marriage. All of her marriages ended in divorce.

"The thing about men that's most interesting is that they're much more vulnerable than women think," she once said, trying to analyze her real feelings about them. "Women are a great deal tougher than men. Maybe it's because we've always had an outlet—being able to cry when we were little girls. It was okay to cry if we fell—someone would always comfort us—whereas a little boy is trained not to cry. Consequently, men have no outlet for their emotions. I admire a man who can cry. I feel sorry for men a great deal. I think they've got it pretty tough—it must be hard to cope with all these ballsy women!"

As the quotation noted, on the one hand she liked strong men, on the other she liked men who could cry. Obviously she frequently had trouble making up her mind about exactly what she *did* like in a man. Perhaps, one of her critics once said, that was the reason she kept getting married so many times.

Since Joan has been involved in so many marriages and divorces during her lifetime, she could be looked on as an expert in the situation.

"I don't think many women would divorce their husbands

on the strength of one instance of infidelity. I think divorces happen from a breakdown in commmunication, and sexual liaisons with other people are just part of the breakdown. I think it's very hard for a couple to remain together and monogamous and not to think that other people are attractive; obviously other people *are* attractive. Just because you decide to have steak for dinner doesn't mean that you're not going to fancy lobster or pot roast another night. But it's the way our society is structured. I don't know the answer."

Nevertheless Joan categorically stated once that men were the cause of most divorces.

"I think the strength really has to come from the man—I think that is true in most marriages. The first one to start straying is the man, although it could start with a woman."

She never made any bones about it: she herself frequently engaged in infidelity. She freely confessed that she had an adulterous affair with Ryan O'Neal while she was still married to Anthony Newley; her excuse was that Newley was cheating on her anyway. Was it a case of "Don't get mad, get even"? If it was Alexis having the affair, she would certainly have done it for revenge, her favorite motivating force. But then, Joan was never *really* Alexis and vice-versa.

It should be noted here that Joan claimed in *People* on February 10, 1986, that she had *never* committed adultery and thought that it was "destructive." Nevertheless, her autobiography, *Past Imperfect*, described her adulterous affair with Ryan O'Neal. Indeed, she told *Playboy* in 1984 when asked about her affair with O'Neal:

"I enjoyed being an adulteress at that time because my marriage was falling apart, and I was taking a certain vengeance for the fact that my husband was not being faithful. And fidelity to me is rather important, actually. It sounds a bit square, doesn't it?"

She believed always in a good marriage.

"I believe that what people need—what everybody is looking for—is a mate, a partner. That's the most fulfilling of all relationships. You can be tremendously fulfilled by your children, but the most wonderful relationship is with a mate—if it's good. If it's bad, it's the worst, absolutely the bottom."

Joan disagreed with a *Redbook* writer that actresses were more promiscuous than other women.

"I think a lot of actresses have fewer hangups about romance and affairs than the average person. I mean, acting is the world's oldest profession, or the second oldest profession, I'm not sure which! We were all considered to be rogues and vagabonds and whores a hundred years ago. I think that perhaps there's still a little bit of that idea in society.

"It is true that to be an actor you have to be more emotional, and you need to have a great deal of vulnerability. And I think possibly because of the emotion and the vulnerability, and the fact that one is thrown into contact with an enormous number of members of the opposite sex who are, I would say, the top caliber of attractiveness, it is probably easier for actors and actresses to become involved. The word *promiscuous* is one that I don't use very often because I think it's a bit of an old-fashioned word—a sort of fifties word. But actors are very complex. They're all searching for happiness in some way. Many of us became actors because we really didn't like who we were and wanted to play another role. That really isn't true of me now, but I think probably at one point it was."

Even in her fifties, Joan Collins was proud of her figure—and with good reason. She could put some twenty-year-olds to shame. She was so proud of her figure that she became the talk of the town in Hollywood when she posed for a nude layout in *Playboy* in December 1983. Once again she had shown that women in their fifties could still be erotically desirable.

Later on, in an interview that was published in the same magazine, she said that she had been pleased with the layout.

"I've gotten a lot of letters from women over thirty-five

who said, 'Hurray! You've shown everybody that women over a particular age can still be attractive—particularly in this magazine of all magazines!' "

Joan continued her discussion: "It's one thing to be in *Harper's Bazaar* or *Vogue,* which caters to the older woman, but *Playboy*—*Playboy* appeals to young guys. Also, I found everyone in Hollywood talking about it—I was the talk of the town for a month. Bette Midler went on the Johnny Carson show and did a whole thing about how great my body was, and everybody applauded. Then I went on the Merv Griffin show and the Carson show with Joan Rivers, and they both did a whole thing about how I looked pretty good."

Pretty good: Joan Collins, like her fellow Britons, sometimes delights in understatement.

During her interview with *Playboy,* Joan exposed her ribald sense of humor for the first time in magazine format, sounding for all the world like a character out of a Jackie Collins soft-core porn novel. Here is an example of her off-the-wall humor:

JOAN: Linda [Evans] is sick. She had her eye scratched
by a cat. I talked with her today. She was sleeping
with her cat. (Pause) I guess that's what you get for
playing with your pussy.

She told the interviewer that she felt her nude layout in *Playboy* helped boost her career and made her more popular. Her father, son, and daughters approved of her posing. The day the magazine containing her spread came out, twenty-five members of the "Dynasty" crew approached her holding their copies of *Playboy* open to her layout. She commented to the interviewer, "God, it was like a great phalanx of walking *Playboys!*"

She said she had no regrets about appearing nude in a magazine. Why should she? She had always flouted convention. In her own words:

JOAN: When it [the nude layout] appeared, I said to a
friend at a party, "I think I've decided to become
notorious." And he said, "What do you mean, decided? You've always been notorious." Listen, if I
hadn't looked good in *Playboy*, I wouldn't have
done it. I'm far too vain. I've too much pride and
I'm much too intelligent to stand there with fat
arms and a big, fat belly. To me, I've got a great
body. Sometimes it looks terrific, and if it's photo-
graphed right, it can look absolutely great. So I
thought, Fuck it, what the hell? Before it came
out, people who heard about it said, "Oh, Joan,
shocking girl! There she goes again, always doing
the wrong thing, always shocking everybody!" But
it's like having an affair. That sort of talk means
nothing to me. I do what I want.

Joan scotched the rumor that there was envy among the
members of "Dynasty" when she told the interviewer:

JOAN: The tabloids make up these ludicrous stories about
how I've been out with Linda Evans's boyfriend—
totally untrue—or they report that I say things
about her and she says things about me. I've never
said anything against Linda. I adore her. We have
a lot in common. We're survivors in this business.
We both started off with the stigma of being beautiful sex objects. We live on the same street. We
both drive Mercedeses. And we both believe that
anything is possible if you believe strongly enough
in it.

Later in the interview, Joan Collins declared that she
liked "women with balls, with guts"—which is probably why
she can empathize so well with Alexis.

She revealed that in 1978 she had written her autobiography, *Past Imperfect*, which came out in America in 1984,

because she needed money. Her agent, Swifty Lazar, wanted her to do the book because nobody as young as she was at the time had written her "memoirs" at such an age. She also wanted to explore the idea that it is all right for men to have multiple sex partners but not for women. The book became a *New York Times* best-seller and named many of the famous men with whom she had slept.

Joan cut offending passages from the British edition and rewrote the book for American consumption after the hue and cry raised in Britain had warned her of the book's possible fate in the States. She was so nettled with the reaction of her fellow Britons that she turned down a $100,000 advance from Warner Books to print the book as it appeared in Britain again in America.

She refused this big advance, she explained, "because of the absolute fucking outcry from everybody in England about this 'shocking' book. And those people know me! The English have known me since I was sixteen—I've always been sort of a household name in England, even when I was not as successful. I thought, they do this to me in England, God knows what they're going to do in America, which is a much more puritanical country. I mean, the British have three newspapers that feature nude girls every day and report the sexual exploits of everybody from prime ministers to pop stars, and there's a great deal of advertising based on sex. So I was astonished at the flak I took just because I talked rather frankly about sex and about women's attitudes toward it. God, did I get flak! I got insulted on television shows. I mean, they made me cry. It was as if I had done something obscene. And all I was doing was being honest."

Joan confessed that she was secure about her looks and her acting talent but insecure about her intelligence.

"I'm not as well read as I'd like to be. My children are shocked by me. They say, 'Mommy, why do you read *Vogue* and *Harper's Bazaar* when you could be reading . . .?' I say, 'Look, I have to read my scripts, I have to work, I don't want to educate my brain! My relaxation is reading *Vogue* and

Harper's Bazaar and *US* and *People*, thank you very much.'
So I'm insecure about that. But not insecure enough to do
something about it."

Why should she develop her mind when the rest of her is
so well developed? She joked with her interviewer about her
shyness and told of a meeting with Woody Allen:

JOAN: I saw Woody Allen not long ago coming out of
Elaine's with his head down, being escorted out by
Elaine. I went up to him and said, "Mr. Allen, I
just wanted to say hello because I admire you and
think you're a great talent and brilliant and I really
empathize with you about a certain facet of your
character, which is that you're shy—because I'm
shy, too." He looked me over and said quietly,
"Well, you could have fooled me."

Joan conceded that she came off as strong and tough until
she would meet a certain man she might like—at which
point she would turn weak and become clinging.

"Yes, I would say that I do. And I hate myself for it, but
it's perfectly true. Basically, I become a wimpy clinging
violet. At least, that was the way I used to be. My head
rules my heart a lot more now. I'm much more logical. I
hate the word *calculating*, but I mean, once burned, twice
shy, right? I've been married [four] times and have had
quite a few relationships. Maybe one gets more discerning as
one gets older. When I'm a free woman, I have less temper
tantrums. I'm much more calm and relaxed. So maybe I'm
really meant to live alone. I just don't understand men. I just
fail to understand them. Maybe they're not sensitive enough."

Like most Hollywood actresses, Joan Collins went into
analysis. As she put it, "I went into analysis because it was
the thing to do, like getting your nails wrapped. I found out
I had some kind of built-in distrust of men because of my
father. And I found out that I was a pretty nice person."

Despite the fact that she owed her fame and stardom to

television, she has always detested it. Without television, however, there would be no "Dynasty," and no Alexis, and Joan Collins would be in the loathed unemployment line or at best an obscure actress. Be that as it may, she vented her wrath on television in this typically irreverent statement:

"TV is such crap. It really is. The average family in America has dinner together, maybe with the TV on, then goes and watches TV from seven until ten. People don't play games, they don't sing songs, they don't have conversations. The art of conversation is lost. There's not enough stretching of the mind. And television actors all look alike; I can't tell half of them apart. They've all got that blow-dried hair. It's extraordinary."

But she felt it was the same in England.

"I am nauseated by the attitude of people in my country, too. All they want to do is lie around and watch television. They don't want to work, they expect the state to support them. We're all so fucking soft, it makes me puke. See, I believe in things like conscription. I think all young men should be taken at sixteen or seventeen and slung in the army for a couple of years to shape them up."

About the impact she made as Alexis in "Dynasty," she said: "I'd seen "Dallas" a few times, "Hart to Hart," "Charlie's Angels," and I realized all those women, as beautiful as some of them were, dressed and acted pretty much like everybody else did. I thought, I must put into this part [of Alexis] a European kind of attitude and a certain way of dressing, a certain *look* that is not a la mode right now. I wanted to make a statement with my clothes. In the forties and fifties, women looked great, with suits and hats and gloves and expensive jewelry. So I started to develop a look, and a lot of my success is based on that. Now I hear that there's a bunch of older actresses who watch me in 'Dynasty' and make favorable remarks. They probably don't realize that they're watching somebody who watched them as a child and is doing today what they were doing in 1950."

Joan was talking about the Alexis look: If you've got money, flaunt it. In other words, if you can afford the best, wear the best. It's great to wear pricey clothes and strut around with your wrists and neck dripping with priceless gems.

The Alexis look—everybody wants it, but only a select few can afford it. Alexis would not be caught dead in clothes off the rack at the May Company. Her overriding ambition is pride. Expensive clothes fulfill that ambition, hence they are perfectly in character for Alexis.

All Alexis cares about is herself and her children. She is devoid of moral sense. Everybody else can to go hell as long as she gets what she wants. Her philosophy of life is social Darwinism with a vengeance. Only the strong survive. Get out of my way or I'll trample you into the dirt. I'll destroy you with my billions of dollars if you stand in my way, because I am the most powerful woman on earth.

No wonder everybody hates/loves her!

As for Joan Collins herself, she is not always like Alexis. Some days she wears blue jeans.

Chapter Twelve

Spinning Alexis Off

The success of Joan Collins's role as Alexis in "Dynasty" was not lost on her new husband, Peter Holm. Almost immediately he saw that Joan's ability to portray Alexis and the type of woman Alexis was could be used to initiate other business successes.

One of the first and most notable of these spin-off ventures was the television miniseries "Sins," for which Joan and her husband acted as executive producers. The result of their activities aired on CBS-TV in February 1986.

It was Holm who took the ball firmly in hand and ran it down the field in this rather tricky endeavor, with blocking all the way by Joan, of course. She mentioned him in an interview early in 1986.

"I think Peter is tremendously strong. I admire his strength; I admire his resilience; I admire his invincibility. He's like me in that he will never give up. I told him quite clearly at the beginning of our relationship that I wasn't ready to get involved, but he didn't take no for an answer! He's very clever, quite brilliant in business. He's extremely adept in

197

dealing with people and handling situations. We blend very well. And he's gorgeous."

She told a magazine writer for *McCall's*: "Peter organized the whole thing ['Sins']. He told me 'Stop being an actress for hire! You know enough about the business. Let's go out and make something of our own.'

"My agents at the time told me that the networks didn't take kindly to actresses becoming producers and running the ship, but I said, 'I want to have control, a lot more creative control.' And that is, indeed, what I had on 'Sins.' "

Joan also discovered something important about her own clout. "It finally penetrated my thick skull that maybe I have some power after all."

The seven-hour CBS-TV miniseries "Sins" was shot in Paris and Venice during a gruelling series of location sequences. Even Peter Holm was cast in it in the role of a reporter. He had little to do or say.

"Peter is very good with deals," Joan said later, "so he was involved in that side, and I was more involved with the casting, script, and the day-to-day producing chores. He wasn't interested in what color dress I was wearing, and I wasn't interested in how much that dress cost.

"I've never been happier on a project, and that includes 'Dynasty.' "

She explained that she had not let success turn her head too much. "I don't think I've changed much. I was outspoken when I didn't have a nickel in the bank. I have a nicer car [a bronze 1984 Rolls-Royce instead of her twelve-year-old Mercedes] and I have a phone in the car. But I still think the same way, and I feel the same. The only way I've changed appreciably is that I'm better in business. I have confidence in myself as an entertainer and a human being, but I was pretty confident before. At my age, you don't make major changes in your attitudes and values."

CBS executives were so eager to have "Sins" that they gave the thumbs-up signal on the $14 million miniseries just thirty-six hours after Joan Collins had presented the idea to them.

She boasted that in "Sins" she would wear no less than eighty-seven costumes created by Valentino and Michel le Frene—specifically for *her*. Actually, the final number was somewhat less than eighty-seven—it was thirty-five—but, really, that was quite enough.

The story from which "Sins" was made appeared originally in a paperback novel written by Judith Gould and published by New American Library in 1982. Actually, "Judith Gould" turned out to be not one person, but two writers: Rhea Gallaher, Jr., and Nick Bienes. The story about the pseudonym casts an interesting light on the publishing business. Gallaher and Bienes said they had chosen the nom de plume "Judith Gould" because they had been assured that they would stand a much better chance of selling their book (to the publisher *and* to the public) if they used a pseudonym that combined two magic elements: (1) a woman's name and (2) a Jewish name.

The screenplay for the miniseries "Sins" was assigned to Laurence Heath. The director would be Douglas Hickox, and the producer Steve Krantz.

As for the story itself—well, it was one of those *epics*. Spanning forty-two years between 1943 and 1985 (right up to the date of the show, almost) it starts out during the turbulence of World War II and progresses through the next four decades of postwar boom and bust and boom again, in typical film travelogue-fashion—first Paris, then the French Riviera, then Venice, and finally New York.

Central to the long-winded and peripatetic story is the heroine—Helene Junot—played, of course, by Joan Collins. The miniseries is, in the rather arch comment of one critic, "the story of her survival and her clothing."

In brief, here are a few of the salient plot elements that decorate the hyperkinetic story line:

There's a flashback to Helene's youth in occupied France, where a sadistic Nazi beats and tortures her pregnant mother— and kills her. Of course, this motivates Helene to exact revenge.

Helene is raped by Nazis as she flees France. She is forced then to spend her postwar days as a servant, and it is as a servant that she meets Hubert the Hideous, played by Neil Dickson, who has been spurned by Helene; Helene then takes on Hubert's father rather than the Hideous.

The father is Jean-Pierre Aumont—certainly a better choice for Joan in the way of men. However, the father is a bit on the sick side, too. As he peels off her dress and slaps her around, he characterizes her viciously as "Whore! Slut!"

But Helene escapes from his clutches and finally meets David, played by James Farentino.

"For the first time in my life, I realize what love is and how beautiful it can be," she says to him. But of course David is killed when he goes as a military adviser to—are you ready for this?—a small country in Southeast Asia called Vietnam!

But Helene has a lot of Alexis in her, as well as a lot of Joan Collins. She starts sewing clothes and winds up with the most powerful fashion empire in Europe and is probably the richest woman in France. But when she tries to parlay her fashion money in magazine publishing, she almost comes a cropper. Because Hubert is waiting for her— and so are all those other people she hurt on her way to the top. Practically everybody in the cast wants to take a shot at her. "It gets so bad," one critic wrote, "you practically have to take a number and wait your turn to threaten this creature."

The cast includes Timothy Dalton, Marisa Berenson as Helene's magazine editor, a fag photographer played by William Allen Young. Even Gene Kelly is a composer who marries Helene—but is finally discovered by Hubert the Pervert, who tosses him off an apartment balcony.

Helene eventually falls in love with Joseph Bologna, playing an architect. But wait. He has a heart condition. After bedding down Helene, he drops dead in the morning. His vindictive wife, Lauren Hutton, hires a killer with a murderous Doberman programmed to bite off Helene's face.

And life goes on.

In the reviews Joan Collins made out relatively well, in spite of the kitschy opulence of the story line and costuming.

"Written by Laurence Heath and directed by Douglas Hickox," wrote Tom Shales of the *Washington Post*, " 'Sins' has such distinctions as a haunting title tune sung by Carly Simon, and, of course, acres of lush scenery, mostly European. Collins seems to be having her usual high time. 'What are parties for, except for people to be bitchy?' she asks rhetorically in Part 1; that seems to be her philosophy of performance, and 'Sins' is her party."

But he also added: "Of course it is seven hours of television without even a wisp of substance. Collins seems to have learned from 'Dynasty' producer Aaron Spelling: Assume the audience is a real dope. The tone is set in the very first shot, when the camera pans down the Eiffel Tower, very slowly, down, down, down, until we can see it all, and the magnificent city around it. And then on the screen one word is superimposed. The word is PARIS. The only thing that can come between a viewer and enjoyment of something like 'Sins' is an ounce of intelligence."

John Corry had a slightly different reaction. " 'Sins' isn't improbable or unlikely," he wrote in *The New York Times*. "It's something grander than that: preposterous, say, or absurd. At the same time it's not really about what it's supposed to be about; it's really about Joan Collins and her Valentino clothes. On 'Sins,' a seven-hour, three-part miniseries, they wear one another.

"And 'Sins' isn't good, great, or uplifting television; it's just television. Actually, it's like the star herself. She is a professional, although we don't expect to see her as one of Chekhov's three sisters. We don't want to, either. The high point of 'Sins' may be when the camera closes in on Miss Collins, and we see her playing a character in her twenties.

Can she do it? Is it believable? After all, Miss Collins is fifty-two. Yes, it is believable, and hooray for Miss Collins."

As for why Joan Collins *liked* to do projects like "Sins," she herself said: "Well, I consider myself an entertainer first and an actress second. I have no longing whatsoever to appear in the flour sack. I will leave 'The Burning Bed' to Farrah Fawcett, thank you. Some people make things that are loved by the critics but no one looks at. I'll take an audience."

Joan admitted that she was done in after making "Sins" and confided to a crowded press conference: "I lounge about and look at TV all day when I'm not working, but it seems I'm always working. I can read a script, the newspaper, and look at television all at once."

She liked having the power and control over a project as she did over "Sins." In contrast to her work on that project, "I'm just an actress on 'Dynasty,' " she said. "What I say doesn't have much clout. If I were the producer, some things would be changed. The scripts this year [1986] haven't been too good."

In "Sins," as elaborated, Joan played a girl who rises from Nazi oppression to become a famous model and then to become the publisher of a $20 million fashion magazine.

Joan once told reporters, "I liked the idea that my character, Helene Junot, was not a bitch. I wanted to get away from the 'Dynasty' character a little. This woman is the heroine."

Reminded by reporters that Helene uses blackmail against her husband's murderer, steals her friend's husband, and tramples competitors ruthlessly, Joan objected:

"Well, she only does what she has to do. She's a strong, assertive woman. That's not the same thing as a bitch. I like to play assertive women. This woman is seeking revenge upon the Nazi who murdered her mother and incarcerated her brother. She's justified in doing anything, in my opinion. And, besides, CBS wanted a *little* bitchiness.

"They like the 'Dynasty' character and I didn't want to

shortchange them. So, I play this woman very soft and vulnerable for the first hour, and then she does what she has to do. If a man did the same thing, no one would call him a bastard, so why call her a bitch? I don't like weak women. I think Krystle is a wimp. I wouldn't want to play that part."

Reporters wondered why Joan went with "Sins" to CBS instead of ABC, which airs "Dynasty."

She admitted, "Well, ABC had this project with Joan Rivers they wanted me to do—a two-hour movie in which I play her twin. I wasn't her *identical* twin. I like Joan Rivers a lot, but I didn't want to do it. I wanted control of the project, whatever I did. The hiring of the actors. The costumes, everything."

The gag idea of having her Joan Rivers's twin seemed excessive to her. On the other hand, she did not want to do a miniseries based on one of her sister Jackie's books because she felt that "that would be *too* close."

The miniseries "Sins" did extremely well in the ratings, in spite of being clobbered by the reviewers. It was a sign that a great deal of money could be made by Joan Collins and Peter Holm by playing off the drama of Alexis in as many different guises as might prove possible.

Because of her hard-nosed authority while making "Sins," some of the people under her decided that she was becoming "difficult" to work with. On that subject, Joan was questioned by several interviewers. "I do require that people not working be put off the set because I can't concentrate. Who can do a love scene with a dozen, or a hundred, strange people gawking at you?"

There was more talk about monetary spin-offs from the Alexis character. Revealing that she felt no regrets about doing television commercials as another aspect of her wide-ranging business interests, she pointed out:

"All entertainers are commodities. We are sellers. But I choose to make fun of myself. I make fun of myself in those commercials, and you know, the contest in which the winner can either take a million dollars or have dinner with me?

Now, you've had dinner with me, but I don't seriously think you wouldn't have taken the million dollars if that was the alternative.

"That contest is a little joke. I think the image I portray is kind of funny. I think that it is a bit larger-than-life and what I'm saying really is, 'I don't take this very seriously, folks, so you don't have to take it that seriously either.' "

Among the commercials she began making at this time, she appeared for Sanyo selling microwave ovens and refrigerators, and even began peddling a Joan Collins line of eyeware. These spin-offs of the Alexis image were all part of Peter Holm's efforts to exploit her professionalism as much as possible.

Joan never lost her sense of humor. Even during "Sins," after she had shot more then eleven takes in a Rolls-Royce with her costar Timothy Dalton, she said dryly: "We've been in this car so long I feel like Marlon Brando and Rod Steiger in *On the Waterfront.*"

But something did get to her, especially when it came to the clothes she wore. She got very testy on the set of "Sins" when she saw that another actress was wearing the same color as she was. She explained her aggravation this way:

"We said at the beginning of this picture that we were not going to have any of the actresses in the same scene wear the same color, which is what we do on 'Dynasty.' The first shot Marisa [Berenson] and I did, they had us both in red and we were a bit clashy. And I saw we mustn't do that anymore, and, as producer I feel it's one of my jobs—and it's not just me. I wouldn't want to have Marisa and Lauren Hutton in a scene together in the same color. Today was the third time it happened, and I said so."

Even John Corry had noticed. "Miss Collins should not be in the orange-red Valentino she wears in Part 1," he wrote. "In a scene in the office of the publishing empire, the senior editor (Marisa Berenson) is wearing the same orange-red. Is this a mere trifle? So what if it is? It's the kind of trifle you don't want to find in 'Sins.' "

He was right.

Sometimes it bothered Joan Collins when people stared at her when she was working, but other times she made light of it, realizing that it was all part and parcel of her profession.

After shooting one of the scenes for "Sins," she was required to take part in a photo session for publicity stills. Looking out at the huge crowd that had gathered to watch her, she laughed and said: "Watch the monkey in the cage! Doesn't anybody have anything better to do except watch me take stills?"

To a *TV Guide* reporter, she pointed out once that she had played characters other than the Alexis type in her long career in films. "I've played nurses and nuns, mission workers and secretaries, travel agents, mothers, certainly. . . . I don't like portraying women as victims."

As Joan became more business-oriented, she found herself more and more the victim of criticism about this facet of her personality. She found it necessary to defend herself.

"Lately I've had a lot of flak thrown at me because I have become more money-oriented. But in my career, I've been through some dry periods. In 1977 I was lining up for unemployment in Santa Monica. I've had business managers who left me broke more than once. Money is an important part of this business. I don't think I want to end my days in the Motion Picture Home—as wonderful as it is.

"In the past I was never smart with money. I was always grateful to be working. I had the reputation of being the cheapest buy around, known for working cheap."

In the spring of 1986 she launched a new collection of headgear. These hats were Alexis-type creations that women in the suburbs could afford to buy. They were imaginative, and were called the "Joan Collins Hat Collection."

She also got out a line of McCall's fashion patterns, a line of costume jewelry, and for Revlon, her own perfume called "Scoundrel" and "Scoundrel Musk" to accompany it.

Besides these businesses she also had the "Joan Collins Home Video Selection." This was a selection of films that had been personally chosen by her—according to the Paramount releases. A la Alistair Cooke for *Masterpiece Theater*, she introduced each of the films herself with a few words of buildup. The first three were *Once is Not Enough*, *The Carpetbaggers*, and *The Last Tycoon*.

According to the PR puff aimed at the Video Software Dealers' Association, "Joan will tell your customers why it's the kind of film they can enjoy again and again. And she'll throw in some spicy inside Hollywood information now and then, because . . . well, just because she's Joan Collins."

Gemini-Star Productions was set up with Joan Collins's money by Peter Holm to handle side-issue projects that came up. One of them involved the marketing of the paperback edition of her racy autobiography, *Past Imperfect*. The same unit also produced a miniseries about Maria Callas, the opera star who was the mistress of Aristotle Onassis—who was, in effect, replaced by Jackie Kennedy.

Involved in as many different businesses as she was, Joan Collins decided to shun such items as lingerie, fortune cookies, and beer. That troika might prove to be an interesting threesome whose implications a psychologist might like to explore. Why, for example, did she not want her name associated with beer? Cookies? Lingerie?

One of Joan's quirks was the fact that she would work only for male photographers. Once Judy Bryer, her right hand, tried to explain why she refused to work with women lensers. "Because she needs to flirt with the camera," Bryer explained. And flirt she did, with photographers like Mario Casilli (who did *Playboy* centerfolds), Reid Miles (who did *Saturday Evening Post* covers), and Harry Langdon, a fashion photographer bearing the same name as a famous movie comedian of an earlier day.

Despite her other businesses, Joan Collins admitted once and for all that television was her forte.

" 'Dynasty' is a good show to be on. With ten of us, I only work two or three days a week. Television is where I've found my niche. I've signed a contract to do the show for two more years—1988 is a long way away, and by then I'll have done it for seven years. I might even go on longer, providing it's not too bizarre."

She also admitted that she owed some of her recent success to Peter Holm, her fourth husband.

"Peter is Swedish and has no guile or deviousness," she said. "He calls a spade a spade. When he came into my life, he saw people pulling me in different directions. He totally reorganized my financial life so that now I'm pointing where I want to go. I'm reasonably bored by business. Peter likes working on the finicky negotiations."

She knew working with him "would be stressful on 'Sins' because we are both combative. We felt if we got through the miniseries without tearing each other to shreds, we'd be able to get through being married."

Joan had always avoided overworking and spreading herself too thin—and wanted to keep it that way. "I think of myself as a cake, and there's these slices that go out. But at the same time I have to have a slice of myself."

She felt that doing commercials was acceptable for actors because Laurence Olivier legitimized them when he did his for Polaroid. Among her commercials was one hyping Health & Tennis Corporation of America's line of health clubs, though she herself exercised a scant fifteen minutes a day.

In her $3,000,000 Coldwater Canyon manse, which used to belong to Joan Cohn and Lawrence Harvey, Joan Collins announced to seventy-five friends in August 1987 that she would venture into still another business. She said she was going to try her hand at writing a novel, following in the steps of her sister Jackie.

More about this later.

Getting back to the Joan Collins miniseries "Sins," it had created such a ratings miracle on CBS when it was run in early 1986 that both CBS and the Joan-Holm combination decided to make another one. To write an epic more or less resembling "Sins" but not really copying it, they hired televison writer Peter Lefcourt, who had won an Emmy for his work on "Cagney & Lacey" scripts to adapt a novel by Stephen Sheppard called *Monte Carlo*.

In order to cash in on the interest spurred by "Sins," it was decided to get the project going as soon as possible. Joan's hiatus from "Dynasty" occurred exactly one year later than the hiatus during which she had shot "Sins." The show would be shot then, and so speed was essential.

By now Joan was pretty sure she had her finger on the pulse of the public. What people want, she had decided by this time, were movies—films—that were "entertaining, adventurous, romantic, with the elements of wonderful locations, exciting situations, beautiful sets, and nice clothes."

The problem with *Monte Carlo,* as it stood, was that it did not have enough of a role for Joan Collins to play.

"CBS would not have been interested in having me do a project in which I only had a fairly minor part, which I can sort of understand."

And so Lefcourt was instructed to combine the characters in the novel of an English spy and a Russian chanteuse. So this character became one of the first singing spies in contemporary fiction.

"Looking at them," Joan said later, "I thought it would be an interesting story point . . . an extremely sophisticated glamorous entertainer, a sort of Dietrich type—though I don't look, sound, or act like her—who's working desperately for the Allies."

And so Katrina Petrovna was born—a woman who managed to serenade Nazi and Fascist generals so that she could sing to the Allied forces. And, in so doing, Joan would be able to rescue an American pilot, knock out an officious Italian officer with a mickey finn, and fall passionately—but reluctantly—in love as she continued to change her costumes thirty-six times.

Lefcourt was asked to read the basic novel in March, and one day later agreed to do it. Within a fortnight he had done a first draft of the first two hours of airing time. But haste had made waste. CBS loathed the story. Lefcourt did a rewrite. CBS still hung by its thumbs, stalling. In fact, the network almost pulled the plug on the whole project—but kept in there because of Joan Collins's clout with the viewing audience.

More rewrites. By now the network insisted on a strong male counterpart for Katrina Petrovna. In the bag were Sam Elliott, Treat Williams, and Keith Carradine. But enthusiasm was not waxing. In fact, the list also included George Hamilton. Hamilton had appeared on "Dynasty," and this bothered the CBS moguls who did not like the implied cross-plug. Also, Hamilton had appeared in a number of freaky gag movies—he was extremely good in *Love at First Bite*, his satire on the Dracula story—and might suggest tongue-in-cheek to the viewers. And, in show business terms, "satire is what closes on Saturday night."

But in the end it was Hamilton who was cast as Harry Price, the writer who lives by his wits and on the money of "interested" women. According to one source, the other actors were not available. "I live near the airport and I have my own wardrobe," Hamilton later said—tongue, as usual, in cheek.

There were several days to go before shooting—and the second female lead had not yet been cast. Finally Lisa Eilbacher, who had great reservations about doing the role of Maggie, the pleasure seeker on the prowl, caved in and signed on, although, in her own words, "The last thing I wanted to do was a miniseries."

When she arrived at wardrobe and found out what she was going to wear, Lisa looked at the sky: "Thank God I'm an actress who doesn't care what I'm wearing. My job is to worry about the acting."

Lauren Hutton, one of the principals of "Sins," signed up for a minor role. Because of the shortness of time, Anthony Page, the director, complained that he did not have time to go over the script.

"It's not really the story; it's the dialogue. Usually I have a lot more time to work with the writer in polishing the script.

Quite honestly, I think this script needs a lot more developing than it's reached even now. I'm still writing notes about it."

Finally the novelist Stephen Sheppard, who had written the book, was brought in to do some rewriting. Page didn't like the author rewrites and threw them out. Now Joan Collins decided that *her* part suffered from underwriting. *She* brought in none other than the best friend and partner of her second husband Anthony Newley—in the person of Leslie Bricusse—to beef up the lines!

About this time even Hamilton the laid-back was getting concerned, although of course he spent most of his time in the sun acquiring that famous George Hamilton bronzed look.

"I suntan in my tuxedo," he yawned one morning. "They don't use makeup on me; they just polish me like a statue." But he was wondering about the filming that had just started. "I feel like I'm in the back seat of a Ferrari going 150 miles per hour and there's somebody at the wheel but I'm not it. I think a lot of people think they're driving the car."

Even Lauren Hutton said, "I kept hearing there was massive confusion. I felt like I was going off to join Custer. But now that I'm here, I find that Tony Page is a wonderful director. It's fun, so far. And he's smart enough, when you invent little funny lines, to let you use them."

Nevertheless, with all the worry and all the temperament among the cast, the miniseries, which would be a four-hour production—was finally brought in. Also in the cast was the English actor Malcolm McDowell, playing the mercenary Irishman Quinn; he had had the misfortune to slip in a sequence being shot on a boat, and continually cursed the heat of the Riviera most of his time there.

Although Joan and her husband Peter Holm were executive producers of the miniseries, they were actually overseen by the show's main producer, Martin Abrams.

"When they made *Casablanca*, I'm told that they worked this way every day," Abrams said. "They were rewriting pages and the actors and directors didn't know which way they were going the next day. Those are obviously not the circumstances anybody chooses to work in, but we should only be so lucky to be compared to that film."

Well, in the end, they weren't.

The film aired less than a year from its predecessor, "Sins," with, unfortunately, almost disastrous ratings. Most of the critics dismissed it as fluff.

It was, according to John J. O'Connor, in *The New York Times*, "balanced by the director Anthony Page on a thin line between being outlandish and being obscene. It manages, in the end, to be merely silly."

O'Connor was annoyed at the heavy German dialect of Pabst, played by Peter Vaughan, with lines like: "'Ve crush you like so many ants."

"Eventually, of course, Katrina and Harry will get together and no one will be surprised to learn that Hamilton and Collins are not Gable and Lombard. There is, admittedly, a certain grim fascination in watching two actors over age forty-five devote so much effort to trying to look fifteen years younger than they are."

He added, "Miss Collins . . . seems to have finally reached the stage in her career where she looks totally unreal. She is a walking air-brushed photograph. . . . While the actresses around her are never allowed to look more than downright drab, she sails through 'Monte Carlo' in more than three dozen costume changes, stopping every once in a while to whisk the plot up to date."

Could the disaster in the ratings in this "Sins" look-alike have been caused by the personal cracking up of the marriage between Joan Collins and Peter Holm? It is difficult to tell.

Nevertheless, it was obvious that shortly after the airing of "Monte Carlo" things were not the same at the Holm home—to overstep the bounds of conventional diction.

Perhaps it was time once again to review the marriage vows to see if possibly somehow each or both had erred somewhere along the line.

Chapter Thirteen

Irreconcilable Differences

Nothing in the life of Joan Collins so resembled a soap opera as her divorce trial in 1987, in which she finally broke the ties that bound her legally to Peter Holm. It was a feast for the media. The tabloids simply ate it up. They could not get enough of the juicy details. Los Angeles television stations flooded the airwaves with actual film taken at the divorce trial. Often the trial was the lead story of the day.

As testimony dragged on, the trial seemed unbelievable and melodramatic in certain of its aspects. Parts of it seemed staged, as if it really were an episode of "Dynasty."

The key to the marriage seemed to be the so-called pre-nuptial agreement that Joan was said to have forced Holm to sign before she would agree to marry him. In fact, its very existence may have been one of the reasons for the failure of their marriage. At least it was one of the reasons that it started off in such a rocky state.

As has been pointed out, they spent most of the two-and-a-half years they lived together before the marriage discussing

213

the prenuptial agreement. Joan Collins's lawyer at the divorce trial once said, "I never yet saw a prenuptial agreement that didn't wind up in a divorce. With Joan and Peter, I think they were doomed from the start."

The settlement hearing took five days. Tears welling in her eyes, Joan announced: "I've been taken advantage of by men since I was twenty." For his part, Holm demanded more than $2,600,000 from his wife, to whom he had been married a mere thirteen months.

Holm wanted the prenuptial agreement invalidated at the divorce trial; Joan Collins wanted it upheld. The agreement stated that Holm was to get a 20 percent take of his wife's earnings from the time they were married.

When she filed for divorce, Joan said that she was suffering from "extreme stress and anxiety." One reason for her misery was Holm's assertion that the mysterious bag he invariably carried around with him held explosives.

At the settlement hearing, Holm confessed that his wife had threatened him with divorce before, but he said that he thought she was only acting—and so he disregarded her demands. He told *People* magazine days before the trial, while he was living in Joan Collins's Bowmont Drive house in Beverly Hills resisting eviction by her representatives, that the divorce took him completely by surprise.

He flipped a crumpled-up $20 bill to a reporter outside the house. Could the man help him get his electricity turned back on? he asked.

"Everything was lovey-dovey. We'd had a few arguments. We agreed to meet for lunch and talk things over. Instead, someone from her attorney's office was at the restaurant. He handed me something and said, 'These are divorce papers.' I was stunned and flabbergasted."

Holm demanded a hefty and mind-boggling $80,000 a month in temporary support from his wife. He also wanted a fifty-fifty split of all the communal property, maintaining that the prenuptial agreement was not binding. He also wanted half of the $5,200,000 that Joan Collins had earned since their wedding.

That was all Peter Holm wanted.

In his suit, he claimed that he needed $80,000 a month to live in the manner to which he had become accustomed by being the husband of Joan Collins. The media had a field day as they went over Holm's so-called needs per month, which were listed on paper as follows:

1. For rent, $6,500.
2. For household salary, $7,000.
3. For groceries, $9,000.
4. For telephone bills, $1,300.
5. For TV, cable, and video supplies, $670.
6. For audio supplies, $400.
7. For lease of the BMW, $635.
8. For the CSI, $3,900.
9. For clothing and accessories, $12,000.
10. For entertainment, $6,000.
11. For travel and lodging, $4,000.
12. For household supplies, $700.
13. For cash draws spent on personal items and purchases, $8,000.
14. Etc.

Joan Collins's lawyer, Marvin Mitchelson, labeled Holm a "con man."

As the trial started, the press was in full attendance, taking down every word, photographing as much as it could of Joan and Holm both in court and arriving and leaving. When the trial continued, becoming more ridiculous and preposterous day by day, the media began to make fun of every nuance.

And then—

Soap-opera time!

A mystery witness appeared on the stand! Wearing a white babushka, and a white dress that looked sprayed on with a zipper down its front, and displaying leopard-print spikes on her shoes—the "mystery witness" took the stand.

How could anyone overlook the resemblance between her and Alexis at Blake Carrington's trial when Alexis made her debut on "Dynasty"?

The crammed courtroom vibrated in surprise as the mystery woman opened her mouth to speak. Who was she? Soon they found out.

She was Romina Danielson, a twenty-three-year-old brunette sexpot.

Why was she there?

She used to be married to a friend of Peter Holm's, an eighty-year-old real-estate developer named Axel Danielson.

On the stand, Romina mumbled in squeaky tones that she had been Peter Holm's lover during his marriage to Joan Collins.

Sensation! Gasps! Excitement!

All but inaudibly Romina described her affair with Holm. "Peter called me his passion flower. . . . He told me the color gets deeper and deeper red if the flower has not been pulled from the ground. He said I haven't blossomed yet."

She was blossoming in the courtroom. There wasn't a sound in that packed courtroom. Mouths hung open, eyes bulged, hearts stopped.

Romina went on in a hushed voice to explain how Holm had cleverly contrived a gambit to remain with Joan Collins for a short time and then take a quick powder, lugging off jointly held property with him.

Romina's testimony did not last long. It took her only ten minutes to tell the story. Her last words were, "We continued our . . . sexual liaison through 1985. There came a time when I thought I was pregnant."

At that moment melodrama took over drama. Soap took over reality.

Unexpectedly, but almost as if on cue, Romina Danielson looked stunned, her eyes rolled up into her head, and she slumped in her chair, on the witness stand. She had fainted dead away.

The spectators sat in shock and disbelief.

By one reporter's account, Joan Collins was watching this all with glassy eyes, then, suddenly, she smiled and bucketed out of the courtroom past the wilting passion flower without giving her a second glance.

Then the courtroom exploded. Romina soon came around and tugged at her skintight dress to free her heavy breasts so she could breathe. Attorney Mitchelson and a female sheriff ran over to her side to give her first aid or whatever they could to help.

When the cameras closed in on her, it was too much for Romina. At her wits' end, she found she could take it no longer. She screamed hysterically until a pair of hastily summoned paramedics bundled her out to a waiting ambulance.

"I didn't *believe* it," Mitchelson said later. "I couldn't have scripted that scene any better."

Mitchelson was not alone in his view. A lot of people could not believe Romina's actions. Many thought it was staged from point A to point Z.

Next day Romina was called to the stand for cross-examination by Holm's lawyers. As luck would have it, she was indisposed and could not appear in the courtroom. Judge Earl F. Riley struck her testimony from the record.

However nobody at the trial could forget Romina, "The Other Woman," in a soap-opera divorce trial held to free Joan Collins of her manager-husband Peter Holm. Joan must have wondered at some point in the proceedings whether or not Esther Shapiro and Aaron Spelling might somehow be orchestrating the trial from behind the scenes.

But Joan harbored no grudges against Holm publicly. "I wish him well," she said. "He's a stubborn man."

Holm received $1,300,000 and $700,000 in support during the thirteen months of his marriage to Joan Collins. That in itself was nothing to scoff at—even for a rock star.

Judge Riley ruled in Joan Collins's favor, however, by finding the prenuptial agreement valid.

This finding did not sit well with Holm. Despondent, he said that he could not understand the outcry in the press against his demands of $80,000 a month in support from his ex-wife.

Sections of his declaration in support of his request of spousal support appeared in the *Washington Post* on July 24, 1987. They ran as follows:

"One afternoon in July, 1983, I met Joan Collins," Holm wrote. "She noticed me and through a third party invited me to escort her that evening to a world premier showing of the film *Superman*. We shared a wonderful evening. After the screening we went to the most famous and chic London discotheque, Tramps, where we danced all through the night."

He went on to describe their life-style when they were together. It sounded like something out of "Dynasty":

"We use private jets on occasions such as the trip to Las Vegas for our wedding and to Acapulco on vacation. Also while in Europe we used private jets to travel within the continent. We used a private helicopter when in France to commute from Nice to our home in Port Grimaud as it saved us fifteen minutes, had we traveled by car. . . .

"We were always part of the local Hollywood party scene and attended, for example, parties at the homes of, or with: Johnny Carson, Roger Moore, Linda Evans, Jackie Bisset, Sammy Cahn, Michael Caine, Dyan Cannon, Alan Carr, Barbara Carrera, Diahann Carroll. . . .

"Because of this life-style we always have to wear very expensive designer clothing and jewelry, and use and employ limousine services, luxury cars, and private drivers.

"We entertained in our Bowmont home on the average of once every ten days and held a major event every month. We employed extra staff, caterers, valet parking, and extra security for these parties. The practice was to cater to our friends' expensive tastes in both food and drink. Provisions would be brought in such as Russian caviar, smoked salmon,

champagne, and vintage wines and liquor by the crate. . . .
Throughout our marriage I have dressed stylishly. I have
spent large sums updating my wardrobe during our marriage
in order to enhance my wife's and my public image. For
example, I spent approximately $20,000 per month on cloth-
ing and accessories. . . . Our life-style demands that we
wear quality clothing at all times, including expensive leather
and fur jackets, ties, watches, shoes, and silk shirts. For
instance, I wear $2,000 leather jackets, $400 crocodile shoes,
and tens of thousands of dollars worth of jewelry. . . .

"While our income and expenses may seem extraordinary
to the average person, the fact of the matter is that to us, it
is our normal way of life, and is typical of those depicted in
the television series 'Lifestyles of the Rich and Famous,' on
which we have been featured several times."

Indeed, Joan Collins threw one of her famous parties even
as she was in the process of shedding husband Holm. She
called it her "Get Rid of Peter Party." She invited more than
a hundred guests, who included Aaron Spelling, Alexander
Godunov, Marvin Davis, Allan Carr, Dyan Cannon, Angie
Dickinson, Marvin Mitchelson, Pamela Mason, Joe Bologna,
and David Niven, Junior. Niven brought T-shirts to the party
with slogans like "Holm Sweet Holm," "A House Is Not a
Holm," "Holm Wrecker," and "Holm Savings & Loan" printed
on them.

Obviously, Joan's divorce did not cause her to lose her
vaunted sense of humor, although it did cost her a pretty
penny.

The Joan-Holm divorce made history in that it was the
largest request by a man for alimony from his wife in the
records of the court. Expensive divorces are a matter of
course in Hollywood, but this one took the cake and even
raised the eyebrows of the jaded Hollywood community.

Holm was initially reluctant to ask for support—at least,
according to him—because, he said, the request would "dam-
age my reputation and soil my name." He felt he would
become the butt of Hollywood abuse. He was right.

In fact, the trial, like a "Dynasty" trial, was primarily concerned with money. Joan claimed Holm ruined their marriage by spiriting away $1,000,000 that she cannot locate anywhere in her effects. Holm denied the charge.

Her exact words concerning that suspicious bag that Holm was always carrying around with him were: "He carries a two-foot-long padlocked bag. Whenever I ask him what is in the bag and why he carries it, he replies, 'Explosives and gold bars.' "

A terrorist? A practical joker? A nut?

No wonder Joan Collins got a restraining order from the court to keep Holm at least a thousand feet away from her home and her place of business: the "Dynasty" set. Joan also claimed Holm gave her heart palpitations.

Strange malady.

Joan Collins was not alone in her less-than-flattering view of "Holm the Home Wrecker." One of his erstwhile girlfriends, Shirley Coe, had this to say to a reporter about Holm:

"The only things he's interested in are money, sex, and prestige—in that order. He's a greedy bastard and money-mad." Hardly a gilt-edged recommendation for a husband.

Joe Collins, Joan's father, agreed with Coe about Holm. "I never liked him from the beginning." He also said that he did not think the divorce would deter his daughter from marrying again. As he put it, "I think she will have another husband soon. You see, I think my daughter likes lovemaking."

Joan Collins herself was sad that the marriage had not worked out. "I believe in marriage, old-fashioned marriage," she said in a prepared statement, read by her attorney Marvin Mitchelson in Superior Court in Los Angeles. "It makes me very sad and regretful that this marriage did not work out at this time in my life."

She said later, "Men have a tendency to change when they get married." That perhaps explained why she had been forced to obtain a divorce from Holm.

For his part, Holm played to the media by pulling a number of PR stunts. One of them involved standing outside the courtroom and holding up placards demanding his rights. One read:

JOAN, YOU HAVE *OUR* $2.5 MILLION, 13,000-SQ. FT. HOME WHICH WE BOUGHT FOR *CASH* DUR-ING OUR MARRIAGE. I AM NOW HOMELESS. HELP!

The placards had no effect on Joan Collins, who sniffed that the only reason she married Holm was so that he would not feel like a dog trailing behind her.

Eager for publicity, hoping for a movie career, Romina Danielson, the Italian-Iranian "Other Woman" appeared as a guest on "The Late Show" on August 17, 1987, shortly after her stint as a witness at the trial.

She wore a tight black leather dress that looked as if it had been taped onto her voluptuous figure. In attempts to draw attention to her full breasts, she kept yanking at the top of her low-cut dress with her fingers, purportedly trying to cover her cleavage.

On the show she demonstrated to the audience how she had fainted and, to put it mildly, did not make a big splash as an aspiring actress. She managed to mutter a few mono-syllables but basically remained tongue-tied throughout the interview. Her only memorable line was: "Where am I sup-posed to look? At which camera?"

One could not blame Johnny Carson for saying that he would never have that airhead [Romina] on *his* show.

Romina could not understand why Carson called her an "airhead." According to her, her former husband Axel Danielson "never really wanted to have sex. He especially loves my brains."

Regarding Joan Collins, Romina told a reporter, "If I were Joan Collins, I would have seen through Peter in a minute." In Romina's opinion, "He was too weak, too foolish, too much a loser." Like a blossoming Alexis, Romina added, "I never let feelings get in the way of what I want. I only admire men who have power and brains."

Holm also took to playing to the media and tried to advance his cause with television appearances. For instance, he showed up on "Donahue" on July 27, 1987.

In that encounter, Holm held the view that he deserved more money from Joan Collins because of the fact that he boosted her career as well as her paychecks during his time as her husband-manager. According to him, neither Joan nor he were very well-off financially when they met. She had only an old Mercedes for a car—worth about four or five thousand dollars—she had owed twelve years' back taxes in England. It was his idea that she do the miniseries "Sins."

He told Donahue, "I was the one who not only helped her, I was the one who initiated it all, and said that, you know, instead of Joan just sitting and waiting around, being an actress, waiting for roles, let's create something that is made—tailor-made—for you." Which turned out to be "Sins."

Holm asserted that the production of "Sins" made the "Dynasty" producers nervous; they thought Joan might leave them and go to CBS, the network that aired "Sins." As a result, ABC upped Joan's salary to $95,000 a week. Holm revealed to Donahue:

"Yeah, they certainly did get nervous, because what we did was, at the strategic time—after 'Sins'—tell them that we should have a raise. And it worked. The raise was an $8,000 bonus, and we got $95,000 in salary, which Joan got per week."

At one point in the interview, Donahue observed that Holm did not look upset or depressed about the breakup of his marriage.

Holm answered, "Well, it's all relative, isn't it? I mean, if these figures were divided by thousands, you know, on that relative issue, it would be fair what I'm asking for."

Evidently Holm was suffering financially more than he was suffering emotionally.

Later in the show Holm defended himself against Joan's charge that he physically hit her.

"You've got to have the full story," he said, "because you

Joan had explained her reluctance to get married again in
these words: "I never met a man yet who was able to take
care of me." Now she apologized to the American people for
the fact that her trial had cost the taxpayers of the country so
much money.

Wearing a white jacket and a miniskirt, she had only this
to say of Peter Holm: "I think he's a bit of a loser."

Joan Collins never did have much sympathy for losers.
She had dumped Ron Kass after his successful career hit the
skids, and she had cut and run from the delightful Maxwell
Reed who was spending most of his time in unemployment
at the time she left him.

About a month after the trial, Romina Danielson was in
the newspapers again. The *Star*, a Rupert Murdoch tabloid
circulated in supermarkets and some newsstands, carried a
story under the headline: "How Peter and His Passion Flower
Cheated on Joan Collins—and Schemed to Rip Off Her $
Millions."

The story went on to "imply," as Romina put it, "that she
was a thief." Immediately she and Caryl Warner, her lawyer, filed an action in Los Angeles Superior Court for defa-
mation of character against the *Star* for printing the story
that had caused such "traumatic shock to her mind and body."
She wanted punitive damages of $100 million.

A day later, she, her lawyer, and her ex-husband Axel
Danielson, called a special press conference in Beverly Hills
to announce the filing of the suit. They were learning the
game of public relations fast. She told the members of the
press who had bothered to show up that it had been enough
of an ordeal to tell the world that she was Peter Holm's
mistress, as she had done during the divorce trial of the
Holms, but it was much worse to be accused publicly of
theft—as she had been in the *Star* article.

"After all," she said. "I'm not a rip-off. If nothing else, I
helped Joan Collins's case."

Holm, too, helped his ex-wife's case. On October 7, when
he had promised that he would be in court to push for his

$80,000 monthly alimony suit, he failed to show up. He telephoned from somewhere in southern France, pleading that he had become too ill to attend court in person.

Judge Earl F. Riley muttered that Holm seemed to be doing nothing more than "playing games" with the court. He struck his case from the calendar. This was the coup de grace. Holm had inadvertently—or advertently—buried forever his plea for $80,000 a month in alimony.

Marvin Mitchelson, Joan Collins's lawyer, promised the court that he would seek evidence from France that Holm was actually remarried several days before to a Los Angeles woman named Cathy Wardlow, former secretary to Jerry Buss, owner of the Los Angeles Lakers basketball team. If this proved true, it would render the question of Holm's alimony moot.

Meanwhile, Holm's attorney Frank Steinschriber of Sherman Oaks resigned from Holm's case, complaining testily that Holm had "never told me during the last several months where he's been."

In addition, Judge Frances Rothchild issued a bench warrant for Holm's arrest because of his failure to appear in court.

Then on October 12, Romina Danielson and Joan Collins were seated at adjoining tables at the Polo Lounge in the Beverly Hills Hotel. Joan had four men with her at her table—Romina had five. One up on Joan for Romina! The two women, it was said, even chatted a bit together:

"No hard feelings. Cheers. Ta. Blah blah blah."

Romina later said on a television show that she thought the seating was a plot engineered by the management to generate free publicity for the Lounge. She also blamed her notoriety in the Holm vs. Holm divorce action on a greedy Swedish journalist who had sold his information about her affair with Holm to Joan's lawyers. She also said that she did not like being called "Passion Flower."

Things seemed to be winding down.

In fact, no one had come up with a topper for the casual

throwaway line Joan Collins herself had uttered so spontane-
ously as she stood on the steps of the court just after her
divorce had been granted.

Asked by a nearby member of the press corps when she
would start looking for another husband, Joan turned casually and said with a beautiful smile:

"I don't need a husband. I need a wife."

There was a postscript to the story:

In February 1988 both Joan and Holm finally met face to
face in a Los Angeles court to settle the last details of their
divorce—the property settlement over which they had been
wrangling for fifteen months.

Before Superior Court Judge Kenneth A. Black, in a closed
courtroom session, the following final decision was made:

Holm would get a total of $180,000 from Joan Collins,
including $98,000 in "management fees" and $82,000 in
"property settlement," as well as a $40,000 custom-built car
called a Spartan. In all, Holm would thus get about $1
million in lieu of the $80,000 a month in temporary spousal
support, or about 20 percent of the $5 million that Joan
Collins had made during their thirteen months of marriage.

Joan would get sole possession of a co-owned French
house in Port Grimaud, France, with an estimated value of
$400,000, and the return of a hefty load of furniture and
paintings valued at about $100,000 that Holm had manhan-
dled from Joan's house in Beverly Hills. Also she would be
able to write off the $98,000 paid to Holm for "management
fees" as an income tax deduction.

Both sides claimed victory.

Holm's lawyer, Frank Steinschriber, denied that. "Nobody's a winner here. They're *both* angry."

Chapter Fourteen

Joan Collins on Parade

Quite soon after the brouhaha of the Holm divorce simmered down—or possibly even before the proceedings got under way—Joan Collins had, in her usual fashion, focused her attention on another man to carry on in the absence of the husband she was shedding.

News items began appearing in gossip columns and magazines. One of them appeared in "Chatter," a regular magazine column compiled by Tim Allis.

"After her celebrated divorce from Peter Holm," the short item said, "Joan Collins vowed never to remarry. No one heard the message more clearly than Bill Wiggins, 41, a British property developer who knows his place. Of their London fling he explains, 'She was going to be here this summer for three months, anyway. I was only incidental—like music.' There was some harmony maybe, but nothing too close."

Clever stuff—but what did it mean? What fling? How serious? Who knew? Nobody but Joan herself—and she wasn't talking for publication.

In the late months of 1986, when Joan was working hard not only on "Dynasty" but on "Monte Carlo" and other projects, sad news had been passed on to her. Ron Kass, her third husband and the father of her daughter Katy, died in October after what the newspapers called a "six-month battle with cancer." He was listed as the producer of *The Stud* and *The Bitch,* and also the producer of a documentary titled *Naked Yoga,* which had been nominated for an Oscar.

Not much of his later months of travail were known to Joan. It might have been the onset of his illness back in the tempestuous days of their last years together that had caused him to let the bills pile up and to ignore the details of his business.

No one would ever really know.

Peter Holm seemed never to rest. During the period he had been "ill" in southern France, he had apparently been hard at work on another venture that would allow him to cash in on his close relationship with Joan Collins. During the divorce proceedings when his name had become a household word—although cussword would be more like what that word resembled—he had pounded out four pages of single-spaced material purporting to be a "tells-all no-holds-barred" outline for a book on what it was like to be Joan Collins's lover—oh, and husband as well.

The "proposal"—as such a pitch is called in the book business—was circulated to a number of publishing houses, but no one had seemed ready and willing to put up a huge amount of money for Holm's revelations.

A columnist for *Publishers Weekly* even told a newspaper reporter that Holm himself was a "flash in the pan confusing itself with a shooting star." The proposal, indeed, was called by one reader "sleazy."

"It is a rags-to-riches story of a Hollywood glamour queen who was cash poor, living in a house that was mortgaged to the hilt, driving a fourteen-year-old Mercedes she could barely maintain, and a thirty-six-year-old European former rock star who brought her multimillionaire status in a very short time."

Wow!

The outline continued with information about something that had not been public knowledge up to that point. Holm, the pitch said, had had "a key role in the publishing of Joan's forthcoming novel."

Novel? Was Peter mixing up Jackie with Joanie? Jackie was the novelist; Joanie was the actress.

But, oddly enough, it was true. Joan Collins had indeed been working on a novel for some time, and had been going through negotiations with Swifty Lazar over its publication.

Holm's proposal as it continued: "Swifty Lazar, the superagent, had worked out the deal for Joan's biography a few years earlier. However, Lazar found Joan to be a treacherous business person and deceitful."

Quite possibly this referred to the fact that Joan Collins had indeed refused to have her autobiography—it was *not* a "biography," Petah!—printed in America as it had appeared in England. She had indeed turned down a handsome sum of money offered for it, and had then toned it down to an extent and updated the ending to provide inside information about her work in "Dynasty." But, "treacherous"?

More Holmania: "Peter convinced Lazar that he, Peter, could control Joan's irrational business side. Consequently Lazar agreed to read the chapters, and he liked what he read. Lazar proceeded to get a $1,000,000 advance from Simon & Schuster for the novel."

Okay, but there was more than just that in the pitch. Holm promised to write "a truthful history of extraordinary people living extraordinary lives, surrounded by the rich, famous, and infamous, the movers and shakers of not only Hollywood, but the world."

Plus a bombshell of sorts: Holm promised to blow the lid off the Joan Collins trust for her children and reveal why each child gets a different amount of money. Gasp!—son of a gun!

To get this proposal circulated around New York publishing circles, Holm had hired Joseph Singer, a literary agent, to represent him. In fact, Singer was annoyed at the loud noises made in editorial offices about Holm's "shameless attempt to turn a buck."

"He has a point of view in this," Singer said of Holm. "It's not making money off her—he has a story to tell. He has a lot to say in his own right."

He—or somebody. Word was that Singer had hired a ghost writer to put together a more formal proposal and perhaps get some of the chapters into shape that would blow the lid off. The writer, Singer said, was on his way to the south of France to confer with Holm.

Now, about that Joan Collins novel.

Actually, the deal had been firmed up at the time Peter Holm was peddling his story around New York, and it was finally sold for a British edition in October, shortly afterward. It was Michael Korda, the top editor at Simon & Schuster, who had "'commissioned" the actress to write her own version of life in Hollywood, or present, as Korda put it, an "inside view of Hollywood." So said the news stories that appeared in London.

In the book, the story said, Joan promised more sexy tales, putting her right on the same path followed by her younger sister Jackie in the years preceding. Titled *Prime Time*, the novel "is a story of four television actresses over forty—something I know a lot about."

In fact, Joan admitted: "Jackie teases me a bit about it. But I tell her: 'Come off it, you started your career acting when I was already doing it. Why shouldn't I have a bash at a best-seller?' "

Actually, Joan had begun the book when she was on a skiing holiday with Peter Holm, during the thirteen months of their marriage. And so perhaps Holm did have something to do with the genesis of the book.

"I started it when Peter was out with the kids every morning on the slopes and it became a sort of pregnancy—something I had to give birth to."

Oh, Joan!

In England, when Century Books finally signed up for the British edition, the word went around that Joan Collins might even have Richard Cohen as her editor. Cohen was the man who handled Jeffrey Archer's best-selling books for the same publisher. "If she wanted to stop acting tomorrow," one associate said, "she could have a contract for life."

And so another blockbuster was about to be launched from the publishing industry onto an unsuspecting world.

But Joan was not keeping herself strictly involved with only the electronic and print media. She was still working occasionally on beauty aids. In fact, in October 1987, she helped Elizabeth Taylor launch a product she called "Passion Perfume."

Joan had been in the beauty-aid business for some years, anyway. In 1980, she had published *The Joan Collins Beauty Book* in England, where it had become a best-seller. The book was never picked up in the United States. Nor has it been reprinted here to this day.

"One of the things I emphasize in the book is the importance of experimenting," she once said. "I think all women should be adventurous with new products and application techniques to find out what works best for them. After all, you never know unless you try."

But she did reveal some of her beauty secrets after her phenomenal success in "Dynasty" and after her appearance on the centerfold of *Playboy*.

"I like a lot of makeup," she told a writer for the *Ladies Home Journal*. "I believe in it, for beauty and protection. The elements are truly destructive, and I use makeup as a first line of defense."

The reason she has stayed beautiful for so long, she felt, is that she keeps her face out of direct sunlight. "I still take the sun on my body, but on the face? Never! I always wear a hat and sunglasses. When my body is tan, I use a darker foundation on my face to match up the skin tones."

She explained why her skin is all but poreless. "No matter how tired I am, I never go to bed without removing all makeup. . . . I also use a mild toner and moisturizer to replenish lost moisture."

As for applying makeup, here are the steps she takes. First she tones and freshens the skin. A clarifying lotion dabbed over her face and neck with cotton can accomplish this. A light lotion form serves as a moisturizer. She smooths on the preparation with her fingertips and cotton.

Then she uses under-eye concealer with a wand. She uses a concealer that is a lighter shade than her foundation. For work in front of the television camera she needs a "rather orange-y" liquid base, which she hates but must use inasmuch as she looks too pale compared to Linda Evans and John Forsythe, who both sport true California tans. When not in front of the camera, Joan Collins uses a tiny amount of pale-colored liquid base because "it looks and wears better, deemphasizing wrinkles."

With her fingers she applies a cream blusher for a foundation, providing highlights for her cheekbones and between her lids and eyebrows. "I've got a huge space up there," she once explained. "I've got to fill it up somehow."

Next she smudges brown kohl in pencil from around her eyes and buffs her face with a transparent powder.

Next comes black eyeliner. She applies it near the top lashes and smudges it in. With a black and brown pencil she darkens her eyebrows. She requires that the pencils "be very, very sharp."

She likes thick eyelashes because she thinks they give her natural sultry look a luminous aura induced by the forest of long black lashes shading it. For television she wears false lashes; for her personal life she wears merely a pile of black mascara.

Now to her lips. She outlines them with a shade darker than the actual flesh color and does not apply it with a lipstick but rather with a lip wand.

Finally, under her brows, over her cheeks, across her forehead, and on the chin she applies a light pink powder blush for "that healthy look."

When she is alone, she uses no makeup at all, and if she goes out in this manner, nobody recognizes her.

Joan Collins frequently worries about her weight in relation to her height. She has always wished she was taller than her five feet six—More like her sister Jackie, who is three inches taller. She also usually wishes she weighed about eight pounds less than she does.

About dieting, she once admitted that she ate "a little bit of everything . . . as many raw salads as possible, some red meat, vegetables, fruit, a little pasta, occasionally French fries and a Coke. I believe it's the amount you eat, not what you eat, that's important. As you get older, you need to eat less."

She once described her fashion style as "eclectic. Perhaps it's something to do with being a Gemini. I love clothes; I'm a hoarder. I keep everything and wear everything . . . jeans, full-length evening dresses, gypsy looks, beautifully tailored suits. And I adore strong colors . . . red, turquoise, black. I'm not shy about fashion, or even subtle. That's not my style."

Food can be a problem. She once admitted that she did not like "rabbit food." "I simply *loathe* carrots and lettuce. I love good, and good-tasting food. I don't eat shellfish because I am allergic to it. And I don't eat too much red meat because I know what farmers do to fatten up those cows." She added, "Junk food is horrible." She would much rather eat caviar—just like her alter ego Alexis.

Joan's life never provided her with the attention she began getting once she had become Alexis on "Dynasty." It was television—not films or the stage—that made her an international celebrity. And now that it has happened to her, she loves the life-style.

"I was walking out of a restaurant, and suddenly these people kept coming up—not fans, people in 'the biz,' agents, producers, directors, writers, actors—saying, 'Joan, how great it is to see you! I'm so happy about your success!' And I thought, 'Well, gee, my success. When did this suddenly happen?' "

Now Joan must constantly be on her guard against social climbers and people who want to use her to advance their own careers.

"I don't mean to insult them by saying this, but there are people who actually pursue people of ephemeral fame and success, inviting them to their dinners and their parties. And I know perfectly well that it's only because I'm successful in this television series at this moment. But, hell, I'm enjoying it! I'm in a top television show playing a tough, meaty, wonderful role, and I'm not going to go around crying in my beer because people are snapping my picture. When I go into a restaurant now, it's like the Red Sea parts. I'm not going to say that I don't enjoy that. I'm not going to say I'd much rather sit at the bar and wait while the maître d' treats me like some piece of shit. Who am I kidding? I want to go in and get my table. I like it."

But Joan knows that she should not let any of her present fame swell her head. She knows in Hollywood nothing is certain and success is transient. She looks at that philosophically:

"Who was it who said, 'It is better to travel hopefully than to arrive'? Whoever it was was a fucking genius. I don't want to think that I'm at the peak. In my own mind, I'm not. I feel I'm still traveling hopefully, and don't want to get there yet, because my head is not in the right place to be able to handle it all."

As far as her career is concerned: "I'm not going to go haywire; I'm far too old and experienced and clever to do that. I've seen them come and go. I just don't want to get big-headed and become like those surly creatures who make ridiculous demands and have everybody hate them. It is ephemeral, I know it is. My ambition now is to solidify my acting reputation so that I can come out of 'Dynasty' and get other shots. I want to play all those parts I've wanted all those years and haven't been able to get."

While female viewers may become aroused by love scenes

they see on television, Joan Collins while performing her love scenes on "Dynasty" does not.

"I think there's probably more acting involved in love scenes than in any others, because you have to simulate a certain passion that you certainly don't feel. And I, for one, think that nothing could be more embarrassing than having to play a love scene with somebody you really are in love with. Thank God, I have played love scenes with just good, nice actors who are professionals, and we've both been in the same boat. And, strangely enough, it's the actors who are usually more nervous than the actresses; I don't know why. Perhaps actors think they have more to lose—they don't know whether they should get excited or not get excited, whether they have to cover up or not have to cover up. But in no way is it erotic or exciting at all—certainly not for me. Maybe some actors or actresses find it to be, but I don't."

Looking back on the breakup of her marriage to Ron Kass, Joan once discussed whether or not her appearance on "Dynasty" had anything to do with the divorce. "No," she said. "I think [the breakup] was unfortunately inevitable because of the various problems we had in our marriage. I tried to keep the marriage together longer than most people would have, because I hate to give up. I'm a fighter; I hate to admit failure."

Her definition of man-woman love is:

"It's sharing common interests, growing together. It doesn't mean that you necessarily have to love football because *he* loves football, but it would be nice if you had a sharing of interests. Doing things together and enjoying each other's company are tremendously important. A flame that's just passion will wear itself out. To me, real love is wanting to be with somebody all the time—and not envisioning being with anybody else."

Joan always was in the past—and is now—adamantly against advancing one's career by means of the casting couch—as so many Hollywood starlets have done in the past and continue to do in the present. She said that she had never slept with anybody to obtain a part in a movie.

"The idea of bedding some fat, awful old man to get a part was—is!—abhorrent to me. I'd rather have worked in some shop."

She also said that she has always told her daughters, "Learn from my mistakes. Don't marry young. Don't give your life over to a man. Don't put your personal life in front of your career."

Joan Collins has always been and will always continue to be a fighter. It is not her nature to give in when the going gets tough. After a national tabloid published lengthy unauthorized excerpts from her British version of *Past Imperfect* in 1982, she sued the paper—and collected.

She reasoned: "You just can't stand by and let the world kick you in the teeth. I will not let myself be maligned or victimized." And she can afford the most expensive Beverly Hills lawyers there are now to protect her.

As well as being a fighter, she can also be very humorous. For instance, when asked if money was an issue at a time she was going through some financial crisis of her own, she quipped, "Show me a person for whom money is no issue and I'll show you a billionaire."

She fired off another gibe when asked if "Dynasty" had changed people's reaction to her.

"I call them the 'woodwork friends,'" she sniffed, "the ones who a year ago wouldn't cross the street to say hello. There's a tendency for people in this town to gloat over others' failures—not cheer their successes."

She also joked, "I'm not knocking 'Dynasty'—it's bloody good and it's been great for me, but it is not 'Brideshead Revisited.' Television is ephemeral. I just happen to be the busiest flavor-of-the-month brunette today. There are other mountains I want to climb."

She thinks that there is not much interest in big-time movie stars anymore; the interest, she feels, is now in television personalities. She is proud of being in the acting business and admits it to anyone who asks.

"I think this is a wonderful profession to be in if you happen to be successful. When you think that ninety-nine and nine-tenths of the people in our profession are clawing for a living, to be successful and make money at it, to be able not only to feed and house your family but to go down to Rodeo Drive and drop a couple of thou in an afternoon and live well—*that* is a great bonus. Actually, I'm getting paid for something I have wanted to do since I was eight years old. And I was able to go through the really fallow periods, of which there have been a lot, without clinging to drugs, booze, men, or any of those other things."

She is glad that she never had to resort to drugs. "I am very hot on the old Cristal and white wine. But drugs? No. They're an absolute no. I abhor what they do to people. I was given some cocaine in St. Tropez in the sixties and it just freaked me. I was at a disco and danced until about six in the morning and didn't sleep for three nights. Then I had a postnasal drip for three weeks, and I thought, fuck for a laugh.

"And, yeah, I've smoked a joint, but it has a very bad effect on me. Of course, I wouldn't today—I'm terrified of getting herpes. I never smoke a cigarette from somebody's lips or even drink from someone's glass anymore. There's a moral laxity around. Herpes and AIDS have come as the great plagues to teach us all a lesson. It was fine to have sexual freedom, but it was abused. Apparently, the original AIDS sufferers were having five hundred or six hundred contacts a year, and they are now inflicting it on heterosexuals. That's bloody scary. A good reason for celibacy. It's like the Roman Empire. Wasn't everybody running around just covered in syphilis? And then it was destroyed by the volcano."

Edward Gibbon—where are you?

Joan cannot understand middle-aged actresses who throw in the towel because they think they are getting too old to be in films. In particular she points to the French sex kitten Brigitte Bardot, who is now a virtual recluse. She recently said of her:

"I disapprove of what [Brigitte Bardot] says about herself now. I think it's shocking. . . . Oh, she's so stupid. She says, 'I'm forty-nine years old now and I'm no longer pretty or attractive and I won't be seen in a bikini, because nobody wants to see me. My flesh is rotting. It's so pathetic. I don't think women should think that way about themselves!'"

Joan is critical of Greta Garbo, too, since she, just like Bardot, retired completely from public life when she reached what she considered an "old" age.

"I never thought she was either very beautiful or a very good actress. But she had *mystery*. And that's something I'm not going to have much of if I keep talking like this all the time!"

Joan has stated that even as she got older she was immature, irresponsible. She never acted like an adult. She wanted to play around and have fun and to hell with everything else. She put it this way:

"I've only started to become mature in the past few years. I was really a kid. It must have something to do with being a Gemini. We are just children. Look at Bob Hope, Judy Garland, Marilyn Monroe. There's a tremendous childishness about us."

She recently had this to say about the most important thing she had done wrong in her life. "The biggest mistake that I've made in my life is staying with people I should have got rid of—whether it was a maid, a nanny, a husband, or a lover. I'm not a very good judge of people."

One thing that frightens Joan Collins very honestly is death itself.

"Death scares me. I don't care how long I live, as long as it's got quality. I don't want to spend the last fifteen years of my life sitting in bed watching television, thank you very much. I've got the kind of metabolism that's going to hold up well against the ravages of time. Too much emphasis is placed on chronological age, I think. I would rather be older and look younger than be younger and look older. I think of myself as a woman of thirty-five. That's how I dress, act, behave. Thirty-eight is the dangerous age for a woman; that's when it all starts to fall apart if she doesn't take care of herself."

She keeps herself in shape with fifteen minutes of exercise a day. She does fifty sit-ups, twenty-five push-ups, and some weight-lifting daily. But an hour and a half? No way!

How long will "Dynasty" last? Joan Collins has never said. Obviously she might hope forever. But nothing is forever in this life.

According to Michael McWilliams in a recent *TV Guide* article, "Dynasty" may be fated to go rather soon.

"It's no secret that ABC president Brandon Stoddard has ordered changes in 'Dynasty,' " he wrote in October 1987. "Ted Harbert, ABC's vice-president for motion pictures, says he wants to make 'Dynasty' 's character 'more believable' and 'to put less emphasis on the glitz and glamour.' "

Nevertheless, it was glamour—Joan Collins's glamour—that put the series on the top after it had faltered the first time. McWilliams predicted that the return of Jeff and Fallon (John James and Emma Samms) from the spin-off on "Dynasty"—"The Colbys"—would probably not make a big difference. "Those two haven't been fabulous since James was young and Pamela Sue Martin played Fallon," he said.

McWilliams liked the second season of "The Colbys"—it "contained some of the finest hours of soap opera I've ever seen"—but he didn't like "Dynasty" at all, since it was "mechanical and absurd." And it continued to go downhill.

"And the one person who could save it—Joan Collins— went down with the ship," he wrote. "'She became a parody of herself, both on- and off-screen, and began to show her age. It's been a grand ride, Joan/Alexis, but it's time to move on to something else."

Overall, McWilliams predicted: "If it keeps slipping, 'Dynasty' will be canceled at the end of this season."

Does that worry Joan Collins?

Not particularly.

It's a great Hollywood guessing game trying to figure out

exactly how much money Joan Collins does make from her work on "Dynasty." A piece in *Parade* recently suggested that she was paid $95,000 for each hour-long "Dynasty" episode.

But $95,000 a week for the required number of weeks of "Dynasty" per year bears no relation to the amount of money she *really* makes. She is paid for various advertising and promotion deals. She has her finger in numerous pies. She was recently pushing a new line of Alexis lingerie—ending the speculation about why she has never promoted lingerie in the past.

Meanwhile, Joan enjoys life. And her latest boyfriend, Bill Wiggins, continues to show up at the bashes she throws at her Beverly Hills "manse"—as the columnists call it.

"She imported a gaggle of chums from Britain," a recent *New York Post* writeup went, "including her latest beau, Bill Wiggins. And they washed down caviar with champagne, as did Dudley Moore; Farrah Fawcett and Ryan O'Neal; Alana Stewart; Jackie Bisset and her Alexander Godunov; Shelley Duvall; Bianca Jagger; Zsa Zsa Gabor; Shirlee Fonda; and Marvin Mitchelson, who squired his wife of twenty-five years, Marcella. Marcella sported a $650,000 turquoise necklace that MM bought from the Duchess of Windsor's estate. Now you know why some Hollywood marriages last."

Joan Collins has a tough moral fiber within. Born into a show-business family and surrounded from her early years by entertainment celebrities, she knows that the business is one of illusion and fantasy. She has always known that it is ephemeral and without guarantee—in the same way that there are no guarantees in marriage either.

About her career in the Hollywood jungle, she wrote it best in her own autobiography:

"This is the toughest of professions. Very tough. Flavor of the month changes rapidly. Only the strongest, the cleverest and the most resilient survive—but survival is not the only objective. To live as normal a life as possible without letting the enormous pressures that one faces change one's attitudes and sense of reality, without giving in to drugs, booze, sex, flattery, the 'woodwork people'—to keep one's sense of balance—is an art in itself."

At this point in her life, Joan Collins must be considered as expert an individual on the subject of marriage and love and sex as, say, Johnny Carson. She has stated her views on sexual freedom in the following manner:

"I think, in a way, [sexual freedom] was abused by women ten, fifteen, or twenty years ago, feeling that they had to be a good sport and just jump into bed with anybody, because of the sexual revolution. Hopefully, women are becoming more discriminating now. But the fact remains that young people are young people, and people like to have sex, and people will continue to have sex. Some people will continue to have it with as many people as they want to have it with, and some people won't because of these horrific things— AIDS, herpes . . . they're pretty scary. I mean, when I was a young girl, there were two things [you worried about]: getting pregnant and getting venereal diseases. But people are dying from sexually transmitted disease, and that's an extremely frightening situation."

She once told *McCall's* that, in spite of the fact that she had loved many men in her lifetime, she *hated* infidelity in a marriage. This is the way she phrased it:

"I hate cheating. I think that, if you're going to be with somebody, you have to be with them completely. If you're not with somebody, you can do exactly what you please, but, if you *are* with somebody, monogamy makes a relationship more meaningful."

An observer of her several marriages and divorces in fact agrees with Joan's assessment of her firm belief in monogamy. "Certainly, she believes in monogamy—while it lasts. I think she *needs* marriage, needs a man around to make her life fulfilled. And, yes, while she loves that man, she refuses to be with other men. She is *not* promiscuous in the general sense of the word, because she operates within her own parameters of faithfulness.

"She is faithful to the man she loves—in her own fashion, if you will. She considers a marriage as binding until it becomes a mockery. Infidelity or betrayal to her *makes* marriage a mockery. For her, at the point of infidelity it is all over. Life might be said to be a series of little marriages to Joan Collins, each beautiful and manageable so long as it is not betrayed or made into a bad joke."

Thus it is within the parameters of her life-style to appear nonmonogamous, but to be, in her own heart and mind, totally monogamous—to make, as she puts it, "a relationship more meaningful." Until there is cheating—and then that marriage becomes meaningless.

So far she has lived by that moral code, and it appears that she will continue to do so in the future. More power to her!

Bibliography

Newspapers and Magazines

Allis, Tim. "Chatter." *People*, (date unknown).
Associated Press. "Joan Collins's Divorce from Holm Is Complete." *Los Angeles Times*, August 26, 1987.
————. "Joan Collins May Appear." *New York Daily News*, September 6, 1987.
————. "Joan Collins Wed Fourth Time, in Vegas." *Los Angeles Times*, November 7, 1985.
————. "Joan Collins Wins Suit on Prenuptial Agreement." *The New York Times*, July 25, 1987.
"Belize Knows Joan Collins's Batting Average." *World Paper*, February 1987.
Bennett, Lisa. "Joan Collins's Ex-Husband Sings the Blues for Donahue." *Stamford Advocate*, July 28, 1987.
Birmingham, Stephen. "*Dallas* vs. "*Dynasty*": Which Show Is Better?" *TV Guide*, October 15, 1983.
————. "Is *Knots Landing* Now Better than *Dallas* and *Dynasty*?" *TV Guide*, November 30, 1985.

245

Bolstad, Helen. "The Lady is Dangerous." *Photoplay*, January 1957.

Bosworth, Patricia. "The Allure of *Dynasty:* A Shiny, Sexy Celebration of Venality." *Working Woman*, March 1985.

———. "Past Imperfect" (review). *Working Woman*, May 1984.

Bunzel, Peter. "Walters Grills the Stars, They Escape Unscathed." *Los Angeles Herald Examiner*, April 9, 1984.

Caulfield, Deborah. "Fast Lines and High Times of Joan Collins." *Los Angeles Times*, May 12, 1985.

Chambers, Andrea, rpt. by David Wallace. "Jackie Collins Husbands Her Energies to Turn out Steamy Hollywood Sagas." *People*, January 12, 1987.

Christie, George. "Nothing Matters When You're in Love." *Photoplay*, April 1960.

Clarke, Gerald. "Daytime's Steamy New Soap." *Time*, August 3, 1987.

Clement, Carl. "She Learned to Say No!" *Photoplay*, May 1957.

Cohn, Al. "Divorced Joan Collins Spurns Marital Reruns." *Newsday*, August 26, 1987.

Cole, Clayton. "Two Faces for Joan Collins." *Films and Filming*, December 1955.

Collins, Jackie. "Why Do We Love the Queens of Evil?" *Redbook*, February 1987.

Collins, Joan. "A Determined Actress Pulls Her Daughter from the Depths of a Coma." *People*, November 16, 1981.

"Collins Kicks up Her Heels." *New York Daily News*, October 20, 1987.

Collins, Mrs. Elsa. "My Daughter Joan." *Photoplay*, January 1957.

Conconi, Chuck. "Joan Collins, Unprotected." *Washington Post*, December 6, 1984.

Corry, John. "Joan Collins in *Sins*, a Mini-Series." *The New York Times*, January 31, 1986.

Daley, Steve. "Even Joan Collins Can't Divorce Herself from TV's Summer Circus." *Chicago Tribune*, July 31, 1987.

Danbrot, Margaret. "Linda Evans's Super Style." *Ladies Home Journal*, April 1984.

Davidson, Bill. "Now I Can Be a Tough Cookie." *TV Guide*, June 18, 1983.

———. "The Possibilities of More Lust, Power and Intrigue, Seemed Endless." *TV Guide*, November 16, 1985.

———. "Today's Main Event: Heather Locklear vs. Joan Collins." *TV Guide*, December 27, 1986.

Davis, Ivor. "Cover Q & A: Joan Collins." *Los Angeles*, February 1986.

———. "The Selling of Joan Collins." (*Unknown*, date unknown.)

"Diahann Carroll and Joan Collins Add Intrigue to TV's *Dynasty*." *Jet*, May 7, 1984.

"Diahann Carroll and Joan Collins Renew Their Feud in *Dynasty*." *Jet*, September 29, 1986.

"Divorce: Granted; Joan, a One and Only." *USA Today*, August 26, 1987.

Dougherty, Steven. "Tell It to Joan Collins." *People*, February 17, 1986.

Downing, Hyatt. "Cool, Crazy and Jolly Exciting." *Photoplay*, November 1955.

Eisenberg, Lawrence. "For *Sins* Imagine Joan Collins Limiting Herself to a Mere 84 Costume Changes." *TV Guide*, January 25, 1986.

Elwood, Roger. "At Home with John Forsythe." *Saturday Evening Post*, January 1984.

Estrin, Eric. "*Dynasty* Remembers Rock Hudson." *TV Guide*, April 12, 1986.

Esterly, Glann. "Singing a Different Tune Now." *TV Guide*, December 19, 1981.

Finke, Nikki. "Male-Imony: A Reverse Support Case; the Joan Collins-Peter Holm Divorce Trial Stirs Interest over His Demand for a Monthly Payment of $80,000." *Los Angeles Times*, May 27, 1987.

Forrester, John. "Joan and Jackie Collins." *People*, December 3, 1984.

Friedman, Jack, rpt. by James Grant. "Slithering into the *Dynasty* Plot, Kate O'Mara Makes Her Mark as Joan Collins's Twisted Sister." *People*, April 7, 1986.

Gardner, Marilyn. "Mannequins' Touch of Gray Hints at Shifting View of Aging." *Christian Science Monitor*, August 6, 1987.

Gendel, Morgan. "Joan Collins Seeking Divorce." *Los Angeles Times*, December 9, 1986.

Giordano, Patrick. "Joan Collins." *People*, January 17, 1983.

Goodwin, Betty. "I Still Do Some Foolish Things." *TV Guide*, November 10, 1984.

Grobel, Lawrence. "*Playboy* Interview: Joan Collins." *Playboy*, April 1984.

Haller, Scot, rpt. by David Wallace. "Scenes from a Sisterhood: Joan and Jackie Collins Turn Sex and Passion into a Family Plot." *People*, November 12, 1984.

Haun, Harry. "A Free Soul." *New York Daily News*, August 5, 1987.

"Health and Tennis Adds Joan Collins to Its Dynasty." *Adweek*, November 4, 1985.

Hill, Michael E. "Joan Collins; Glamor, Romance, Revenge and Responsibility." *Washington Post*, February 2, 1986.

Hirchberg, Lynn. "Joan Collins Needs Twelve Inches." *Rolling Stone*, March 29, 1984.

Holden, Stephen. "Joan Collins Stars in 'America's Vixen.'" *The New York Times*, November 2, 1984.

"Holm Also Calls in Sick." *Los Angeles Times*, October 8, 1987.

Hoover, Eleanor, and Doug Lindeman. "Divorcing for Dollars." *People*, September 10, 1987.

"In the Matter of Joan Collins vs. Peter Holm." *Washington Post*, July 24, 1987.

Jarvis, Jeff. "Reveling in the Lap of Luxury; Who Buys the Costliest Clothes in the World? Big Spenders from Princess Di to Rick James to Joan Collins." *People*, October 10, 1983.

Jerome, Jim. "*Dynasty*'s Dynamo; at 49, Joan Collins Has Carried the Dallas Imitation to the Top and Capped a Flashy 30 Years in Showbiz." *People*, December 20, 1982.

"Joan Collins Hasn't Got a Holm Anymore." *People*, January 5, 1987.

"Joan Collins in Victory on Marriage Pact." *Los Angeles Times*, July 24, 1987.

"Joan Collins Stands by Her Man, Peter Holm, Amid Rumors Linking Him to a Diamond Smuggling Caper." *People*, November 28, 1983.

"Joan Collins to Be a Bride." *The New York Times*, December 7, 1986.

Johnson, Lois Joy. "TV's Most Beautiful Women." *Ladies Home Journal*, March 1983.

Kass, Ronald S. (obituary). *Variety*, October 29, 1986.

Kelley, Ken. "The Prettiest Person in *Dynasty* Was—John James?" *TV Guide*, May 14, 1983.

Kitman, Marvin. "Alexis Saves This *Dynasty* and Steals It." *Newsday*, May 20, 1986.

———. "Another Dynasty?" *New Leader*, November 4, 1985.

Lemon, R. "Glamour Girls Off-Duty." *Newsweek*, January 4, 1960.

Litwin, Susan. "Linda Evans: She *Was* Like Krystal—But Is Learning to Be More Independent." *TV Guide*, March 1, 1986.

London, Herbert. "What TV Drama Is Teaching Our Children." *The New York Times*, August 23, 1987.

MacKenzie, Robert. "*Dynasty*" (review). *TV Guide*, February 14, 1981.

Mansfield, Stephanie. "15 Minutes with Joan Collins; a Little Dash, a Little Trash, a Little Salesmanship." *Washington Post*, August 27, 1985.

Maslin, Janet. "Romance and Comedy" (review *Sunburn*). *The New York Times*, August 10, 1979.

Maynard, John. "What's Wrong with Me." *Photoplay*, November 1957.

250   Jay David

McEvoy, Marian. "Fountain of Youth Beauty Book: Joan Collins's Foolproof Over-40 Makeup Guide." *Harper's Bazaar*, August 1985.

McGovern, Michael. "Joan Jettisons Her Mate." *New York Daily News*, August 26, 1987.

McWilliams, Michael. "Is This the End for TV's Prime-Time Soaps?" *TV Guide*, October 25, 1987.

"Meet Two People Who Make Fashion Happen." *Scholastic Choices*, April 1984.

Meisler, Andy. "The Rise and Fall—and Rise Again—of Diahann Carroll." *TV Guide*, March 23, 1985.

Miles, R. "The Many Faces of Joan." *Life*, October 1985.

"Mr. Peepers's Nights: Writing Habits." *New York*, November 3, 1986.

Monte, Don. "John Forsythe Dances on Table at $30,000 Plate-Smashing Bash." *National Enquirer*, July 8, 1987.

Murphy, Mary. "Behind *Dynasty*'s Breakdown—and Recovery." *TV Guide*, May 17, 1986.

Nolan, Tom. "While He's Poisoning His Brother-in-Law, Gordon Thomson Tries to Add *Warmth*." *TV Guide*, November 5, 1983.

Norwich, William. "The Stars Go Shopping for Some Trinkets." *New York Daily News*, August 5, 1987.

Novak, Ralph. "*Past Imperfect*, by Joan Collins" (review). *People*, May 14, 1984.

O'Connor, John. J. "CBS Offers *Monte Carlo*, Starring Joan Collins." *The New York Times*, November 7, 1986.

O'Hallaren, Bill. " 'Humbug!' She Yelled at the Mayor of Los Angeles." *TV Guide*, February 27, 1982.

———. "If Bo's a Perfect 10, Will Linda Be a Perfect 40?" *TV Guide*, June 27, 1981.

"Parties Are Patriotic." *Los Angeles Times*. October 8, 1987.

"Passion Flower Was Outraged. . . ." *Los Angeles Times*, October 1, 1987.

"People." *Stamford Advocate*, July 25, 1987.

Perthen, Amanda. "Writer Joan's Red-Hot Novel Will Net Her a Cool £500,000." (London) *Daily Express*, October 5, 1987.

Price, Susan. "Mother Is a Princess . . . Father Had Four Wives . . . Then There Was the Titled Spaniard . . ." *TV Guide*, June 15, 1985.

Rapattoni, Linda. "Woman Collapses after Telling Court of Affair with Joan Collins's Husband." *Los Angeles Times*, July 24, 1987.

"The Real Joan Collins." *Good Housekeeping*, May 1984.

Reuters. "Collins: No More Hubbies for Me." *New York Post*, August 26, 1987.

"Revlon Enters Musk Market with Spokestar Joan Collins." *Adweek*, March 18, 1985.

Robbins, Fred. "Joan Collins: 'I Feel Sorry for Men.' " *Redbook*, March 1986.

Rosenthal, Herma M. "Confusion—and Joan Collins—Reigns in *Monte Carlo*." *TV Guide*, November 8, 1986.

Roura, Phil, and Tom Poster with Patricia O'Haire. "Joan Asks Quick Divorce, Says Holm Haunts Her." *New York Daily News*, August 7, 1987.

———. "Joan's 'Bye-Bye, Peter' Party." *New York Daily News*, August 4, 1987.

Ryon, Ruth. "Hot Property: Joan Collins Buys Dynasty-Type House." *Los Angeles Times*, May 4, 1986.

Schemring, Christopher. "Joan Collins's True Confessions; *Past Imperfect*; An Autobiography, by Joan Collins" (review). *Washington Post*, April 15, 1984.

Scott, Walter. "Personality Parade." *Parade*, September 20, 1987.

Shales, Tom. "CBS's *Sins*: Joan Collins Adrift in an Ocean of Opulent Nonsense" (review). *Washington Post*, February 1, 1986.

Shaw, Ellen Torgerson. "Joan Collins Takes Over . . . and How!" *TV Guide*, October 23, 1982.

Vincent, Mal. "O'Mara Eyes 'Real Work' after *Dynasty*." (Norfolk) *Virginian-Pilot*, May 24, 1986.

———. "TV's Wanton Queen of Glitz, Joan Collins, Turns Heroine for Role in 3-Part Miniseries." (Norfolk) *Virginian-Pilot*, February 2, 1986.

Wallace, David. "I've Always Spoken My Mind." *McCall's*, February 1986.

Wallace, David. "Joan Collins and Her New Husband Peter Holm Are Partners in Sins, but Her Response to the Poll Proves She Has a Conscience." *People*, February 10, 1986.

———. "On and Off Camera, Joan Collins Helps in the Making of Male Model Jon-Erik Hexum." *People*, October 10, 1983.

———. "Proving the Rumors Right, Joan Collins and Ron Kass Declare Their Troubled Marriage Ex-Rated." *People*, January 31, 1983.

Warren, Elaine. "Backstage with *Dynasty*." *Cosmopolitan*, August 1985.

Weller, Sheila. "Good Old Joan." *McCall's*, November 1983.

Whitcomb, Jon. "On Location with *The Opposite Sex*." *Cosmopolitan*, October 1956.

Wilson, Earl. "Shock Trouper." *Photoplay*, September 1956.

Wilson, John M. "Don't Tread on Me." *TV Guide*, March 10, 1984.

Books

Collins, Jackie. *The Bitch*. London: Pan Books, 1979.

———. *The Stud*. New York: New American Library, 1969, 1978, 1984.

Collins, Joan. *Past Imperfect: An Autobiography*. New York: Simon & Schuster, 1978, 1984.

Collins, Joe. *A Touch of Collins*. London: Columbus Books Ltd., 1986.

Kercher, John. *Joan Collins*. New York: W. H. Smith, 1984.

Robert Levine. *Joan Collins: Superstar*. New York: Dell Publishing Co., 1985.

Sanderson, Eddie. *Joan Collins: Portraits of a Star*. New York: Fireside, 1987.

Scheuer, Steve H., ed. *TV Movie Almanac & Ratings: 1958 & 1959*. New York: Bantam Books, 1958, 1959.

———. *Movies on TV: 1972–73 Edition*. New York: Bantam Books, 1972, 1973.

Shapiro, Esther, ed. *Dynasty: The Authorized Biography of the Carringtons*. Garden City, NY: Doubleday & Co., 1984.

Thomson, David. *Warren Beatty and Desert Eyes*. Garden City, NY: Doubleday & Co., 1987.

Collins, Joan. *Katy: A Fight for Life*. London: Victor Gollancz, Ltd., 1982.

Television

Hour Magazine. WNYW–TV. October 8, 1987.

Phil Donahue. WNBC–TV (NBC–TV Network). July 27, 1987.